Women Writing Jewish Modernity, 1919–1939

Women Writing Jewish Modernity, 1919–1939

✦

Allison Schachter

NORTHWESTERN UNIVERSITY PRESS
EVANSTON, ILLINOIS

Northwestern University Press
www.nupress.northwestern.edu

Printed in the United States of America

10 9 8 7 6 5 4 3 2 1

Library of Congress Cataloging-in-Publication Data

Names: Schachter, Allison, 1974– author.
Title: Women writing Jewish modernity, 1919–1939 / Allison Schachter.
Description: Evanston, Illinois : Northwestern University Press, 2022. | Includes bibliographical references and index.
Identifiers: LCCN 2021034873 | ISBN 9780810144361 (paperback) | ISBN 9780810144378 (cloth) | ISBN 9780810144385 (ebook)
Subjects: LCSH: Hebrew literature, Modern—20th century—History and criticism. | Hebrew fiction—20th century—History and criticism. | Hebrew fiction—Women authors—History and criticism. | Yiddish fiction—20th century—History and criticism. | Yiddish fiction—Women authors—History and criticism. | Jewish women authors—History and criticism. | Modernism (Literature)
Classification: LCC PJ5029 .S33 2022 | DDC 892.43099287—dc23
LC record available at https://lccn.loc.gov/2021034873

For my children, Lev and Simone,

who always surprise me.

CONTENTS

ACKNOWLEDGMENTS

This is a book about the difficulties women face when they write and the many ways their labor goes unacknowledged. I began writing it after the birth of my two children, concluding during an international pandemic marked by school closures and the cessation of childcare. On both ends, writing this book could not have happened without a supportive partner willing to share the work of parenting and the remarkable efforts of my children's school to reopen safely during these challenging times.

The seed for this book was planted by Chana Kronfeld when she introduced me to Leah Goldberg's prose fiction, leading to our decades-long dialogue on women writers. Although I began writing this book long after my days at Berkeley, it is very much a product of the intellectual community that she helped nourish there.

I am lucky to have found a welcoming and generous group of colleagues at Vanderbilt, which has been my home for over a decade. My colleagues in Jewish studies, English, and Russian and East European studies have graciously read and commented on my work, offering support, encouragement, and advice, as well as intellectual and culinary sustenance. Among them are Dana Nelson, Mark Wollaeger, Colin Dayan, Mark Schoenfield, Jay Clayton, Nancy Reisman, Rick Hilles, Emily Greble, Vera Kutzinski, Houston Baker, Jennifer Fay, Scott Juengel, Jessie Hock, Alex Dubilet, Akshya Saxena, Candice Amich, Haerin Shin, Shaul Kelner, Ari Joskowicz, Julia Cohen, Jay Geller, A. J. Levine, Phil Lieberman, David Price, David Wasserstein, Matthew Worsnick, Lutz Koepnik, Bradley Gorsky, and Irina Denischeko. Emily Greble—neighbor, friend, and colleague—has read countless pages of this book, while our children played on the roof of her shed. For the past eight years Samira Sheikh has been my writing partner. Her friendship and care have kept this book alive. I am grateful to her for offering her dining room table when the pandemic found me without a home or work office.

This book developed in conversation with many extraordinary scholars. Na'ama Rokem, Maya Barizlai, and Shai Ginsburg read and helped me think through early chapters of the book. Maeera Schreiber offered careful close readings and support when needed. I regularly turned to David Shneer ז״ל for all things Soviet and I dearly miss him. I received important feedback at different stages from Natasha Gordinsky, Lital Levy, Adriana Jacobs, Shachar Pinsker, Mikhail Krutikov, Anita Norich, Zohar Weiman-Kelman, Shira Robinson, Wendy Zierler, Giddon Ticotsky, Harriet Murav, Anna Torres, Tamar

Hess, Barbara Mann, Sasha Senderovich, Rebecca Walkowitz, Robert Adler-Peckerar, James Loeffler, Barry Trachtenberg, Karen Underhill, Ken Moss, Jonathan Freedman, and Karolina Szymaniak.

Jordan Finkin and I have been collaborating for the past few years on translating Fradl Shtok's collected stories. Reading Shtok's words and bringing them into English has often felt like conjuring the dead into a delightful literary conversation. I am grateful to have gone on that journey with Jordan and am indebted to him for his countless suggestions and insights into Shtok and Hebrew and Yiddish literature.

I have benefitted from the help of research assistants who have made international research possible when I couldn't travel. Zach Mazur is the source of all things Polish in this book. Yael Flusser tracked down vital sources for me in Israel. In addition, Hannah Hicks assisted me in trying to locate Fradl Shtok's medical records. Alex Oxner and Mimi Brown helped with research and managing my bibliography.

I thank Vanderbilt University for supporting the writing of this book. I am especially grateful to have received a Research Scholars Grant and the Chancellor's Faculty Fellowship, which gave me time and resources to complete my research. I also thank the Simon Dubnow Institute for funding a summer of research and writing in delightful Leipzig.

Allison Brown carefully read through and helped incubate the book into the form it takes today. She is an extraordinarily generous and insightful reader. Daniela Blei's copyediting assistance and historical suggestions greatly improved the manuscript.

I am also grateful to Trevor Perri and Anne Gendler at Northwestern University Press, who embraced this project and helped bring it into fruition with much careful attention.

A version of chapter 1 appeared in article form as "Orientalism, Secularism, and the Crisis of Hebrew Literature: Re-reading Leah Goldberg's *Avedot*" (*Comparative Literature* 65, no. 3 [2013]). A modified version of chapter 6 appeared in Hebrew as "Minority Cosmopolitanism in Elisheva Bikhovsky's *Simta'ot*" (*Meḥkere yerushalayim be-sifrut ivrit* 30 [2019]).

I am grateful for the loving support of my family. I thank my mother, Laura Schachter, who has always believed in me and supported my work. We have missed her presence since the pandemic began, and I look forward to handing her this book in person. Ben Tran read every word more than once. As we motorbiked through Hanoi in the waning days before the pandemic would force us home, we spoke excitedly about collaborative projects and new adventures. Even as we are now homebound in Nashville, I still feel as though our life is a surprising adventure that I am lucky to share with him. I look forward to seeing where the next years take our family.

Finally, I want to thank my children, Lev and Simone, who have joined me on this book-writing journey and have kept me honest at all times.

NOTE ON THE TRANSLITERATION

For Yiddish I have used the YIVO transliteration system. For Hebrew, I have used a simplified version of the ALA/LC system. In transliterating the names of Hebrew and Yiddish authors, I have where possible tried to choose the name as it appears in the records of the US Library of Congress, unless that spelling diverged from the one used by scholars of Hebrew and Yiddish literature for the most commonly cited authors (such as Dvora Baron, where the Library of Congress has Devorah Baron, and Fradl Shtok, where the Library of Congress has Fradel Stock). The most difficult spelling for me to decide upon was Debora Vogel, as opposed to Dvoyre Fogel (her transliterated Yiddish name) or Devorah Fogel (per the Library of Congress). I chose to use the Polish spelling of her name, which she herself went by her entire life in Poland, and which scholars use internationally, although not always in the United States.

Women Writing Jewish Modernity, 1919–1939

Introduction

Women, Modernism, and Jewish Modernity

On May 23, 1939, the Lwów-based modernist Polish and Yiddish writer Debora Vogel composed a letter to Aaron Glanz-Leyeles, a New York Yiddish modernist poet and editor, describing her deepest frustrations as an artist. "I also have this talent in me, but it has not been able to find its full expression," she writes, "because . . . because—I'm going to make a risky statement—because of the miserable fortune [*shlemazeldikn mazel*] it is to be a woman."[1] Vogel had produced two volumes of poetry and one of prose montage works. She also worked tirelessly in Galician Yiddish circles and in collaboration with Ukrainian and Polish writers to nourish a multiethnic and modernist literary and artistic cultural scene in Lwów. Yet as a woman in 1930s Yiddish literary culture, she believed that her talent could not come to fruition. After her death at the hands of the Nazis, Vogel's work would go largely unread, overshadowed by her close friend, Bruno Schulz, the Polish modernist Jewish writer.

Recent attention to her work, including translations into German and English, show Vogel to be a powerful intellectual and innovative avant-garde artist. We cannot know what might have been had Vogel been able to develop her talent unhindered by sexism, war, and racial ideology. Only if we read and consider her work, however, can we recognize her contributions to Jewish cultural modernity. Writing avant-garde Polish and Yiddish modernist montage prose and poetry, she examined the commodification of women's bodies and aesthetic experience in the twentieth century and envisioned new democratic modes of representation that would bring peripheral and minority experiences to the fore. Her work, along with that of other Jewish women writers, redefines our understanding of European Jewish cultural modernity, highlighting the intertwinement of new forms of Jewish culture and new modes of women's political and cultural belonging.

Women Writing Jewish Modernity examines the work of five interwar women writers: Fradl Shtok, Dvora Baron, Elisheva Bikhovsky, Leah Goldberg, and Debora Vogel. Bringing together voices of Hebrew and Yiddish women, the book uncovers a transnational Hebrew and Yiddish feminist modernist aesthetic. I chose these women writers because in their work they each self-consciously reflect on the role of women as artists in the twentieth century and seize the authority of prose fiction to narrate women's lives. They were writing in an era when the literary emerges as a key site of a new secular cultural authority, seeking to supplant the authority of Jewish law to govern everyday life. Born in the Austro-Hungarian and Russian empires, these women lived and wrote in Poland, New York, Mandatory Palestine, and later Israel. Placing them in conversation with one another, I show how they engaged the central political, social, and aesthetic movements of their lifetime. These women shaped new social, cultural, and literary experiments to reimagine the basis of Jewish culture beyond the traditionally male, homosocial world of Jewish letters. Rather than exploring Jewish life through changing paradigms of Jewish masculinity and male angst, they probed the porous boundaries between Jewish and non-Jewish culture, asking pointed questions about the necessity of such boundaries. They identified as minority writers in worlds where minority identities were rapidly remade with the breakdown of the Austro-Hungarian and Russian empires and the rise of new nation-states. As such, they portrayed the tension between minority particularity and the universalizing force of modernity through women's intimate desires and their artistic practices. Their work reflects on the very terms of storytelling in the twentieth century. Recovering their voices is not merely an additive project, but rather a generative enterprise that requires transforming our narratives of literary and cultural history—and of modernity itself—to include their capacious visions of modern secular Jewish culture.

Women's experiences are central to understanding Jewish minority life in Europe, although they have been absent from the central narratives of Jewish history. We cannot simply recover their voices and imagine that those narratives will change. Instead, we must document the labor conditions under which women struggled, along with the social violence that hampered their careers and expelled them from the literary record. Only then can we reorient the very grounds of our understanding of modernity. *Women Writing Jewish Modernity* draws connections between the social forces that marginalized women's artistic expression and the aesthetic projects these women undertook. It documents both possibilities and the melancholy "impasses" to feminist revolution that Ewa Ziarek identifies in her study of Anglo-American women writers who "explore the tenuous possibility of women's aesthetic innovation in relation to unbearable historical losses and damages inflicted by racist and sexist violence."[2] These impasses and dreams of possibility are shared by modernist women writers across the globe, who, like the women writers in the book, harnessed experiences of both loss and possibility as the grounds for their imaginative work. *Women Writing Jewish Modernity* illuminates how Hebrew and Yiddish women writers embraced the power of literary narrative to enact social change, even as they acknowledged the limits of their projects.

The 1920s and 1930s saw new political possibilities for women and minorities. During this period, new forms of national identity and minority rights emerged: the Polish Minority Treaty redefined the concept of national minority in Europe; the postwar Mandate system created the political possibility for a Jewish national homeland in Palestine; Soviet minority policy offered a new model of national minority identity that was meant to ultimately subordinate itself to socialist internationalism; and rising national movements, including Zionism, amplified the power of territorial nationalism as a key concept of communal identity. At the same time as these political concepts emerged and evolved, women gained hard-fought enfranchisement across the globe, including in the Soviet Union, Poland, the United States, and the Assembly of Representatives in Mandatory Palestine. These new rights and political movements promised new freedoms, but those freedoms were contingent on the social conditions that structured women's and minorities' access to the privileges of citizenship and the protections of the law. For example, in Poland or in the United States, women may have had the right to vote but were unlikely to hold high political office. Women faced challenges in gaining entry to male-dominated fields of knowledge and were stymied by the inequitable divisions of household labor that would prevent them from pursuing independent careers. Jewish men celebrated women's education and literary achievements so long as they restricted themselves to women's subjects and inspired male creativity. Jewish women trained in Europe to be equal partners with men in the newly founded labor collectives in Palestine, only to discover rampant inequities once they arrived in their new homes in the Middle East. For example, Dvora Baron's work showed the contradictions at the core of the new society being built by Zionist socialists in Mandatory Palestine, exposing the unexamined exploitation of women's labor.

The women writers in this book responded to these historical conditions, writing modernist prose fiction that dramatized the social conditions of women artists in the twentieth century, while also seizing for themselves new forms of social authority. In prose they could explore Jewish and non-Jewish romantic relations, amplify the tensions between languages and national strivings, and articulate Jewish women's frustrated desire to become artists and gain recognition for their work. They highlighted the ways women's desires were demonized and commodified and how their labor was devalued. They experimented with modernist techniques to explore tensions between the inner lives of women and the social demands that silenced those lives. Exploring new forms of desire, aesthetic practices, and political communities, they imagined modes of Hebrew and Yiddish writing that could encompass women's experiences. They also envisioned new forms of Jewish collectivity and Jewish minority culture that did not rely on the patriarchal privileging of male authority, European Orientalist ideologies, instrumentalized female desires, and all-male narrative perspectives. This book recovers their lost vision of Jewish modernist literary possibility.

The women in this book were also part of a much broader international flourishing of interwar women writers and artists who generated new avant-garde and feminist projects. Even as women initiated and participated in modernist circles, their contributions have been elided. Thus for example, until recently there has been little examination of women's participation in movements such as Dadaism and surrealism. As Ruth Hemus explains, "Many of the best-known accounts of Dada were, and remain, those written by the male Dadaists themselves," who failed to acknowledge the work of the women artists in their orbits.[3] Hemus opens her book with a moving 1924 letter from Céline Arnauld to Tristan Tzara, in which Arnauld chastises Tzara for not mentioning her in his history of the movement while generously acknowledging his male rivals. Women's participation in modernist arts was erased as "both the authors of original manifestos and the literary historians of modernism took as their norm a small set of its male participants, who were quoted, anthologized, and taught as geniuses." Women writers "were often deemed old-fashioned or of merely anecdotal interest."[4] In dismissing women writers, male artists and critics, I argue, were responding to the threat that women posed to male cultural authority. These masculine narratives about modernity and women's writing have not only obscured women's participation but also impoverished our understanding of modernism and its relationship to radical gender transformations. Contemporary feminist critics continue to observe how, despite the importance of feminist political ideas for modernist innovation, women's contributions continue to be sidelined in studies of modernism. As Anne Fernald avows, in her extended critique of what has been termed the new modernist studies, "No new work on modernism should go forward without serious engagement with women and feminist theory. To understand the uneven, surprising, and profound impact of modernity, we must remember, despite our theoretical, practical, and somatic sophistication, that gender played and continues to play an enormous role in defining social roles and economic opportunities."[5] Urmila Seshagiri identifies an "aporia between feminism's vitality for modernism, on one hand, and the scholarly neglect of that vitality, on the other."[6] Feminist scholars have illuminated the links between the political movement for women's equality and suffrage and the work of the modernist avant-garde, and we need to listen to this work and take seriously the centrality of women to the history of modernism.[7] In offering an account of women and Jewish modernism, this book contributes to the larger project of theorizing modernism and writing its history from the perspective of women writers and artists who catalyzed the aesthetic and political transformations of modernism.

We know little about the women writers, artists, and intellectuals who participated in the modern Jewish revolution. Their absence in the literature on modern Jewish culture means that we understand less about Jewish modernity than scholars realize. As Paula Hyman eloquently wrote in 2000, "Although the discussions about the 'women question' and the activities of women have been largely ignored in Jewish historiography, they are part and parcel of the emergence of modern forms of Jewish consciousness and culture in two ways. As historical agents—professionals, educators, and activists—women shaped 'Jewish modernity' within the boundaries of their different societies. As the subjects of communal debate, they became the touchstone of just what modernity would mean."[8] Hyman stresses how women occupy a historical blind spot, emphasizing that until we bring women's historical experience into view, the meaning of Jewish modernity for Jewish men and Jewish women will not be fully understood. Just as scholars of Europe have conceived of modernity in masculine terms through "an equation of modernity with a masculine sphere of rationalization and production," so too have scholars of Jewish cultural modernity.[9] Yet women, Hyman reminds us, shaped modern Jewish historical experience as intellectuals, artists, mothers, or labor activists. Twenty years after Hyman's sage words, modernity in the Jewish context remains largely synonymous with changing forms of masculinity.

All too often, Jewish male difference has displaced discussions about women. In part, this derives from European racial ideologies about Jews. Nineteenth-century European writers portrayed Jewish racial difference in terms of male sexual difference, depicting Jewish men as effeminate, sexually ambiguous, and perverse.[10] As many critics have noted, Jews internalized these racialized depictions, producing a new ethos of Jewish masculinity embodied in representations such as the "new Hebrew man" or the "muscle Jew."[11] Scholars have accepted this narrative of Jewish masculinization to describe the gendered transformations of Jewish modernity, effectively erasing the complexity of women's historical experiences and reducing narratives of Jewish gender to narratives about Jewish men. In researching and writing this book, I came to realize that the study of Jewish modernity, including the study of Jewish masculinity, not only is impoverished without Jewish women's experiences but also presents a fundamentally one-sided, flawed understanding of Jewish culture in the twentieth century.

Moreover, the underlying assumption that has governed the field of modern Jewish culture and literature is that women are absent for good reason: they weren't as talented, productive, or significant. Thus women writers are missing from syllabi and from literary and historical scholarship. Many remain untranslated. This continues to make it difficult for new generations of scholars to recognize the full extent of the Jewish cultural revolution that took place during the interwar period, when Jewish women experimented with new aesthetic practices, embraced new communal affiliations, and upended the gendered social order. Women writers in interwar Europe responded to the changes that modernity brought in ways that often differed from men, not least because for many women, modernity's disruption of religion's gender hierarchy was a source of possibility, not anxiety. Women took advantage of openings for women in cultural production: they composed poems, wrote plays, published novels, and founded literary journals. They achieved all this as male authority was being reconfigured in new secular institutions, and as the relationship among religious, cultural, and political identity was reconfigured in the interwar period.

Over the past three decades, feminist scholars have uncovered an array of women writers who played key roles in modern Jewish culture.[12] Despite their contributions to Hebrew and Yiddish literary history, women writers continue to be excluded from normative accounts of modern Jewish history and culture. Look at the standard syllabi, particularly in the field of Yiddish, and you will see that progressive scholars teach not a single text produced by a woman, or dedicate only a single day to women's poetry.[13] Mention a Jewish woman writer to a colleague, especially a prose writer, and you will often be asked, "Is she *really* good?" Behind this question lies the insidious assumption that any gesture to include women on syllabi or reading lists panders to a feminist recovery project that cares nothing about literary value. Noting the absence of women from Jewish intellectual history, the feminist poet and critic Irena Klepfisz asks pointedly, "Did Eastern European women really not think or write? Did they not have ideas? Were they not part of the intellectual Jewish life of the last 1,000 years? Did a mere handful write only poetry and the rest never have any thoughts about their lives, about the Jewish community, about the broader world?"[14] Nearly three decades later, these questions still resonate. The project of recovering women writers has been devalued in Jewish literature as a feminist venture that destroys aesthetic standards. This view of recovery as additive but not generative has to do with the lag between the emergence of feminist theory in the 1970s and its arrival in Jewish literary studies. Recovery feels antiquated because it has been achieved in many more mainstream literary fields, even as the work of recovery for Jewish literature is far from over. However, recovery is also inadequate to the task at hand when it merely adds texts to syllabi or single chapters to books about men, rather than transforming the very grounds of our understanding of the past. We cannot just add a chapter, an additional week on a syllabus to fix the problem. Instead we must read women's writing and assimilate it into the core of historical and cultural understanding.

The writers included in this book received exceptional acclaim on the one hand, but their prose oeuvre has yet to be integrated into narratives of Jewish literary modernism on the other hand. When remembered, they are recalled primarily as poets or, in the case of Baron, as an author of lyrical prose. Categorizing them as "poetesses" ignores their prose and thus elides their work to redefine Jewish minority identity and culture. Although their poetry might be occasionally included in an anthology, their intellectual and literary achievements have not been integrated into our understanding of modern Jewish literature and cultural modernity. As I discuss in chapter 1, male writers and literary critics wrote their female counterparts out of the prose canon because the women threatened this emerging sphere of secular masculine authority. Women recognized literature as a new arena of secular authority that could compete with the authority of traditional Jewish textual authority—what I term in chapter 1 the Talmudic regime. *Women Writing Jewish Modernity* illuminates how women's prose fiction experimented with and opened new possibilities for imagining Jewish futures and shaping an emerging secular Jewish culture.[15] Women writers explored the intersection between labor and aesthetics, envisioned nonnational forms of cultural belonging, and sought to break down rising ethnic and national divisions.

At the end of the nineteenth century through the first decades of the twentieth, East European Jewish women struggled to gain a foothold in a cultural milieu undergoing revolutionary changes. Women should have found an easy place in a literary culture that rejected traditional social and gender norms. They did not. This is a repeating theme in their lives—freedoms are tantalizingly just beyond their reach. They turned to literature as a modern tool to transform their lives and realize some of these unfulfilled gains. Many educated women recall how reading sparked their intellectual curiosity and catalyzed a desire to realize their artistic, intellectual, and political dreams. Yet they confronted barriers to achieving these aspirations. The Russian revolutionary Eva Broido (b. 1876) describes how she longed to continue her studies, but women were not allowed entry to the Russian university system. "The thirst for knowledge and learning," she observes, "for self-improvement and a free unfolding of one's personality, however vague and aimless, was so typical of all of us, that the then current ludicrous term 'a young girl of striving' described the condition most aptly."[16] Broido captures a moment when new educational possibilities ignited in women the desire to become writers, intellectuals, and artists. However, unable to enter and succeed in these fields because of their gender, they were reduced to their desires, as "merely" strivers. Sadly, the character of social change did not match women's ambitions. In her memoir *No Time for Tears*, Mary Asia Hilf (b. 1874) describes how despite her advanced studies in Russian and German literature, when she attended her brother's all-male literary circle, they asked her to sit in a corner.[17] The prominent feminist and Zionist activist Puah Rakovsky (b. 1865) recalls her extraordinary educational and intellectual journey to divorce her husband and become an educator and activist: she had to resort to threatening her family that she would convert to Christianity if they did not assist her with the divorce.[18] All of these women struggled with the realization that even as new professions, new rights, and new social roles became legally open to women, de facto social realities prevented women from gaining equal access to these new possibilities.

A YIVO collection of youth autobiographies contains memoirs written by "striving" young women who dreamed of becoming writers and artists.[19] One moving account by "Esther" (b. 1920), a young woman born into a Hasidic family in a small Polish town, captures these struggles. Esther's family enrolled her in a newly founded Bays Yaakov school in her town. Her traditional learning prompted her to find a way into her local Polish elementary school, where she distinguished herself as an outstanding student. Through Polish books, she discovered new worlds of experience and erotic desire that left her questioning her traditional Jewish world and longing for more freedom as a woman. Stymied in her attempts to continue her education because of her father's reluctance to educate girls and later because of her family's deteriorating economic condition and the rise of antisemitism in Poland, she writes, "My soul aspires to distant horizons, yet I remain in this little world of narrow duties."[20] She composed poetry and two novels in Polish that were never published, and yet she concluded her autobiographical essay on a hopeful note: "I think: How limited my aspirations are! I desire nothing more than to have a room of my own. For me this is typical: a great, beautiful, idealistic thought runs into a material obstacle. But this in turn provokes fresh ideas."[21] Esther alludes to Virginia Woolf's feminist essay *A Room of One's Own* and its dictum that a woman must have money and a room of her own if she is to become a writer. Woolf's description of how women's material conditions prevent them from realizing themselves as writers resonated with Esther's struggles for economic security and freedom to pursue her artistic dreams. Esther's material circumstances, however, were magnified as a Jewish woman alienated from the Polish culture that educated her. She was a woman writing in a minority language at a moment of enormous political strife. Writing her autobiographical essay in Yiddish, she seeks to rescue herself from these conditions. Her story echoes the struggles of Debora Vogel, another Polish Jewish writer, who embraced Yiddish as a tool of feminist self-expression. History thwarted both their ambitions: Esther composed her essay in 1939, as Hitler was poised to invade Poland, and her fate is unknown. But her story is similar to others told in countless memoirs of Jewish women who did or did not succeed in their literary careers.

The modernist women writers I analyze in *Women Writing Jewish Modernity* channeled their "striving" into the creation of prose fiction in Jewish languages, and they did so while coming up against similar obstacles. These women responded to the political and social transformations of their historical moment by engaging in ambitious prose experiments to challenge the patriarchal norms that defined the roles of art, artists, and minority literature. They envisioned new forms of Jewish collective attachments, resisted the pull of national languages, and interrogated the boundaries of Jewish and non-Jewish cultures. They wrote about the conditions of art in a time of radical social transformation. The book addresses these women's relationship to aesthetics and to politics in two parts. Part 1, "Aesthetic Authority: The Role of Women as Artists," focuses on how women writers imagined themselves as artists and embraced aesthetic labor as political. In chapter 1, "The Disruptive Power of Prose," I offer a literary historical account of women's participation in the rise of modern Jewish-language prose fiction, showing the prominent role that modern prose fiction played in these communities and highlighting how Hebrew and Yiddish literary historical models have erased women's participation in both languages. The chapter illuminates the influence of Gustave Flaubert's nineteenth-century novel *Madame Bovary* on Jewish writers, who turned to the novel to rethink the relationship among women, desire, and aesthetics. Chapters 2 and 3 examine how Fradl Shtok and Dvora Baron seized the authority of prose fiction for themselves, embracing Flaubertian narrative techniques and overthrowing the aesthetic hierarchies that govern the relationship of art and life. These chapters highlight how their works reclaim women's domestic experience as aesthetic, showing the ways the authors conceptualize their aesthetic labor through portraits of women's unrecompensed domestic labor.

Part 2, "New Languages for New Collectivities: The Role of Literature in Cultural Identity," connects my analysis of women's aesthetic labor and literary authority to the social transformations unfolding across Europe and in Mandatory Palestine, including the breakdown of empire and the rise of new nation-states. All of the writers in the book grapple with the shifting grounds of citizenship, national belonging, and transnational forms of identification in the interwar period. In chapter 4, "The Minority Literature Question: Literature and Political and Cultural Belonging in the Interwar Period," I theorize the intersections between the new political order, minority culture, and women, highlighting how women created and participated in new cultural and political arenas that shaped revolutionary discourses. They both engaged with and challenged minority and national forms of identification as these very categories were being renegotiated in the wake of World War I. In turn, women seized on the freedoms afforded by the social revolutions of the period, which offered new forms of autonomy and independence. Yet they also struggled to overcome patriarchal structures—both Jewish and non-Jewish—that limited and constrained them. Chapters 5 and 6 examine the potential of Hebrew culture in interwar Europe, highlighting the unresolved tensions between Jewish and non-Jewish culture through the vexed romantic relationships between Jews and non-Jews. Goldberg envisions a non-Orientalist future for Hebrew literature that would emerge from a new community of women readers and writers. In contrast, Bikhovsky imagines a nonnational or cosmopolitan Hebrew emerging from the pen of a non-Jewish woman. Chapter 7 connects the aesthetic questions in part 1 to the minority national questions raised in part 2. In this chapter, I show how Debora Vogel's prose montage, with its attention to women's experiences, creates a democratic, minority aesthetic that rejects national chauvinisms.

Portrait of a Woman Writer

Looking at the works of these five women writers in concert reveals that their stories are not the exception but represent a norm for women writers and artists in this period. In bringing them together, I identify the patterns and structures that shaped women artists' lives and work, as well as their later reception. A careful look at the overlap among these five women tells a different narrative of Jewish modernity; these women did not experience the quintessential Jewish male narrative of the alienated son, who breaks from his father's faith and seeks new community amid male friends but remains lost and disconnected. What sets these women apart is not a break with family and tradition but their struggle to seek recognition in modern societies that devalued women's labor and created institutional and material roadblocks for women writers seeking publication and recognition.

Embracing prose fiction, they assumed new authoritative voices to describe their reality and the future world they might inhabit. They located aesthetic possibilities in women's everyday lives, describing the work of the woman as artist. Many of these writers turned to Flaubert as an important precursor to their modernist project, even as they critiqued his demonization of his famous protagonist, Madame Bovary. Their attention to the everyday also belonged to a broader modernist tendency in European and Anglo-American writing of the period. In their oeuvres they reflected on the conditions of Jewish minority life in Europe and represented alternatives to Jewish collectivities, both national and international. They turned to Jewish languages as the medium of their art, against the grain of the realities they described. For example, Bikhovsky portrays the Russian-speaking Moscow art world in Hebrew, whereas Vogel captures 1930s Poland in Yiddish. Using prose to document the Jewish minority culture's intimate connections to non-Jewish cultural forms, they also attended to the tensions between language and culture.

These women make up two generations. Fradl Shtok, Dvora Baron, and Elisheva Bikhovsky were born between 1887 and 1890. Debora Vogel and Leah Goldberg were born more than a decade later, in 1902 and 1911. These two decades defined differences in access to education and intellectual outlets. Shtok and Baron came of age in the provincial regions of the Russian and Habsburg empires, and they rebelled against small-town Jewish social norms. Their careers and work were shaped by this fading traditional world. Born in 1888, Bikhovsky straddled both generations, in part because as an outsider to Judaism, she was not restrained by its conventions. A child of prerevolutionary Russia, she too experienced limits to women's freedom, even if she was raised in a more cosmopolitan milieu than both Shtok and Baron. In contrast to Baron and Shtok, Goldberg and Vogel enjoyed wider access to a European education. Both pursued their studies and received doctorates: the former in Oriental studies from Bonn University in Germany and the latter in Polish literature and philosophy at Jagiellonian University in Kraków, Poland. The decade that opened these doors to them meant that they could publish works of literary criticism and actively participate in the intellectual and philosophical debates of their age, and yet each remains unassimilated into cultural histories. In these two generations, I identify a Hebrew and Yiddish modernist feminist aesthetic in the twentieth century.

These authors embraced multiple languages, moving between Jewish and local national vernaculars. Their multilingualism was both a sign of their rootedness in the multicultural Russian and Habsburg empires, even after these empires' demise, and their engagement with new national ideologies that were attached to language. Baron and Shtok wrote in their native language: Yiddish. Baron soon switched to Hebrew, which she learned studying alongside the young boys in her father's school. At the age of thirty-nine, alienated from the Yiddish literary world, Shtok attempted to transform herself into an English-language novelist, publishing her only English-language work, a novel titled *Musicians Only*, in 1927. She did not succeed in making this transition and receded from public literary life. Baron, like many male writers, received a traditional education in Hebrew. After she emigrated to Palestine, she chose Hebrew over Yiddish. Rejecting Yiddish and embracing Hebrew were fraught choices for women differently than for men. In her short fiction, Baron captures the divide between Hebrew-literate daughters and their Yiddish-reading mothers, most memorably in her story "Geniza" ("Burying the Books"). Moreover, in her short story "Ziva," she conceives of the ways women are excluded from the newly forming Hebrew public in Palestine.[22] Both Shtok and Baron perceived the gendered limits of their literary languages, and both suffered as a result.

Bikhovsky, Vogel, and Goldberg adopted their chosen literary languages in late adolescence and early adulthood. Goldberg studied Hebrew after her family returned home to Kaunas from their exile in Russia during World War I. According to her account, her father was a Yiddishist and did not initially realize he had enrolled her in what had become a Hebrew gymnasium.[23] Bikhovsky was born into a non-Jewish, Russian-speaking family of British descent and started her career as a Russian poet. In 1913, at the age of twenty-five, she enrolled in night classes at the Society of Lovers of Hebrew in Moscow.[24] These classes would transform her life, leading her to marry a Jewish Zionist activist and emigrate to Mandatory Palestine. Debora Vogel (Dvoyre Fogel) was raised in a Polish-speaking and Hebraist milieu. She adopted Yiddish during her university years, when her close friend and fellow student Rachel Auerbach encouraged her to embrace the language and engage in intellectual Yiddish circles.[25] For these three women, language choice—and here I truly mean choice—guided their literary works and shaped their lives. Each turned away from the surrounding vernacular and official state languages at a moment when language became a site of great political contestation. Language was linked to the minority and national contexts they found themselves in and at times fought against. Moreover, they chose languages that separated them from their families and childhoods, in their attempts to imagine alternate forms of community.

Alongside language difficulties, they also faced barriers. Despite early recognition, Baron, Shtok, and Vogel encountered obstacles to publishing their writing. Baron's first book-length collection appeared in 1927, when she was forty years old. She was stymied by the decisions of male editors, including her husband, editor in chief of the Hebrew newspaper *Ha-poel ha-tsair* (The young worker), who promised to publish a collection of her stories and then prioritized other writers. After the publication of her collected stories in 1919, Shtok was outraged by the reception of her work and, I suspect, by the arrogance of a male Yiddish literary culture that could not integrate women into its inner circles. She never published another book in Yiddish. Vogel, too, had difficulties finding Yiddish publishing venues for her avant-garde writing, a source of great frustration for her in the 1930s. She could not support herself and her family with her writing, and she became discouraged by the failure of the mainstream Yiddish literary world in Poland to recognize and value her work. Bikhovsky's literary career fell apart after the death of her husband, when she abruptly lost the ability to earn a living from her writing and was ostracized as a gentile foreigner to Hebrew literature. Success or failure for these women depended on the men in their lives and whether they were married, even if they had a room of their own.

These writers also had to confront what one eighteenth-century British writer referred to as the "matrimonial trap"—the expectation that aristocratic and "genteel" women participate in an institution that took away their economic liberty and personal freedom.[26] Marriage shaped women writers' experiences in ways that did not touch their male counterparts. Women shouldered the social demands of motherhood and domestic life, labors that took them away from their literary pursuits. As Christine Delphy reminds us, it is the "labour market itself" that pushes women out of the public sphere, forcing them into unpaid domestic lives as wives and mothers, to deal with the "stream of daily trifles."[27] Their publishing successes, often ephemeral, and their failures could be tied directly to their husband's will. Dvora Baron worked side by side with her husband in editing *Ha-poel ha-tsair*. But he refused to support the publication of her books when he had the resources at his fingertips. Elisheva Bikhovsky's husband, by contrast, built a publishing house to support her writing career. As a result, she was the first woman to publish a collection of poetry in Palestine, and the first to publish a novel there. Bikhovsky granted his non-Jewish wife a form of legitimacy that disappeared with his death. Fradl Shtok's marriage, ending in divorce, did not provide her with a stable home from which her career might flourish. Debora Vogel longed to marry her close friend and intellectual interlocutor, Bruno Schulz, but her parents opposed the match, and she later married an architect. Her intimate friendship with Schulz nurtured both of their literary careers. Vogel, however, was hampered by her life as a married, respectable woman and mother and bemoaned the "domestic trifles" that occupied her time.

How do we calculate the violence of a literary field that circumscribed women's contributions and withheld artistic support? Of these five authors, three withdrew from their literary communities. In 1922, once she and her husband resigned as editors of *Ha-poel ha-tsair*, Baron famously departed public life. She refused to leave home and often her bed. Although she continued to actively participate in literary circles, it was only by permanently retreating to her home that she could produce her work. After the publication of her first book, *Gezamelte dertseylungen* (Collected stories; 1919), Shtok moved away from the Lower East Side and cut her ties with colleagues and editors; she all but disappeared from the Yiddish world. Tragically, Shtok was institutionalized in 1966 and died alone at Rockland State Hospital in 1990. Bikhovsky was a celebrated writer in Hebrew literature, but following her husband's death in 1932 she fell into obscurity, living in dire poverty until her passing in 1949.[28] Whatever her commitments to Hebrew were in the 1920s and 1930s, the death of her husband broke those ties. She was vilified by critics for her simplistic poetry and nonnative Hebrew. She, too, cut ties with the Hebrew literary establishment and, in 1947, requested refugee status from the British government, declaring that she had "positively no vital interest in the life of the Jewish community of Palestine" and explaining that she had "no property or business of any kind, no family or other intimate relations, no regular professional work, and no part whatsoever in the manifold activities of the Jewish population here."[29] Fleeing a literary world that refused to welcome them on their own terms, these women faced grave consequences: mental illness, poverty, and social isolation.

Vogel and Goldberg confronted different challenges, beginning their careers in 1930s Europe under the shadow of fascism. Although Debora Vogel remained active in Polish and Yiddish literary circles in the 1930s, she felt her literary world narrowing. Her writing was too avant-garde for Polish Yiddish publications and too "Jewish" for the socialist publications she had previously relied on, and she was desperate for her work to appear in the New York modernist literary publication *In zikh* (In oneself). Goldberg fled Europe for Palestine, ensuring her safety as the rise of Nazism curtailed her future in Europe. Goldberg also explicitly disavowed an identity as a woman writer, and argued in a 1977 interview that she "never felt a special difficulty pursuing her literary path because she was a woman."[30] Despite these public statements, in her prose she quite explicitly describes the challenges that women faced in becoming writers. Goldberg still waits to be assimilated into Jewish intellectual history as a major scholar and intellectual, as well as a novelist, poet, and playwright. Jewish literary studies must reckon with this history of social violence against women writers, which forced women into public retreat and, in some cases, left them impoverished and alone.

The women writers I study take as their subject the idea of writing and the making of art. They explore these concerns through their female protagonists' erotic desires and aesthetic tastes, distinguishing their writing from male writers' fascination with their male protagonists' erotic and spiritual despair. Many of these women writers' protagonists reject the traditional structures of courtship and marriage by pursuing transgressive relationships with non-Jews. These relationships do not merely serve as a shared thematic but also function as the means through which female authors conceptualize the social role of the modern Jewish author and the political valence of modern Jewish writing. Shtok and Baron describe women in the shtetl who suffered unhappy marriages, burdened by domestic labor. They each embrace the aesthetic as a site of self-transformation for women who lack access to power. Bikhovsky, Goldberg, and Vogel portray women's struggle to become artists in literary worlds that devalue their contributions. All three depict the sexual and artistic politics that abounded in European metropolises, whether Moscow, Berlin, or Lwów. Both Goldberg's and Bikhovsky's novels interrogate the vexed relationship between modern secular Hebrew and a Christian Orientalism. They grapple with the relationship between a Christian Orientalizing instrumentalization of traditional Hebrew sources and a Jewish secular transformation of Hebrew at a moment of rising antisemitism, as Jews were articulated as a distinct Other in the political consciousness across much of Eastern Europe. In doing so, each harnesses the Jewish minority crisis as a potential model for modernist experimentation and for thinking about new forms of minority belonging that resisted the chauvinistic consolidation of national identity.

The authors central to this book embraced prose in a variety of forms: revising Flaubertian narrative techniques, overthrowing the aesthetic hierarchies that govern the relationship of art to life, disarticulating Hebrew and Yiddish from both religious practice and the national project, and envisioning women as makers of modernity. As they engaged with the political fervor of the interwar period that gave rise to forms of nationalism, socialism, and feminism, they produced works of art that self-consciously linked the aesthetic to the political and the domestic. Some offered sharp critiques of territorial ethnonationalism, recognizing the dangers it posed to the future of Jewish life, whether in the guise of Jewish nationalism or European nationalism. Reflecting on the role of the woman writer, they saw that the creation of modern Hebrew and Yiddish literatures was inseparable from the transformation of the gender order, and they understood that women, outside of traditional Jewish textual authority, were in a unique position to develop new ways of reading and writing.

In reading these five women's modernist projects in dialogue, this book destabilizes the idea that Jewish literary modernity was a conversation among men about women, with a few women writers listening in while hiding behind the curtain. When we read women, the grounds of our literary understanding shift, and we can see the political ambitions of their aesthetic projects to break down the boundaries of art and life and to bring about new social possibilities for women. In bringing together the work of these women, I create what I hope is only the beginning of a new cultural narrative that refuses the now all-too-familiar masculinist doxa of modern Jewish life—that for Jews, becoming modern was a project about becoming men. Reading these women writers and their extended reflections on the social, aesthetic, and political dimensions of prose showcases a world of women's intellectual liveliness, of robust historical and political visions, and of literary innovation. These women revolutionized the very terms of Jewish fiction at a pivotal moment in Jewish history, and this book tells their story.

Part 1

Aesthetic Authority

The Role of Women as Artists

Chapter 1

The Disruptive Power of Prose

Though not widely discussed in Jewish literary history, the fact is that Gustave Flaubert served as an important literary authority for Hebrew and Yiddish writers. Censored by French authorities for its improprieties yet hailed by critics as the culmination of novelistic realism, Flaubert's *Madame Bovary* (1856) has long been a touchstone of European literary modernity. Set in provincial France during the first half of the nineteenth century, the novel describes the travails of a young woman married to a provincial medical official. Impelled by the novels she reads, Emma Bovary dreams of a better life, enacting those dreams through her adulterous desires and consumption of goods on credit. Her material and sensual desires lead her to bankruptcy and suicide. With *Madame Bovary*, Flaubert revolutionized the realist novel through his innovative use of free indirect discourse, or what Dorrit Cohen terms "narrated monologue," a technique that allows the narrator to render "a character's thought in his/her own idiom while maintaining the third person reference and the basic tense of narration."[1] It is, according to Frances Ferguson, "the novel's one and only formal contribution to literature," and has come to be a defining feature of modern prose fiction.[2] Free indirect discourse allowed Flaubert to depict the intimate interior world of his protagonists from an ironic distance, blurring the boundary between the author and his creation. Through this narrative portrayal of his novel-reading protagonist, Flaubert also captured the gendered anxieties that arose around the relationship between women and reading beginning in the eighteenth century, when male authorities harbored anxieties about the dangers novel-reading posed to women, who were singled out as the readers most likely to confuse the fictional worlds depicted in novels with their everyday lives.[3]

Jacques Rancière identifies *Madame Bovary* as the apotheosis of aesthetic modernity; the novel emerges from the democratization of art, which made art indiscriminately available to all and all things available to art. Rancière locates aesthetic modernity not with the turn to an antimimetic art but with the emergence of the realist novel, such as Flaubert's, in which the borders between art and life dissolve, when a new literature "blurs the distinction between the realm of poetry and the realm of prosaic life."[4] Flaubert's realist turn divorced language and representation from previous hierarchies of authority: "No more the old hierarchy of ranks, no more the old privilege of the acting word uttered by the master, the priest, or the general, but the new power of a meaning written in the very fabric of 'real things.' "[5] Rancière's insight about the novel's relationship to a new secular authority resonates with the experience of modern Jewish writers, who wrested Hebrew from the hands of religious authorities and transformed the language into a medium of secular literature. It also sheds light on the way Yiddish writers sought to remake themselves as secular authorities on modern Jewish life. In the Jewish case, this revolution can be understood in terms of the secularization of reading and interpretation and the rise of new forms of prose fiction.

In Flaubert's portrayal of Emma's reading practice, male writers identified their own anxieties about women's changing relationship to reading and textual authority, as well as to desire and consumer capitalism. Women writers were drawn to his strong and complex female protagonist, whose inner life distilled larger social forces, even as they critically evaluated Flaubert's mocking of Emma's dreams. As Hebrew and Yiddish prose fiction in the early twentieth century turned to the interior worlds of its protagonists, Flaubert provided a third-person narrative technique for realistically portraying a character's inner world. We can see the influence of his writing in the use of free indirect discourse in works by Dovid Bergelson, S. Y. Agnon, Fradl Shtok, and Dvora Baron, among others.

This turn to Flaubert was part of a radical shift in Jewish literary culture that began in the late nineteenth century as Hebrew and Yiddish writers embraced prose genres, including the novel, the sketch, the short story, and reportage, to produce literature that was divorced from the authority of Jewish law and that could serve an emerging community of readers. Relying on the narrative tools of European realist fiction, including third-person narration, realist techniques of description, representations of psychological interiority, and plot development, authors sought to create a national literary culture on par with other European nations. They also sought to harness the world-making potential of prose toward national ends, as Na'ama Rokem explores in the context of Hebrew and German Jewish prose fiction.[6] This wave of prose fiction was preceded by an ideologically driven satiric prose prevalent in the Haskalah—the Jewish Enlightenment—and by Yiddish *shund* or pulp fiction. Of course popular fiction in Yiddish did not disappear with the arrival of these new forms of prose. The new wave of twentieth-century prose fiction, however, was distinguished by its openness to and deep interest in the everyday world of Jewish experience and by its newly formed reading and writing community, which included both men and women.

The male writers who dominated this movement—S. Y. Abramovitsh, Sholem Aleichem, and I. L. Peretz—imagined themselves in multiple roles: secular rabbis, ethnographers, and social commentators. In a world torn asunder by the breakdown of empires and religious communities and the arrival of new systems of knowledge, they positioned themselves as new social authorities. Women writers also seized upon the potential of prose fiction to disrupt older power structures and endow themselves with new forms of cultural authority. Embracing authorship, women viewed their role as equal to men's in the literary regime, and the male literary establishment instinctively viewed their participation as a threat.[7] Male critics and writers were threatened by women's access to prose, which challenged their newly constituted secular male authority.

Women and Jewish Literary Authority

To understand the significance of women's participation in Jewish literary modernity and the threat it posed to the status quo, we must examine how the breakdown of traditional Jewish practices contributed to a reorganization of Jewish literary and cultural authority, including the rise of secular prose fiction in Jewish languages. This shift in authority can be seen in the changing status of two different gendered frameworks of reading and interpretation: what I call the Talmudic and literary regimes. I use the term "Talmudic regime" to refer to Jewish religious authorities and their interpretations of Jewish law governing daily life, and as shorthand for the vast traditional Jewish library to which Jews turned to understand and interpret their daily lives. The Talmudic regime, dominated by male authority figures and rooted in the interpretation of traditional texts, is sometimes described as the way of the Shas (the six orders of the Mishnah and the Talmud) to capture how "traditional community life in Yiddish-speaking Eastern Europe was organized around the centrality of rabbinic law and lore, codified in the six so-called Orders of the Mishnah, which form the core of the Talmud."[8] By contrast, I use the term "literary regime" to describe the production of literary texts not governed by Jewish law and practices, even if they are still influenced by them. As Jordan Finkin observes, "The sacred literature is both an end in itself and a powerful source of fresh cultural creativity," a source on which the literary relied.[9] While both regimes are invested in representing aspects of everyday life, the Talmudic seeks to govern those practices through Jewish legal doctrine and traditional social norms.

As interpreters of the Talmud, male rabbis and scholars gained social capital through their knowledge, accruing the authority to interpret and regulate Jewish daily life, from the preparation of kosher foods to intimate details concerning women's menstrual cycles or men's nocturnal emissions. Their Talmudic system of representation determined a gender hierarchy that affirmed men's dominance. Meanwhile, women were officially excluded from religious textual knowledge even if they might gain access to it in private.[10] The gendered dimensions of the Talmudic regime were part of what Naomi Seidman calls the "sexual linguistic system" of Eastern European Jewry: this system correlated Hebrew with men and Yiddish (the lower-status vernacular) with women, even though men and women used both languages.[11] The emergence of prose fiction created and addressed new communities of readers, produced new writers, and freed Jewish languages from their traditional religious function to dramatically transform the Jewish linguistic polysystem. By the early twentieth century, Yiddish was no longer considered the domain of women, and Hebrew no longer implied an all-male audience.

The literary regime, unlike the Talmudic regime, marks a mode of writing that invites a man, woman, or anyone to become both writer and reader. It is a representational space where diverse behaviors and desires are allowable and can be made visible. The rise of both Hebrew and Yiddish prose fiction during the Eastern European Haskalah in the mid-nineteenth century introduced new forms of literature that challenged traditional social, cultural, and literary hierarchies, including the all-male organization of textual authority. This secular literature was "preceded by centuries of belletristic writing in Hebrew, first in Spain, then in Italy and Northern Europe" that was primarily poetic and not prose fiction.[12] Most of the earliest practitioners of modern Hebrew and Yiddish literature represented the educated elite of Jewish culture: men who had studied in yeshivas (Jewish academies of learning). In the second half of the nineteenth century, these primarily male writers broke from traditional Jewish practices, sought non-Jewish educations, and began to produce literary fiction in Hebrew and Yiddish. Many were also influenced by the educated women in their lives.[13] They transformed the traditional Jewish library into a resource for a secular and national literary culture. However, they remained embedded in the system of Talmudic interpretations and linguistic divisions even as they disrupted them.

As educated men, they had privileged access to the sources necessary to take up this project, and this access shored up their new secular authority. This project of creating a modern Hebrew and Yiddish literature rested not only on women's inclusion as new readers but also on their exclusion. This was true not only for Hebrew, but also for Yiddish. As Irena Kelpfisz argues, Sholem Aleichem consolidated the patrilineal narrative of Yiddish literature to show "that contemporary Yiddish literature was not a continuation, but a break from its illiterate and women's roots," creating "a male literary dynasty which mirrored the rabbinical scholarly dynasties whose legitimacy and fame were rooted in Hebrew. Just when Yiddish was being championed as an authentic national *mame-loshn* [mother tongue], Sholem Aleichem declared—and everyone agreed—its literature now belonged to the fathers."[14] Klepfisz's keen insights on Yiddish literary history remind us of the until recently unexamined gendered assumptions that organize both these literary histories.

Alongside these men were women writers whose families educated them in traditional Hebrew texts or opened doors to their literary educations in Yiddish and European languages. They too published works in Hebrew and

Yiddish journals in the nineteenth century. Yet these women have been sidelined, leaving the impression that prose of the literary regime was a man's realm. Although women have been written out of mainstream accounts of the Hebrew renaissance, they produced poetry, commentary and even novels. As Tova Cohen observes, women *maskilot* (adherents of Jewish Enlightenment) were not as rare as has been assumed: "Maskilot read Hebrew literature, wrote in Hebrew, considered themselves part of the Haskalah movement, and even had some of their writings published in maskilic Hebrew journals."[15] Women wrote prose fiction in Hebrew and Yiddish in the nineteenth century. Sarah Feige Meinkin Foner (1854–1936), a product of the Haskalah, published the first novel in Hebrew by a woman, *Ahavat yesharim o-hamishpachot hamurdafot* (A righteous love, or The persecuted families) at the age of twenty-six in 1880. Set in Milan during the Napoleonic era, the novel is a love story between Finalia, a highly educated young French woman, and Victor, an Italian Jew. As Wendy Zierler explains, the novel has many flaws: "Its plot is fantastic, its character development sketchy," and it includes "errors in style and grammar" that offended contemporary reviewers.[16] The Hebrew writer and critic David Frischmann wrote a scathing and sexist review, demeaning the novel and women's writing. Yet as Zierler notes, the novel's weaknesses could be found in much Hebrew fiction of the Haskalah. Chava Shapira (1878–1943) published her first Hebrew story collection in 1909, kept one of the first known Hebrew diaries by a woman, and wrote Hebrew literary criticism.[17] Norma Fain Pratt, Irena Klepfisz, and Anita Norich have written about or translated late nineteenth- and early twentieth-century Yiddish women writers.[18] The Yiddish prose writer Yente Serdatzky (1877–1962), born a year earlier than Shapiro, left her family to pursue her career in Warsaw in 1905. She immigrated to the United States in 1907 and published widely, briefly working on the *Forverts* staff until clashing with its editor in the 1920s.[19] Rokhl Brokhes (1880–1945), another early pioneering Yiddish author, published her first story in *Der yud* in 1899 to great acclaim. Hardly any of her work appeared in book form. She is one of the few women writers who did not emigrate from European soil. This first wave of women's literary flourishing was ambivalently received by the male establishment as a sign of the blossoming of a modern national literary community.

By the first decades of the twentieth century, women wrote and published in larger numbers than ever before. Yiddish women writers seized upon this new literary regime as an opening to challenge patriarchal authority. They wrote and published Yiddish prose in the nineteenth century in *Yuntif bletlekh*, *Hoyzfraynd*, *Der yud*, and *Der fraynd*, and in early twentieth-century periodicals such as *Di tsukunft* (The future), *Dos naye land* (The new land), *Forverts* (Forward), *Fraye arbeter shtime* (Free workers' voice), *Der veg* (The way), *Tsushtayer* (Contribution), and *Der idisher kempfer* (The Jewish fighter); and after World War II, in periodicals such as *Di goldene keyt* (The golden chain), *Sovyetish heymland* (Soviet homeland), and Kadia Molodosky's prewar and revived postwar journal *Svive* (Surroundings).[20] In the first decades of the twentieth century, editors of anarchist and socialist papers published the work of women prose writers. As Norma Fain Pratt contends, "Women's literature was both a symbol of modernity and a way of increasing circulation. Women wrote about women, a subject which sold papers."[21] Yente Serdatzky, Rokhl Brokhes, Miriam Karpilove, and Fradl Shtok all published books in the first decades of the twentieth century.[22] At the same time, women writers were marginalized from literary circles, excluded from authoritative roles, and erased from literary history. Their narrative fiction was ignored, assumed to be superficial *shund* (pulp fiction) or not artistic enough to demand attention. Norma Fain Pratt notes that although growing demand in the Yiddish press for short fiction in 1915–16 opened doors for women writers, "most of the literary careers of young woman writers, although received with some initial enthusiasm, really never matured."[23] There are several reasons for the failure of women to thrive in the literary scene: a lack of critical attention, barriers to sustaining an independent living, and economic pressures pushing them toward marriage. Many women writers found themselves isolated from any literary community. This isolation also found expression in their writing. Klepfisz notes that unlike Sholem Aleichem's monologues, which directly address a sympathetic reader, many of the early women writers' stories "simultaneously focus on speech and silence. Rather than monologues, many are soliloquies which do not demand response," and she hypothesizes that this aesthetic isolation was a reflection of these women's lived experience.[24]

Women poets, including Rokhl Korn, Kadia Molodowsky, and Ida Maze, did sustain correspondence and friendships, though these have gone largely unexamined by scholars.[25] Their ability to create and shape community, I suspect, was a product of their public recognition. Korn and Moldowsky, for example, corresponded frequently in the 1960s and 1970s about Korn's contributions to Molodowsky's literary journal *Svive*. In sharp contrast to their prose contemporaries, women poets were part of the larger, if contested, public conversation about Yiddish modernism, and they were recognized by the Yiddish poetic establishment in the early twentieth century and canonized in Ezra Korman's 1928 anthology *Yidishe dikhterins* (Yiddish women poets).[26] Although women were not seen as central to the Yiddish literary tradition, they were recognized as part of the literary present, even if their importance (or lack thereof) was debated. The Yiddish press in the 1910s and 1920s contains many debates about the status of women's poetry, with Aaron Glanz-Leyeles and Melekh Ravitch, for example, expressing their anxieties about women's writing.[27] Kathryn Hellerstein wrote the first literary history of Yiddish women in 2014, and her work grapples with the complicated legacy of a women's poetic literary tradition.[28] As a result of the attention paid to women poets, Yiddish women's poetry has been widely translated and anthologized, such as in well-known collections of Yiddish literature by Irving Howe and Eliezer Greenberg and Joseph Leftwich. Many of the women who appear as poets also wrote prose, much of which has gone untranslated.[29] Poetry was thought to be more appropriate for women, who would restrict themselves to women's concerns, whether love or nature.

Women's near complete absence from histories of Yiddish prose fiction attests to the social and political significance of prose in Yiddish culture and the threat women posed to male writers. In the nineteenth and early twentieth centuries, many male Jewish writers believed that central to the project of creating modern Yiddish literature was the transformation of Yiddish from a language associated with Jewish women to a language of Jewish men. In the premodern period, Yiddish texts were often published with an explicit address to women, even if the intended audience included men. This "legal fiction" provided an alibi for men who did not have the requisite Hebrew literacy.[30] Hebrew textual mastery was a prominent symbol of Jewish masculinity, so to admit to reading in Yiddish instead of Hebrew was a threat to masculine identity. In the modern period, the traditional association of Yiddish literature with a female audience adhered to Yiddish, and the male writers of the modern Yiddish renaissance struggled with the shame of writing in a so-called woman's language. As Naomi Seidman explains, "The 'femininity' of Yiddish was a problem, above all, for men and masculinity,"[31] and had little to do with actual women as readers or writers of the language. These anxieties are encapsulated in I. L. Peretz's speech at the 1908 Czernowitz language conference, where he stated that modern Yiddish literature emerged only when Jewish writers divorced Yiddish from both clericalism (i.e., Hasidism) and women's texts, allowing Yiddish to evolve from a *mameloshn* (mother tongue) to a *shprach* (language).[32] Worries about modern Jewish self-fashioning were bound to the rise of modern Yiddish prose fiction and to the threat that women posed to the male literary establishment.

Male insecurities and fears shaped women's literary and artistic lives. Women's writing would challenge the social norms and gendered divisions of labor that granted men social authority. Many women directly addressed the injustices women faced, whether Dvora Baron depicting domestic violence, Fradl Shtok describing young women longing for education, or Yente Serdatzky and Miriam Karpilove portraying the ways radical political movements in the early twentieth century, under the banner of free love, exploited and abandoned women. Male editors limited women's access to publishing venues, preventing them from sharing their literary ambitions and erasing their contributions from the literary record. Women like Shtok fought against a traditional male model of cultural production that denied women material support and institutional recognition. Women's literary networks were thinner, and women were less likely to be part of formal literary institutions, to write and publish memoirs, or to preserve their records. So many women's careers were cut short before leaving a documentary trail. Scholars often come to these women long after surviving friends and relatives offer personal histories. The absence of women in Yiddish literary history is also a product of these archival silences.[33] What records and documents have survived remain to be pieced together to bring these women's stories to light.

Similarly, the central narratives that shape our understanding of modern Hebrew literary history also obscure women's participation in Hebrew prose fiction. These narratives are based on the biographies of male writers who broke from their fathers' traditions and struggled to remake themselves as writers and intellectuals, often called *talush* (uprooted). Alan Mintz, for example, in his elegant study of Hebrew autobiography, argues that the modern Hebrew novel emerged through the work of male Hebrew writers who embraced "the autobiographical mode" to capture the internal psychic crises they faced as they abandoned their fathers' faith but could find no coherent modern substitution, and were thus left with a profound "intellectual and metaphysical negation" and heightened feelings of alienation and loneliness.[34] Modernist scholars have extended this line of inquiry to look at the journey of male writers, for example, along "the productive axis between the 'house of study' and the *Kaffeehaus*."[35] This biographical axis, though a useful frame for reading men's work, necessarily excludes women, who could not enter the house of study. Men played a key role in the establishment of modern Hebrew prose, but if we rely on their biographies as a critical lens to understand Jewish modernity, then we replicate the exclusion of women from male literary and intellectual circles. What of women whose itineraries went from the domestic comforts of home to the café, never stepping foot in a traditional institution of learning? Moreover, when women do register in this history, they do so as poets whose works were received as "feminine" and domestic; as Miki Gluzman has argued, such stereotypes "of women's writing in general are so prevalent that the ideology underlying their production has very nearly attained invisibility."[36]

Women Hebrew prose writers, with the exception of Dvora Baron, barely register in normative Hebrew literary histories before the 1950s and 1960s. They are visible as poets, as in the cases of Leah Goldberg and Elisheva Bikhovsky, but not as prose writers. Although we have several important works of Hebrew feminist literary criticism, a comprehensive history of women's Hebrew prose contributions has yet to be written. We know that women participated in the Haskalah and the Hebrew renaissance in Europe, in Hebrew culture in Ottoman and Mandatory Palestine, and in nascent Israeli literature. These women include Foner in Europe; Nehama Pukhachewsky and Hemda Ben Yehuda in Mandatory Palestine; and the many *maskilot* who embraced a variety of genres in the nineteenth century, including Miriam Markel Mosessohn.[37] The overarching historical arguments remain unchallenged, and despite a surge of scholarship on Hebrew and Yiddish literary relations, we lack a clear understanding of the role women played, particularly in the realm of prose fiction.[38]

The following two chapters intervene in these lopsided and incomplete accounts of Jewish literary modernity. They illuminate the intersecting literary histories of Hebrew and Yiddish modernism through the lens of women writers who shared a serious literary engagement with Flaubert and embraced the critical potential of prose fiction. In these chapters I track how Fradl Shtok and Dvora Baron seized upon new secular forms of literary authority to produce an important body of prose writing. Baron and Shtok were keenly aware of the gendered dynamics of the literary cultures in which they participated. Their work meditates on the limits that prevented women from becoming artists and how they harnessed the power of prose fiction to challenge those limits by documenting women's aesthetic desires. Each engages in a critical dialogue with the gendered norms of both Hebrew and Yiddish literary history through her prose fiction. Both women understood that prose played a social role in Jewish culture as a site of male literary and cultural authority, and both document and challenge that authority. Baron offers a critique of the gendered norms of labor Zionism, and Shtok asks us to recognize the exploitation of women's artistic voices.

Writing respectively in Yiddish and Hebrew, Shtok and Baron found in realist prose a form whose attention to ordinary life and the social dimensions of subjectivity allowed them to comment on the gendered and communal boundaries that regulated women's lives and to recast the figure of the dreaming, desiring woman as an artist in the making, with her aesthetic engagement a form of labor.

Chapter 2

Fradl Shtok's Aesthetic Desire

In 1907, Fradl Shtok emigrated to New York from Skala, a small town on the eastern border of the Austro-Hungarian Empire.[1] Upon her arrival in New York, she associated with the modernist writers of Di Yunge, publishing her poetry to critical acclaim. Moshe Bassin included eleven of her poems in his authoritative 1917 anthology, *Finf hundert yor yidishe poezye* (Five hundred years of Yiddish poetry).[2] According to the poet and literary critic Avrom-Ber Tabatshnik, Shtok was "the first Yiddish poetess who stood artistically at the same height as the male poets of her era."[3] Turning her pen to prose, Shtok published short fiction in the New York Yiddish newspapers, including *Der tog* (The day) and *Der yidisher kempfer* (The Jewish fighter). In 1919 she published her first and only collection of short stories, *Gezamlte ertseylungen* (Collected stories). At a time when women's prose writing received little critical attention, her work was widely reviewed by prominent critics, including Melekh Ravitch and Aaron Glanz-Leyeles. By the age of thirty-one she had made her mark on the New York Yiddish literary scene and was recognized as a dynamic woman writer with a productive career.

One of the first poets to experiment with the sonnet form in Yiddish, Shtok published sonnet cycles in the Yiddish press. Her poetry explores complex themes of desire and longing and plays with classical forms and imagery. Her wide-ranging corpus of modernist short stories describes the travails of young women experiencing desire, looking for love, and grappling with disabled bodies, sexual violence, and unwanted marriage—all while suffering a patriarchal tyranny that they feel they must resist. Reviews of her work were colored by male critics' prejudices toward women's writing. For example, in his review of her collection, Glanz-Leyeles acknowledged Shtok's promise, praising the stories, even as he lamented that he found the collection as a whole "monotonous." Glanz-Leyeles, like many male critics, did not believe that women's everyday lives could speak to larger questions of human experience. In his 1915 essay "Kultur un di froy" (Culture and women), Glanz-Leyeles famously opined that Yiddish literature required more women to inspire and invigorate the male poet and help him "find his real place, find himself."[4] Apparently Shtok did not live up to this expectation. By 1920 she had all but disappeared from the Yiddish literary scene.

A Portrait of the Artist as a Young Woman

What extinguished this unique voice so abruptly? What drove Shtok to leave the Yiddish literary world and end her career? According to Yiddish literary lore, in 1919, after reading the poet and editor Glanz-Leyeles's review of her collection, she stormed into the offices of *Der tog*, slapped him across the face, and dramatically broke all ties with Yiddish literature. She died sometime in the 1930s.[5] The *Leksikon fun der yidisher literatur* describes her end: "Over time she became melancholic and died in a sanatorium for the mentally ill" (Gevorn mit der tsayt melankholish un geshtorbn in a sanatorie far gaystik-kranke).[6] As early as 1927, Melekh Ravitch observes that Shtok's writing was rapturously received, until one day she disappeared because of "some little incident" in which her "hysteria" won out, proving that she was "more woman than poet."[7]

What prompted Yiddish writers to embrace this legendary story of her breakdown and early death? The premature obituary of the sensitive and beautiful young female artist who cannot survive the difficulties of being a writer reminds us of how the male literary establishment viewed women and linked certain characteristics deemed innately feminine to mental illness. Women were perceived as temperamental, fragile, and threatening to the existing literary establishment, which remained haunted by the feminine associations of Yiddish. Mikhail Krutikov argues that the introduction of female protagonists was an important innovation in early twentieth-century Yiddish modernism."[8] In the hands of Shtok's modernist male contemporaries, however, female characters were more likely to suffer than their male counterparts. "The reactions of women were more spontaneous and ingenious, but also more desperate; they were more likely to choose a deadly revolt, and even risk the ensuing destruction, rather than to work at finding a compromise."[9] Shtok's fate, it would seem, mirrors the narrative trajectory of these female protagonists. Though her life did have a tragic end, perhaps the greatest tragedy is that she was "killed off" long before she died.

News of her death was in fact premature. Shtok did not leave Yiddish behind in 1919, nor did she die in the 1930s. Rather, she continued to write in Yiddish, corresponding with Abraham Cahan and publishing a story in the *Forverts* on November 19, 1942. Shtok's enigmatic life is proof that we do not know enough about Yiddish women writers. Few have substantial archives of their own. Many women writers had short careers, facing insurmountable barriers to publication. Their families and literary communities did not recognize the value of their papers, and poverty, instability, and short careers are not conducive to the preservation of records. Feminist scholars returned to these women writers long after the majority of them passed, and there are few living witnesses to their lives.[10] Shtok's story is one example of the tragic gaps in Jewish literary history.

The narrative of her early death in a sanatorium went uncontested until 2002, when Joachim Neugroschel uncovered a letter Shtok penned to Abraham Cahan, dated October 20, 1942, which included her story "A soykher fun fels" (A fur merchant).[11] Cahan published the story in November of that year; however, no one in the Yiddish literary world appeared to notice that she was alive and writing. Still, the letter to Cahan (see next page) offered some clues to researchers. She signed her name in Yiddish as F. Shtok but included a return address—the Morrison Hotel in Los Angeles—with an Americanized name, Frances Zinn.

Helene Kenvin speculated on JewishGen that Zinn was Fradl's married name and presumed Shtok "had moved from New York to California, married a man named Zinn, and anglicized her name to Frances," eventually dying in California in 1952.[12] Even this appears to be incorrect information.

While lacking a clear picture of Shtok's life as a writer, we can piece together her struggles in the New York literary scene. Relying on official records, I have uncovered a more detailed account of Shtok's life and the challenges she faced in attempting to sustain herself as a writer while battling mental illness. Like many young immigrant women, she lived with relatives in New York: an aunt and uncle. Residing with them in 1915, she listed her profession on the census that year as "newspaper poetry."[13] Despite her rapid rise in Yiddish literary circles and her participation in New York café culture, Shtok was presumably lonely and struggled to find a literary community. As a woman whose literary works were in demand, she could still only locate a place for herself on the margins of Yiddish culture. She was, according to Norma Fain Pratt, "a popular figure in the literary cafés of the Lower East Side frequented by the Jewish intelligentsia."[14] Yiddish writers were habitués of those cafés, including such storied locations as Sholem's Café and Café Europa. These were predominantly male spaces, though the presence of women in certain establishments signaled a café's more radical politics.[15] In general, though, there was a sense that women who "ventured into the café and Jewish politics could not ultimately be part of it."[16] The poets of Di Yunge often referred to themselves as a "new kind of minyan" (an all-male prayer circle), and although there were women writers in that orbit, including Yenta Serdatzky and Shtok, they were never "mentioned socially as one of the group."[17] Pratt argues that not only were women writers excluded from male intellectual and literary circles, but "there was little camaraderie among them, in sharp contrast to the long-term friendships and the intimate groups created by male writers."[18] However, women did form literary friendships, but these tended to be private and are less documented. Men delighted in Shtok's beauty and published her work but never admitted her into their literary circle.

MORRISON HOTEL
TWELVE FORTY SIX SOUTH HOPE STREET
LOS ANGELES, CALIFORNIA

אָקטאָבער 30.

געערטער הער קאַהאַן –

ס'האָבן זיך בײַ מיר אײַנגעזאַמלט אַ פּאָר זאַכן
וועלכע איך וואָלט וועלן איבערגעבן. איך שיק אײַך
אַ דערציילונג. איך האָף אַז זי וועט אײַך געפֿעלן

מיט דרך־ארץ
פ. שטאָק

מײַן אַדרעס:
Frances Zinn
Morrison Hotel
Los Angeles, Cal.

Letter from Fradl Shtok to Abraham Cahan, YIVO Institute. RG 1139, Folder 278.

At the height of her literary career in 1918, a year before the publication of her short-story collection, Shtok married Samuel (Simcha) Zinn.[19] The marriage portended the downfall of her career. Four years later, her naturalization papers list her as divorced and her husband's location as unknown. By 1923, divorced and still writing, she had moved away from family and the Yiddish literary world of the Lower East Side to 502 West 179th Street in Washington Heights. She shared an apartment and literary aspirations with Jennie Bedrick, whom she knew from her childhood in Galicia. When Bedrick witnessed Shtok's naturalization, she stated her profession as stenographer, in contrast to Shtok, who listed herself as a writer. According to Jacob Glatstein, who relied on Bedrick as the main source for his 1965 essay on Shtok, Bedrick published stories in *Fraye arbeter shtime* (Voice of free labor) under the name Sheyndl Bedrick in the 1920s but "took a critical stance toward her own literary career and left the field of Yiddish."[20] She later married, assumed the name Herzog, and worked for Columbia University Press. The two women found some kinship and perhaps literary community in their shared home.

Shtok did not end her literary career in 1919, as many have supposed. She tried her hand as a playwright and sold her play, *Der Amerikaner* (The American), to Maurice Schwartz's theater company, though the play was never performed.[21] In 1927, she published an English-language novel, *Musicians Only*, which the *New York Times* described as "poor art" with "remarkably bad writing," claiming it was only interesting as "an authentic diary."[22] The failure of the novel marks the end of her early writing career. By 1930 she no longer listed her profession as a writer but instead wrote "none."[23] After living with Bedrick, she moved in with her ex-husband on East 8th Street, and then in Brooklyn, where he opened a photo studio.[24] She continued living with him until at least 1940. He eventually remarried and left New York, and the relationship with Shtok presumably came to an end. Shtok's literary ambitions were revived in 1942, when she wrote to Abraham Cahan from Los Angeles with her story "A soykher fun fel." In 1943, according to her application for a social security number, she was living in the Bronx and working for her cousin Louis Stock in the garment industry.[25] By 1966 she was institutionalized at the Rockland State Psychiatric Hospital, where she died in 1990, alone and without any known family.[26]

Her path from writer to garment industry worker went against the grain of Jewish history.[27] Jewish immigrant women typically began their American careers working in the industry, leaving it behind when they married. Initially choosing to be a writer, Shtok bucked Jewish convention for women. She fought to create a literary career for herself, but like many woman writers, including her roommate Jenny Bedrick, she did not succeed in finding a place for herself. Marrying and divorcing, working as a writer in New York, living with roommates and family, she struggled to support herself while grappling with mental illness. Male critics wrote her off as a hysteric who did not have the mental stamina of a true artist, and thus they saw her tragic end as almost predetermined, even as she fought against the odds. Shtok's difficulties were surely amplified by her treatment at the hands of male critics who had trouble accepting women into their circles and who believed that women's pain was a product of their innate hysterical tendencies. These beliefs silenced not only Shtok but countless other women writers, who suffered similar fates and whose stories have never been told. In the past five years, feminist critics have returned to Shtok's poetry and prose to reconsider her place in Yiddish letters.[28]

(Mis)Reading Shtok's Modernist Project

In the 1930s, just as critics envisioned Shtok's obituary, the Yiddish writer and critic Rachel Auerbach posed the critical question of whether Shtok's withdrawal from Yiddish literary circles was the result of the "condition of Yiddish broadly" or of "the conditions under which women writers work."[29] Auerbach was a Yiddish intellectual and writer from the Galicia region of the Habsburg Empire, where Shtok was raised. Auerbach, like her close friend Debora Vogel, received her PhD in interwar Poland, where she was a feminist intellectual and Yiddish cultural activist. A founding editor of the Galician literary journal *Tsushtayer*, she played a leading role in Yiddish letters. In the 1930s she moved to Warsaw, where she published widely in both Polish and Yiddish, and continued to write about women writers. During World War II, she led the soup kitchen in the Warsaw ghetto and documented the hunger and deprivation there before fleeing the ghetto. The remainder of her career was largely devoted to documentation of Jewish life during and before the war, from her home in Israel. In the 1930s, when Auerbach set out to write about Shtok, she did not ask her question naively, well aware of the reception of Yiddish women writers.

By looking at the history of Shtok's reception, we can easily answer Auerbach's question. A telling example is Jacob Glatstein's 1965 essay, "Tsu der biografye fun a dikhterin" (Toward a biography of a poetess), which reads Shtok as a symbol of female crisis. What's especially troubling in Glatstein's biographical study is that he is explicitly not interested in her work or legacy. In fact, to protect her identity and reputation, he employs the pseudonym Anna Tabak. In his own words, she is "a legend," but not, it appears, an artist worthy of analysis or fame.[30] He attributes the information he shares in the essay to Shtok's old friend, Jennie Herzog, née Bedrick. In his account of Shtok's early years—she is orphaned, her father is imprisoned, and she lives with her cold aunt—he argues that her childhood experiences help "partially explain the enraged and zigzag way that she left Yiddish literature."[31] Rather than reading the work, he psychologizes her literary future. What escapes Glatstein's notice is that two promising women (Shtok and Bedrick) from the same town who lived together and shared literary ambitions both embraced authorship and then left it behind. Each fails, whether in anger or not, to succeed in a literary world that did not value their contributions. Examining Shtok and Bedrick together, we can answer Auerbach's question: the conditions under which women wrote limited their ability to flourish artistically. These same conditions also denied them a place in literary history.

The reception of Shtok's work further illuminates the challenges women writers faced in gaining recognition for their artistic achievement and critical acclaim. Although reviews of her collection were not all negative, the failure of male critics to recognize her contributions represents a desire to silence them.[32] Glanz-Leyeles acknowledges her talent even as he condescends to her as a neophyte, declaring that the collection is a monotonous affair. He titles his review "Temperament" and accuses of her being a "temperamental" writer.[33] The single most negative and telling review, however, came from Moshe Olgin, the founder of the communist Yiddish paper *Fray-hayt*. He attacked Shtok's collection for its dispassionate scientific narrative style, accusing Shtok of describing her subjects as through she were observing "microbes in a drop of blood under a microscope."[34] Olgin views Shtok as practicing a form of myopic realism, caught up in scientific detail without any social or historical context: "She blames no one, not the surroundings, not social relations, not the social struggles of the Jews."[35] In Olgin's eyes, Shtok fails to offer a political critique of conditions in the shtetl, because he cannot recognize her feminist critique.

Olgin does not recognize how Shtok deploys free indirect discourse to mediate the porous boundary between women's individual subjectivity and collective social judgment. With this narrative technique, Shtok refuses to pass moral judgment on her characters and resists the normative nature of the social rules that limit women's artistic potential. Olgin's critique of Shtok recalls the criticism leveled against Flaubert for relying heavily on free indirect discourse to move between the perspectives of various characters without passing moral judgment on the adulterous Emma. Shtok's embrace of free indirect discourse challenged traditional forms of authority and imagined new textual arenas that could encompass women's aesthetic experience. Using free indirect discourse, she engaged in a rich intertextual dialogue with Flaubert's *Madame Bovary*, offering a feminist counterpoint to Flaubert's dramatization of Emma's deadly materialism.

Olgin failed to apprehend her modernist style, including her portrayal of the porous boundaries of individual subjectivity, her blurring of art and life, and her intertextual dialogue with other modernist Yiddish writers. Male critics, such as Olgin, demanded that women be compassionate, stick to women's domains, and not attempt to innovate like their male contemporaries. Shtok's modernist style also differed from her male peers: Shtok dared to take women seriously and refused to sacrifice them to the altar of modernity. Critics ultimately ignored Shtok's stylistic innovations, denigrating these elements of her work by refusing to read them in relationship to the modernist projects of her male contemporaries.

In his essay on Gustave Flaubert's novel *Madame Bovary*, Jacques Rancière advances the provocative claim that Flaubert "murders" the protagonist of *Madame Bovary* not because she mistakes literature and life, as many have argued, but because she transgresses the boundaries between them to threaten the authority of her male creator.[36] Emma Bovary must die because she is the dangerous incarnation of a new democratic aesthetics taken to an extreme: by fusing literature and life, and refusing to distinguish between material and aesthetic pleasures, she also refuses to distinguish between the artist and his creation: an adulterous woman from the provinces. A woman like Emma enters into Flaubert's stylized aesthetic only as an example of the wrong way to aestheticize the everyday. Emma refuses to see the aesthetic as a separate realm from the material, for example, purchasing the furniture described in the romantic novels she reads to spark her own passions. If Flaubert's novelistic mantra was to aestheticize everything, Emma's irreverent practice of aestheticization refuses not only the exalted status of art but also that of the artist himself. If there is no difference between art and nonart, then there can be no difference between the artist and his heroine.

Shtok also deployed free indirect discourse, albeit toward ends that differed from Flaubert's. Instead of demonizing the fantasizing woman, Shtok takes seriously her desires, recognizing her potential to become an artist and endowing her with the aesthetic authority to transgress the boundaries between art and life, as well as between Jewish and non-Jewish culture. In her short fiction, she embraces the destabilizing figure of Emma Bovary as a challenge to male literary authority and a model for the female artist. Rather than viewing Emma's desires as dangerous and suicidal, she envisions them as generative. This might explain why male writers were so quick to embrace the untimely account of Shtok's death. Just as Flaubert saw Emma's mode of aestheticization as a threat to the authority of the artist, so too did Yiddish writers see Shtok's irreverent embrace of women's aesthetic desires as a threat to their own authority.

Portrait of the Artist as a Dreaming Woman

In her 1919 story "Friedrich Schiller," Shtok envisions her protagonist Elka as a woman and potential artist destroyed by a world that suffocates her potential. Shtok titles her story after the German poet, playwright, and theorist, whose *On the Aesthetic Education of Man* is one of the central works of eighteenth-century aesthetic theory. In *Aesthetic Education*, Schiller conceptualizes the aesthetic as a state of human development, identifying an aesthetic sensibility common to all, including women, that can be cultivated to produce democratic subjects. Schiller writes, "Follow the path of aesthetics, since it is through beauty that we arrive at freedom."[37] Schiller was a revered figure in Western and Central European Jewish culture, even as the world of European *bildung* he represented was by this point reduced to rubble. His view of the liberatory potential of art inspired young Jewish artists and intellectuals. As Asher Biemann argues, "Schiller was no less revered by the young Jewish rebels than Nietzsche, George, or Bakunin,"[38] and he was influential for Martin Buber and Gershom Scholem.[39]

In the story, Shtok asks what Schiller's cultivation of aesthetic sensibility might look like in the hands of a young Yiddish-speaking woman in the provinces, educated in womanly arts, including declaiming poetry, singing, and producing embroidery, and wonders what freedoms it might afford her. Shtok's story shares Schiller's vision of a democratic aesthetics open to all but takes his aesthetics to an extreme to upend the literary hierarchy of the male philosopher-poet. Elka absorbs the imaginary world of Schiller's poetry and operas, the romantic scenarios, the dramatic settings, and the ardor. She transforms them into a fantasy world that colors her everyday life. The romantic components of his work become the material of her own aesthetic project.

Elka grows up in a rarefied Jewish household with her father and brother. The narrator portrays all three as aristocratic, distinguished from other residents of the town by their perceived intellectual and artistic merit. The opening lines offer a view of Elka from the town's perspective: "'That girl, she's quiet as a dove. She knows all of Schiller by heart.' That's what everyone said about Elka."[40] It is her knowledge of Schiller that sets her apart in the town, marks her as special, and endows her with aesthetic value. If Elka's distinction is in relationship to German literature, her father's distinction is in relationship to his traditional Jewish knowledge: "He was a kind-hearted man, more learned than the rabbi (at least that's what everyone said). He was also vain. It was said he never remarried because no one was good enough" (38). In these contrasting passages we can see distinctly gendered aesthetic hierarchies. Women are valued for their knowledge of European culture and men for their Jewish learning.

Shtok ironizes the family's distinctive learning by attributing it to rumor: "At least that's what everyone said." Is this family merely putting on airs? Does Elka actually know Schiller's corpus? Does her father really know more than the rabbi? The world of the shtetl wields a collective judgment that cannot be corroborated. Moreover, this ironic narration mocks the knowledge that both father and daughter represent. In the world she inhabits, a young woman's intellectual distinction is defined by her ability to perform the work of others rather than her ability to produce original work or engage intellectually with poetry and music.[41]

Shtok employs free indirect discourse to penetrate both her protagonist's thoughts and the social judgments of the community, blurring different subjectivities, individual and collective. For example, she relies on a collective narrative impression to convey the town's view of Elka: "At embroidery class, all of the girls wanted to sit next to Elka. Somehow she held the needle differently than the rest of them. What she embroidered was *aristocratic, proud. Elka had made it.* Wherever she went, pride surrounded her. Anyone who got near her felt it; and what's more, pride suited her. The girls would sing German and Polish songs. But when Elka moistened her lips they all grew quiet" (38). Note the italicized lines that give voice to her classmates' thoughts in a collective form of free indirect discourse. The narrator articulates in plural third person Elka's classmates' collective perception of her skills. This communal view of Elka relieves the narrator of having to pass judgment him/herself and lends itself to narrative irony. There is no objective measure against which to compare Elka. Is she really "aristocratic" in her style, or does she merely stand out in a small village? The tension in the story between the impression of Elka as special and the lack of evidence of her distinction is never resolved. Instead, Shtok highlights the power of language, in the guise of rumor, to regulate women's artistic lives. Throughout her collection, Shtok is interested in this form of collective narration that circulates between the public realm of the shtetl and the interior world of her protagonists, piercing the façade of individual subjectivity and limiting women's vistas.

Elka tries to protect her private desires from the prying eyes of the community whose judgment she fears. The narrator enters her mind to bring her private thoughts to the reader's attention, signaled in the italicized sections. While she publicly performs Schiller, she privately fantasizes about him: "Then she sang one of Schiller's songs. But in her mind Schiller himself was the knight and she the nun who came to him in the valley. She always saw him, Schiller, lying bloodied somewhere in a field as she bent over him, dying with him, quietly . . . No, they got married somewhere off in a church" (38). While her fellow students are privy to her public performance, in her imagination, Elka fantasizes about a romantic relationship with Schiller. In contrast to the rumor about her aristocratic demeanor, we see Elka working through a counternarrative of private desire. Through the fantasy, she becomes an author, writing her and Schiller's romantic ending. The passage ends by repeating: "Dying with him, quietly . . . No, they got married somewhere off in a church." The fantasy is frivolous and absurd, a tragic poetic scene abruptly transformed into a simple church wedding. The repetition throughout the story gently mocks the fantasy that so quickly pivots from death to marital idyll. If the repetition mocks Elka, ironizing her romantic ambition, it is also a site of resistance to social pressures. Unable to escape the social demand for marriage, she tames Schiller into a pliant lover whom she will wed. In her fantasies, she chooses her own mate and marries him outside of Jewish tradition and without censure.

In refusing to murder her heroine, Shtok challenges the tragic end Flaubert scripts for Emma Bovary. Whereas free indirect discourse in *Madame Bovary* establishes an impassible distance between true art and the objects of Emma's aesthetic desire, in Shtok's work, the dreaming woman has the potential to become the artist. Emma's fantasies are often vague and unformed, while Elka, in contrast, concretizes her fantasy by bridging the literary imaginary with her everyday life. To do so, she masters the art of collage. She blends portraits of Schiller and details from his poems and layers them with images from her life. She replaces the poet with the faces and fashions of the few men she and her friend encounter on their walks through town. Among them are an aristocrat, a young man named Zaleski, and a visiting music tutor: "During one of their walks they happened upon the count's young son with his pure face, dressed in green riding clothes, seated on a horse. Elka looked into his eyes and nearly fainted. From then on her Schiller wore the count's green riding clothes and the same pure expression as he bled alone in the field" (39). Notice here how Elka manipulates Schiller like a dress-up doll, changing his clothes and facial expressions. Not only does she transpose the literary into her fantasy, but in a reverse operation, she transposes fantasy into her real life. After each encounter, she envisions her Schiller in the guise of the other men, now dressed in the count's green riding habit, singing Zaleski's love songs, and riding off on the tutor's bike with his rakish cap. He dons the material objects from her everyday world.

Her art of collage and substitution is a democratic practice of leveling social distinction. In the story, Schiller, Zaleski, and the tutor are equivalent, and no distinction can be made among them. Elka blends the poet, the aristocrat, and the Jewish tutor: they are all objects of her desire and indistinguishable from one another. Like Emma Bovary, she merges literature and life, and like Emma, she is as concerned with the material and the erotic as the spiritual. Elka, however, refuses social distinctions, including between Jews and non-Jews, aristocrats and working-class tutors. In doing so, she pushes Schiller's vision of democratic aesthetics beyond what he might have imagined, subordinating him to the force of her desire. In this way, Elka represents the dangerous democratic possibility that extinguishes the difference between literature and life.

Shtok's short story also develops an intertextual dialogue with Dovid Bergelson's *Nokh alemen* (1913; *The End of Everything*), which distills the themes of Flaubert's novel into the milieu of fin de siècle Russian Jewry. Bergelson was a prominent and widely read Yiddish modernist prose writer. A member of the Kiev Group, he moved to Berlin in the 1920s, where he penned impressionist prose fiction that he published in the international Yiddish press in Berlin, New York, and the Soviet Union. He shared Shtok's stylistic debt to Flaubert and her interest in continuing to write about the shtetl from the vantage of a cosmopolitan city.[42] In his novel *Nokh alemen*, Bergelson's heroine, Mirel Hurvitz, is a young woman who refuses to marry. The novel opens with her broken engagement and concludes with her failed marriage to the wealthy businessman Shmulik, whom she divorces after aborting her pregnancy. Mirel does not have any clear aspirations; she doesn't study or pursue any intellectual path. She wants more from life than marriage but has no language to articulate her desire. As in Flaubert's novel, Bergelson's ends with his protagonist's suicide.

Although Shtok's Austro-Hungarian provincial world departs from Bergelson's Russian setting, both writers use the same language to characterize the distinctiveness of their protagonists. Both families have prominent rabbinic pedigrees, both have fallen on difficult economic times in the provinces, and neither can afford a dowry. Thus marriage is proposed as a solution to economic concerns. In contrast to Bergelson's novel, where Mirel travels to live with her husband's family, Arn comes to live with Elka's family. Whereas Mirel wanders freely in Bergelson's novel, a sign of her despair and her privilege, Elka's movements are restricted. She is portrayed as a prisoner without agency and thus a victim of her circumstances. In contrast, Bergelson characterizes Mirel as mired in an ennui she refuses to escape; her troubles are self-inflicted, and she is partly to blame.

Mirel, like Elka, appears special to others, set apart for her elegance and beauty but not distinguished by her intellectual substance. During a party to celebrate her engagement, Bergelson describes how her tired face appears to those present: "To the eye of the stranger she seemed to be no naive girl, but an unusually passionate young wife who'd been living for three or four years with a husband whom she loved to distraction and to whom she unreservedly gave herself with great devotion, that because of this her refined face appeared so weary and pale with exhaustion."[43] On the one hand, Bergelson's description of Mirel recalls Shtok's description of Elka. We see Mirel refracted through the eyes of others. Whereas Bergelson's narrator offers a supposition about the eye of the stranger, Shtok enters into the collective thoughts of the community, and the narrator's judgment is replaced with the community's point of view. Bergelson's narrator purports to know Mirel's true mind, while Shtok's narrator does not. Instead, like Dvora Baron, Shtok boldly plays with the narrative structure of rumor and gossip, challenging the social conventions that underwrite the representation of reality.

In a fascinating scene of reading that gestures to *Madame Bovary*, a despondent, postnuptial Mirel takes to her bed and reads a thick bound book that deals with "women in the middle-ages to more modern times."[44] The scene of reading recalls both Elka's and Emma's literary imagination: "among the medieval castles and the romantic heroines of love poems that filled her book, were Miriam Lyubshitz and her baby, her mother-in-law, Shmulik with his devastated expression, and the little man from out of town."[45] Notice how Mirel blurs the stories from the book and her own life, unable to distinguish among them. In contrast to Mirel's break with reality and her descent into ever greater desperation, Elka's fantasies are rooted in pleasure and joy. If Flaubert allows Emma pleasures from her fantasies, Bergelson removes them, highlighting the bleakness of Mirel's life as she reluctantly agrees to marry to spare her father economic humiliation. Elka and Mirel are sold to the highest bidder. Mirel sees no way out and takes her life. Elka, by contrast, indulges in the creative pleasures of fantasy. Shtok's feminist ending substitutes death and suicide with an imagined marriage in a church.

The social norms of provincial Jewish life also limit Elka's ability to realize her fantasy to become an artist. Elka does not continue her education, does not attend university, nor does she study to be an artist. She stays home to keep house for her widowed father as expected. These gendered demands limit her access to education and her artistic potential. A visiting tutor is invited to town to prepare the mill keeper's sons for their entrance exams; the tutor is described as a bicycle-riding flautist who has the distinction of being able to read sheet music. The narrator describes how Elka and her brother sing traditional Jewish music beautifully, but neither has musical training. When the tutor teaches Elka's brother to read music, he offers a form of artistic literacy denied to Elka.

Instead of studying music, Elka invests her desire in the man who teaches her brother. She blushes when she catches sight of him from afar, "but since she was a quiet, respectable girl, she never saw him up close" (39). Unlike the other men in her fantasies, the count's young son and Zaleski, Elka never exchanges a word with the tutor out of Jewish propriety. This Jewish ethos of modesty means that while Asher learns to read music and becomes a musician, Elka remains at home. She reacts by transforming the music book into a fetishized object that generates her fantasies: "Elka borrowed the book and shut herself in her room, taking in the designs on the cover and the scent of its pages. She went dizzy as the fragrance conjured the teacher before her eyes, walking daintily in his rakish cap, playing his flute. She developed a strong attachment to those sheets of music, staring at them endlessly until her bloody Schiller rose from the field and sped off on a bicycle, with a rakish cap on his head" (40). She cannot read the notes inside the borrowed book; she can only stroke its cover, losing herself in its materiality, a form of aesthetic desire. She elevates the music she cannot read into her own romantic narrative. Elka remains at home to fantasize about music she'll never learn to read while her brother runs off to study the flute in Switzerland. Elka is the stranded female audience for a traveling, male-authored Yiddish culture, a female counterpart to Rokhele in Sholem Aleichem's *Stempenyu* or Shifra in Shtok's story "Komediantn."

Transgressive, Everyday Desires

Elka Judaizes Schiller, indulging in her fantasies on the Sabbath, infusing her Hasidic household, which the narrator describes as a "pious sanctum" (*mokem koydesh*, in the original) with aesthetic pleasure (38). Her family's beautiful cantorial music and Schiller's poetry evoke the same feelings of desire: "That delicate Schiller with his songs and his entourage of young noblemen seemed to suit the quiet Sabbath in the aristocratic house and the proud girl with her freshly washed braid" (39). Elka brings the pleasures she associates with the Christian Schiller into her pious Hasidic household on a holy day of rest. These pleasures suffuse the material objects of her everyday life: "her little box of scented soap, the blue velvet ribbon" (39). These feminine objects are ritual items necessary for her fantasy, propelling her into the aristocratic world of Schiller's poetry.

If the story Judaizes Schiller, it also de-Judaizes Elka. She imagines herself as an aristocratic lady in one of Schiller's poems, or even as Schiller's lover. By marrying Schiller she enters into a Christian, German literary universe. Elka's Sabbath fantasies profane this holy space, as the hymn-singing pious woman dreams on the holiest day of the week of marrying a gentile poet in a church; her fantasy transforms her Hasidic household into an imaginary Christian space, with the Jewish daughter marrying the Christian Schiller inside a church. Her romantic fantasy is also a literary one. Marrying Schiller, she gains entrée into a Christian, German literary universe. He offers her an entrance to European modernity, but it relies on a death remade as marriage.

Playing on the tensions between Jewish and non-Jewish literary culture, the story also reflects on the cosmopolitan readership for these stories and the audience's ambivalence toward Yiddish. Elka is a provincial reader of European literature in German. She contrasts with Shtok's actual readers: metropolitan men and women in urban centers reading literature in the minor language, Yiddish. Shtok's readers could easily look down on a provincial woman who surrenders to her father's marriage demands and, like Emma Bovary, turns her literary predilections into erotic fantasies. Unlike Shtok's audience, Elka is a German-reading woman whose back is turned to Yiddish culture and whose outlook is seemingly "European." For Elka, European literature represents escape and liberation. The story ironizes her European pretensions, at times gently mocking her while granting them a form of creative authority. In this untidy circle of readers, I see ambivalence about European pretensions that are both celebrated and called into question.

Titling her Yiddish story "Friedrich Schiller," Shtok invokes two contrasting worlds, one provincial and Yiddish-speaking, the other cosmopolitan and German. The title points to the distinction between the poet who represents the height of German literary culture and the Jewish vernacular language, with its fraught status in European culture and working-class Yiddish New York. Elka sings Hebrew hymns alongside her brother and father (separated by the walls of her room), recites German poetry, and speaks the Jewish vernacular in her daily life. She breaches the boundaries between the Hebrew hymn and the German poem, between Jew and gentile. If there is no distinction between art and life, then there are no distinctions between sacred and profane texts or, by extension, between Jewish and Christian texts. This breaking of norms and boundaries represents the revolutionary potential of prose—and women, not men, are the boundary crossers.

Elka's fantasies mirror Shtok's narrative strategy of revising and challenging the literary narratives of women's reading and their desires. Will Elka, like so many novel-reading and adulterous women (she only fantasizes of adultery), end her life by her own hand, will horrible sickness intervene, or will her marriage fulfill her romantic fantasies? Elka irreverently produces her own fictions from the remnants of the literary and the everyday, breaking down literary and aesthetic boundaries, which are subordinated to the whims of her desire. Shtok gathers Elka's fictions to transform them into the medium of modernist art. Through collage, repetition, and attention to everyday life, she pushes the boundaries of Yiddish literary norms by portraying aesthetic desires that propel women to new levels of creative imagination. This is the flip side of the democratic project of aesthetic modernity that so terrified Flaubert. The authority of the poet is subordinated to the aesthetic longings of a woman—in this case, a Jewish woman who disrupts the boundaries between Jewish and non-Jewish literary culture, catalyzing a modernist secular revolution.

If mixing registers represents revolutionary potential, then the social norms of marriage represent its opposite. Shtok, like Bergelson and Flaubert, explores the suffocating effects of marriage on her young heroine. She challenges the instrumentalization of marriage plots by male writers, whose female protagonists' lives end after marriage, by envisioning a heroine who accommodates her marriage otherwise. As talk of war circulates in Europe, Jews cross the border in waves, bringing many young Jewish men of marriageable age into town. Elka's relatives press her father to accept a Russian cousin, Arn, as a match for his daughter. Her father dislikes this cousin because he is a boorish youth without Jewish learning and a Zionist. But he acquiesces to the marriage because he cannot afford otherwise. His family reminds him of this: "What d'you think, you're gonna get the Tshortkever Rebbe's grandson? . . . No one's interested in a girl without a dowry"(40). Economic reality deflates the family's aristocratic pretensions. Elka is exchanged like a commodity, sold to the highest bidder. This is the inverse of Flaubert's fascination with materialism. Here it is not the woman whose desires lead her to buy luxuries on credit. Instead, it is the patriarchal family structure that commodifies women and exploits them. Shtok provides a feminist corrective to the demonization of women's desire for commodities: highlighting the ways that marriage as a system transforms women into commodities.

Describing Elka and her father's aristocratic pretensions, Shtok's story also critiques the system of *yiḥus*, a Hebrew and Yiddish term that refers to pedigree or ancestry. In her book *The Marriage Plot*, Naomi Seidman traces the afterlife of *yiḥus* in post-Enlightenment writing, noting its flexibility as a concept that can accommodate both traditional ideas of ancestry and democratic notions of merit. *Yiḥus* is primarily attached to men, however, and is not necessarily achievable by women. As Seidman writes, "For all the differences among these functions and claims, *yihus* should be seen as a relatively unified and coherent social structure and medium of exchange, functioning as a shared currency in which disparate values, classes, and family lines might be converted."[46] It is a system, she argues, that allows money to be converted into learning and vice versa: a system of abstracting and commodifying value on the marriage market. Although the emergence of secular learning opened up a space for women to gain access to intellectual *yiḥus*, Elka's knowledge of Schiller gives her no advantage in the marriage market. Elka is sold to the highest and only bidder, her cousin, because she lacks any dowry. As a daughter, she cannot inherit her father's *yiḥus*. Her value on the marriage market is her dowry, yet due to her father's economic failures, she does not have one. Shtok picks apart the democratic potential of *yiḥus* that Seidman locates in post-maskilic literature, offering a feminist take on its commodification of women.

Elka's father is repulsed by Arn's crass capitalism, which he sees as corrupting the refined and pious atmosphere in the home. Yet such judgment is hypocritical; Arn's trade in livestock is no different from her father's negotiation of the marriage contract. Describing to Elka the great deal he made for a well-bred Tyrolean cow, Arn tells her, "Elsie, it's as fat as you" (41). If Arn's business savvy enables him to trick the Tyrolean cow's owner into selling it cheaply, then what of Elka, an elegant girl from a prestigious family line? Was she also purchased at a good price? Shtok's playful parallel highlights this troubling objectification of women who, like well-bred cattle, are valued for their family line rather than their person. It is hard to not to think of the famous agricultural scene in Flaubert's novel, where Rodolphe's romantic words to Emma are punctuated by a discussion of animals and their manure. In that scene, Flaubert skewers the lack of substance in Emma and Rodolphe's exchange. Shtok uses agricultural figures to a different end, mocking not the bride but the system that devalues her.

The story's conclusion departs from Emma's despair and Flaubert's masculinist vision of aesthetic modernity. Elka's husband approaches his wife while she is lost in an erotic fantasy with Schiller as her lover. At first he misreads the scene: "Arn finally understood that she was longing for him but was too embarrassed to speak up. He sat down next to her, lay his hands on her wig, gave her a little slap on the cheek and whinnied, hee, hee, hee. Then his smooth yellow fingertip slid down her neck and throat" (41). The slap on the cheek and the fingers on her neck are ominous. For a moment he treats her like his recently purchased cow. In disgust, she closes her eyes and cries out, "Friedrich . . . Friedrich . . . Jump down from your horse . . . Don't go . . . Don't go" (41). At first Arn is alarmed by his wife's descent into fantasy. However, she seduces him into the part:

> "Oh . . . Don't stare so brashly!"
> "Who's staring? I'm not staring."
> "Stare!"
> "Now I'm staring." (41)

In this strange scene, her husband agrees to play the role of the German poet, staring on command at his wife, who pretends to be a modest and coy lover. He submits to her fantasy, becoming material for her imagination. The story ends with the same refrain: "Elka closed her eyes again, and there was her Schiller leaning over her shoulders with his pure face, saying farewell, calling her *Liebchen,* and speeding away in his rakish cap. Bloodied. All alone in a field. She quietly died with him . . . No, they got married in a church" (31). Instead of suicide, Elka orchestrates her own erotic fantasy, coaxes her boorish husband to play along, and concludes the fantasy on her own terms: a church wedding.

Shtok offers a second, literary and imaginary ending that displaces Elka's husband and his advances. She rejects the tragic ending that faces so many female Yiddish protagonists by envisioning a gentile Elka who imagines marrying her beloved inside a church. This ending likens Elka's desire to a form of cultural conversion. The story doesn't offer a Jewish ending, and perhaps there is no such thing for a woman who reads gentile literature. Reading Schiller, admiring his portrait, and longing for the various men that surround her, she comes to see herself outside of her everyday context, and in doing so, sees a vista beyond the Jewish marriage plot that confines her. Yet the vista is subsumed into her life as a Jewish woman married to a boorish cattle merchant who whinnies at her like an animal.

If Emma Bovary must die because of the threat she poses to the distinction between art and life and the authority of the male writer, then Elka's survival proposes a different aesthetic practice. Shtok embraces the promise that Elka or Emma might offer to a new organization of literary community that includes women who dream of transforming the aesthetics of everyday life. Shtok acknowledges the very real conditions that structure the aesthetic practices of Jewish women, the reality of marriage, and the limits on education and movement. Shtok's protagonists are oppressed by the social norms of small-town Jewish life that preclude their participation in the world of arts and letters. While her husband attempts to silence her, Shtok allows Elka to speak without fear of death. Shtok embraces European literary culture as the touchstone of her literary project. While one could read this as a form of literary assimilation, whereby a young Jewish woman turns her back on Jewish textual precedents and embraces secular, European cultural norms, Shtok's story enacts a more complex solution to the tension between the universal European literary world and the particular Jewish one. Her protagonists do not fully submit to a European literary regime that also rejected women and subjected them to deadly endings such as Emma's suicide. Elka adapts to her situation by enacting her own erotic fantasies, playing the dominant to her husband as she pretends to submit to him. In this way, she becomes the author of her own desires even as she remains subject to her husband in what is not complete liberation but an opening for women's aesthetic experience.

Desire and the Dangers of Prose in "The Archbishop"

Shtok's story "The Archbishop" foregrounds how prose fiction ignites women's desire and transgresses the social regulation of women's bodies and their sexuality. In this story, Shtok links her protagonist's transgressive desire to a key narrative technique of prose fiction, free indirect discourse, highlighting the disruptive power of discourse that circulates without a mediating authority. Shtok enacts a new way of thinking about reading and desire that moves beyond the now familiar account of the dangers of women's reading. "The Archbishop" dramatizes the power of prose to act in the world, to circulate outside the text, and to wreak havoc on traditional social practices. Yet the story does not imagine these freedoms for its protagonist and ends on a similarly ambiguous melancholic note. Torn between her imagined lover and her parents' desired bridegroom, she can only give mute testimony to the strictures that limit her imagination and the expression and fulfillment of her desire.

Shtok structures the story around two intersecting narratives. The first describes the shtetl's preparations for the arrival of the archbishop, which culminate in a ceremonial encounter between the town's rabbi and the archbishop at the end of the story. The second is a brief meeting between a young Jewish woman, Dvoyre, and a gentile laborer, Lutsyk, which prompts Dvoyre's erotic fantasies. The former is a public event of Jewish-Christian relations mediated by male officials. The latter is a private affair restricted to Dvoyre's inner world. However, Dvoyre's encounter with Lutsyk is catalyzed by preparations for the archbishop's arrival, and its meaning is structured by these preparations. If the public conversation at the story's opening is about the significance of the archbishop's arrival for the town's Jewish residents, the ceremony at the conclusion represents the consummation of Jewish residents' desire in a public ritual that resembles a wedding. This quasi-wedding becomes a mirror image of Dvoyre's secret longing for her gentile laborer.

Shtok's story dramatizes the disruptive force of prose fiction on the authoritative world of Jewish tradition. In his 1948 collection of essays *Qu'est-ce que la littérature?*, Jean Paul Sartre argues that in contrast to the poet, the prose writer is a person who "makes use of words," who understands that words are meant to act.[47] The "committed writer knows that words are action. He knows that to reveal is to change and that one can reveal only by planning to change."[48] Sartre describes prose fiction as a revolutionary, anticolonial project that acts not only in the aesthetic realm but also in the world. For Sartre, it is precisely prose's capacity to represent everyday life that marks its political force. Rancière, building on Sartre's argument, redefines literature's political capacity beyond the transitive use of language that calls for direct political action. Rancière explains that the "historical distinctiveness of literature is not due to a state or specific use of language. It is due to a new balance of the powers of language, to a new way language can act by causing something to be seen or heard."[49] Literature makes these things visible by establishing new systems of literary value. Rancière sees prose fiction's democratic potential in its ability to disrupt the hierarchical distinctions that precede its arrival, to "break with a determined order of relationships between bodies and words, between ways of speaking and ways of doing and ways of being."[50] Literature acts in the world, circulating language and ideas once authorized by institutions like the church, written by men of letters for other men of letters.

What happens to texts when they reach the hands of unauthorized readers, including women? Ewa Ziarek conceptualizes the emergence of a feminist modernist aesthetic that "allows us to examine artistic practice in the context of the politics of capital, race, and gender—which constitute the heteronomous aspect of women's literature—without negotiating its aesthetic specificity—that is, its autonomy."[51] Her approach acknowledges that barriers to women's participation in Jewish literary culture structure their aesthetic practices. Through this feminist aesthetic approach, she illuminates the tensions between the ideals of "democratic freedom" that Rancière and Sartre celebrate and the realities of "imperialist, economic, racial, and gender domination."[52] When we think about prose in the world along Rancière's lines, we cannot ignore that the changing form and meaning of the literary is inseparable from the social forces that produce the literary texts. Shtok highlights the social constraints placed on women seeking to become artists, which do not allow them equal access to democratic freedoms promised by new representational practices. In this story, Shtok forcefully figures a Jewish woman's desire for a non-Jewish man as a disruptive romantic act that threatens the boundaries of Jewish culture while highlighting the limits that prevent Elka from crossing those boundaries.

Shtok also dramatizes the revolutionary potential of prose to incite unregulated and transgressive desires. There are two forms of circulating discourse in the story. The first is the public conversation among the men about the meaning of the new gate being built in town and the archbishop's arrival. The men talk directly to one another, their speech recalling the prose norms of the previous generation of Yiddish writers, from S. Y. Abramovitsh's affable book peddler narrative to Sholem Aleichem's Tevye monologues. Irena Klepfisz argues that "the use of male narrators who had the freedom to travel and observe the world" in the writing of the three patriarchs of Yiddish literature "testified that literature in *mameloshn* [mother tongue] was now rooted in the male domain."[53] The self-reflective storytelling strategies employed by the patriarchs of Yiddish literature relied on the illusion of voice, of conversations among men with women as spectators and objects of discussion. Shtok contrasts these public male voices to her third-person narrator, the very narrator that Moshe Olgin dismissed as a cold-hearted scientist. Shtok employs free indirect discourse to highlight the interpenetration of interiority by a world of social discourse and its effects on women's lives.

"The Archbishop" opens with rumor: "People knew an archbishop was coming to Skala, but they weren't making a big deal about it. It was only after they saw the pine-branch arches being erected for his arrival that they started talking about it in the street."[54] The "collective voice" of the town is voiced by a narrator who tells us what the town thinks. In this story, these rumors are voiced in public by men. There is Motkele, whose brother works in the town hall, Heynikh the matchmaker, Alter the money lender (Dvoyre's father), and Shloyme the "deaf one." These typological male characters of the shtetl engage in a comic exchange that highlights their provincialism. The rumor is that the archbishop's arrival means a new church is being built, which excites the matchmaker because "the town'd be more respectable, more civilized," and the matchmaker knows "how many matches had been nipped in the bud purely because Skale was uncivilized" (31). The matchmaker perceives the arrival of a Christian authority as an aid to Jewish matchmaking that will contribute to the marital value of Jewish brides and grooms in the town. From his male perspective, an authoritative Christian presence does not represent a threat but rather raises the status of the Jews through a sexual dynamic that persists in the story.

The story then pivots from the traditional collective perspective to a modernist appropriation of female subjectivity. Young Dvoyre watches the preparations for the archbishop's visit while standing next to the pharmacy. She spies a young peasant worker whom she recognizes:

> But now Sheyndl had already gone, and Dvoyre was still watching them build the archway. And in point of fact she hadn't even thought about Lutsyk. *So what if Lutsyk appeared on his own. If he appeared on his own, was that her fault? Was it her fault if they were building the archway right by the pharmacy? And if he said "good morning" and tipped his hat to her, was she not supposed to respond?*
>
> "What a shame. So many pine saplings broken," Lutsyk said.
>
> "Yes, a shame."
>
> *Should she not have responded?*
>
> When Lutsyk looked at her, she looked away.
>
> She stood there a minute longer and fled. She felt the whole marketplace could tell she was burning for the gentile. (33)

Note the narrator's use of third person to describe the thoughts circulating in Dvoyre's mind. The ellipses and the repetition of "Was it her fault?" signal that we are in Dvoyre's inner world. The interrogative clauses also heighten the sense that she is under scrutiny. The narrative jumps to the spoken exchange between the two. Lutsyk doffs his hat and says, "Good morning." She does not respond. He wistfully adds, "What a shame. So many pine saplings broken." Dvoyre echoes his words back to him: "Yes, a shame." Lutsyk's casual phrase, "What a shame," materializes her own feelings of shame in the passage. She fears that by acknowledging Lutsyk, she is publicly professing her illicit desire, "She felt the whole marketplace could tell she was burning for this gentile [*sheygets*]." Her private thoughts become in her mind a public shame.

Dvoyre has not made her feelings public. However, the narrator bears her interior thoughts to a reading public. In her essay on the rise of fictionality, Catherine Gallagher discusses how "these modes of access to the inner lives are recognizable signs that an imaginary person is in the making."[55] Citing Ann Banfield and Dorrit Cohen's work on free indirect discourse, she argues that "competent readers understand that the seemingly intimate revelations of the character's depths are also revelations of its textual nature."[56] In reality, no one has such access to another's thoughts, but it is precisely this access that realism relies upon in creating fictional characters. Such access has been theorized in multiple ways, as transparent access to interiority,[57] as a form of surveillance,[58] as a form of "uncounted experience,"[59] and as a means for working through the relationship between the individual and the communal.[60] In Shtok's work, the device amplifies the tension between female subjectivity and collective social pressures. Like Jane Austen, another early innovator of the technique, Shtok is interested in the relationship between individual experience and communal norms. Frances Ferguson shows how Austen uses the technique to highlight the ways individual experience is structured by larger social norms and rules, and how the individual resists those rules: "Individuals can be described as having temporal extension and a traceable history only from the standpoint of the constant comparison of their current situations to a projected communal stance, but individuals would cease to be individuals (would become indistinguishable from one another) if they ever actually coincided with the communal stance."[61] In Shtok's work, there is no delicate balance between individual and community. Instead, free indirect discourse gives voice to darker and more threatening social forms and operates as a site of rupture that creates an opening for transgressive desire to break through. Moreover, in her innovative stories, her characters are acutely aware that their thoughts have been exposed to the community and, by extension, the reader. Shtok locates the source of her protagonist's shame as the narrator's exposure of her private thoughts. It is as though the town's marketplace is equated for Dvoyre with readers who might have purchased Shtok's book in the literary marketplace. Shtok grants her protagonist an unusual measure of literary self-awareness, linking the literary to the actual.

Shtok experiments further in the story, transforming indirect discourse into a free discourse that takes on a life of its own, converting interiority into pure narrative. She dramatizes how prose takes private experience and enters it into the social universe, only to circulate in the world, where it wreaks havoc. As Dvoyre walks away, she hears Lutsyk's words echoing in her mind: "So many pine saplings broken" (33). Separated from his body, his voice looms over Dvoyre: "Everywhere she went Lutsyk's words followed her—over the footpaths, past the sheaves of wheat and rye, off by the mill—and she was ashamed to get undressed in front of his words" (34). Shtok not only separates these words from their speaker as they echo in Dvoyre's thoughts; she also personifies them. They become a ghostly presence following Dvoyre: "They dogged her, burning her shoulders, echoing her footfalls" (34). Dvoyre experiences the disembodied and recorporealized words as a relentless male pursuer whose gaze she cannot escape. She internalizes these words, and they ignite her erotic desire to transgress Jewish sexual and social norms.

As the narrative tracks her thoughts, the boundaries between Dvoyre's thoughts and the words of others, including the narrator, become blurred. A swirl of discourse circulates in her mind, but the words are not attributed to any clear source: "*Wasn't her step beautiful? Graceful? Gazing into her eyes, weren't they beautiful in any mirror? Undo your braid, your long hair, Dvoyre? No, short braids are not beautiful, Dvoyre. Smear creams into them, wash them with yellow wildflowers, then you'll get long braids, long, long . . . And can you sing, Dvoyre? Then sing, but softer, softer, don't screech, that's unbecoming to a Jewish girl. Just a sigh, quietly, hush, to yourself . . .*" (34). These lines oscillate between second and third person. Many sentences are brief commands followed by questions that register uncertainty. Whose uncertainty? Is this the beginning of an erotic fantasy? Are these commands issued by her mother, a lover, both? We do not know. Shtok plays on the uncertainties of this swirling narrated monologue with no clear speaker or addressee. This unregulated circulation of discourse highlights how prose can incite unregulated aesthetic desire as it upends traditional institutions and disrupts the social regulations of Jewish marriage.

As the discourse transforms from speech to narrative, it reaches unintended audiences. Lutsyk's quoted speech to Dvoyre later becomes a line of unquoted narrative: "*So many pine saplings broken*." It is no longer the quoted speech of the gentile laborer, nor part of Dvoyre's interior monologue. The transformation from spoken word to narrative occurs in stages. First, we have the speech from Lutsyk's mouth. The narrator then quotes the lines as they echo in Dvoyre's mind: "Days passed, then weeks, and Dvoyre lived day and night with the words: 'So many pine saplings broken.'" Then the words become embodied: "Everywhere she went Lutsyk's words followed her." Finally, they appear unmoored in the descriptive world of the story, becoming part of the narrative, free discourse without any addressee. This transformation unleashes the potential for prose to take on a power not authorized by the divine or by sanctioned interpreters.

We can see how circulating discourse can also assert new forms of authority in one of the narrative's most perplexing moments, which introduces the threat of conversion and punishment by death:

> *So many pine saplings broken . . .*
>
> The gentile was walking all alone into his village, going home, playing his *drumbe* so beautifully, "Hey, there under the mountain."
>
> Convert to Christianity and die. (34)

No one speaks the line "Convert to Christianity and die." The words do not issue from the peasant but accompany him. This cryptic threat, unattributed to any speaker, is an allusion to Job. In Job 2:9, Job's wife implores her husband to turn against God: "Do you still cling to your innocence? Curse God and die."[62] If Job's wife's words warn of a punishment to come for a crime never committed, in Shtok's story, the punishment is for desire not yet consummated. Desire the gentile, and you will convert and die. Dvoyre's desire for Lutsyk is framed as an act of conversion and cultural betrayal. This is the flip side of circulating discourse, which here allows the community to regulate its borders and impose the threat of death.

The peasant who accompanies these lines appears twice in the story, each time in relation to Lutsyk. Dvoyre first encounters him with a feather in his cap playing his *drumbe*, just after she walks away from her brief exchange with Lutsyk. In this instance, she is drawn to the carefree gentile wandering bard: "She felt a foreignness among the trees, with the gentile who was walking home by himself to his village, but she felt no fear" (33). This "foreignness" doesn't frighten her; rather it mirrors her own estrangement from the Jewish social norms of the shtetl. Violet Lutz reads this whimsical peasant troubadour as a figment of Dvoyre's imagination, "a poeticized memory of Lutsyk" that presents "a counter-idea of identity that seems autonomous, unfettered, and lit by creativity and imagination."[63] In contrast to the peasant's freedom, Dvoyre is a figure of anxiety and unease. The second time the peasant appears, he precedes the story's most cryptic line: "Convert to Christianity and die" (34). Here, unlike the first instance, he is accompanied by fear of conversion, Christianity, and divine punishment. The folk bard represents the radical possibility of rejecting a Jewish match and embracing gentile aesthetic freedoms represented by the peasant's "foreignness" (*fremdkayt*). He also figures the dire consequences of doing so. Should Dvoyre embrace the *sheygets* and his folk rhythms, she can become an artist, but she will also sacrifice herself in the process. Shtok captures the intersections of the revolutionary and melancholic tendencies of modernism described by Ziarek as the condition of women's modernist writing. The woman writer can break free from the constraints that bind her, but the punishment for such rebellion—described here in the language of conversion—is fierce.

Just as Lutsyk's words take on a life of their own, Dvoyre's parents' repeated refrain that she should marry her cousin, Mayer Zisi, also circulate and loom over the story. There is a palpable tension between her parents. Dvoyre's angry mother berates her husband for his laziness and failure to marry off his daughter. The father then addresses his daughter: "And you, child, why don't you want Mayer Zisi, eh? Who are we supposed to talk to, girlie, eh? Who?" (34). The narrator describes how everywhere she goes, people mention Mayer Zisi: "'Mayer Zisi's a good man'; 'Mayer Zisi's a fine man'; 'Mayer Zisi's got quite the Adam's apple and broad shoulders'" (34). These lines form a strange collective monologue, anonymous but voiced. Just as Lutsyk's words circulate in her consciousness, so do her parents' pleading and the townspeople's urgings. However, Dvoyre resists their force, refusing to marry this cousin. Lutsyk and Mayer Zisi are both impossible matches for a young woman who rejects Jewish marital norms but cannot take the risk of transgressing them either.

Shtok frames her protagonist's erotic crisis with the visit of the archbishop to the town, situating her intimate thoughts in the larger context of Jewish-Catholic relations in the Austro-Hungarian Empire. The story connects Dvoyre's romantic woes to broader concerns about the Jewish minority in the empire. The arrival of the archbishop animates her feeling of Jewish belonging, her shared sense of community heightened by a wave of non-Jewish visitors to town. When she feels the presence of the "gentiles" in her "Jewish marketplace," she "felt exactly like someone hosting a bunch of strangers who turn the house all topsy-turvy, guests who bring their unfamiliar things with them and stay for a while" (35). Here, the idea of foreignness returns, but unlike the foreignness she feels while walking with the folksinging peasant, the Catholic visitors appear as strangers, while she is suddenly at home.

Yet despite the clear lines she draws between Jew and non-Jew, the archbishop's procession blurs these boundaries. The Jews watching the procession have difficulty differentiating between the rabbi and the archbishop:

> "Who's coming? Obviously, the archbishop's coming; no, it's the rabbi who's coming, they're going out to greet the archbishop, right there. Stop it, quit your pushing mister—I mean, Alter."
>
> "Who is it, who is it, Reb Motye, can you see him? The archbishop—I mean the rabbi." (35)

As though one could substitute for the other, the observers cannot distinguish between the two men. Both represent religious officialdom. The Jewish sexton arrives, singing the German imperial anthem, which aligns him with the state. There is a blurring of Jew and gentile that mirrors Dvoyre's own desires.

Just as in the opening of the story, Shtok's narrator moves from the public discussion of the men to Dvoyre's internal thoughts, focalizing the remainder of the scene through the eyes of Dvoyre. She watches the rabbi and his retinue walking under a Jewish bridal canopy and the archbishop and his retinue in their capes carrying crucifixes. The rabbi and the archbishop stop before each other: "The Torah opposite Jesus [*Der toyre antkegn yozl*]" (36). Then, in a gesture that astonishes the Jewish crowd gathered, the archbishop bows before the Torah. The male public is titillated by this public performance of respect. Dvoyre sees something else in the encounter: "She watched the old, stooped rabbi as he held the Torah, the Torah in its old velvet mantle embroidered with gold. The velvet and the gold were old and faded but distinguished and respectable like a wealthy old woman with a silk head kerchief, whose nobility and lineage were etched in the wrinkles on her face, in the dust of the velvet folds. 'My girl, why don't you want Mayer Zisi, eh?' " (36–37). Dvoyre sees the Torah through Christian eyes, a symbol of an ancient religion whose authority and importance have passed; an older woman whose reduced circumstances and aristocratic bearing recall her own family's fallen status. What are the words that come out of this older woman, this nearly allegorical figure of Judaism: "My girl, why don't you want Mayer Zisi, eh?" The encounter between the archbishop and the rabbi, with the bridal canopy in tow, signals a marriage of Judaism and Catholicism, a mirror image of Dvoyre's own desire. However, the Torah does not tell her to embrace her gentile lover, but rather mouths her parents' words: "My girl, why don't you want Mayer Zisi, eh?" The old Torah is pitted against the new world of writing that is conjured up in Dvoyre's encounter with Lutsyk and the folksinger in the woods.

What do we make of this strange ending? The rabbi and the archbishop wed, or rather the Torah and the little Jesus statue are joined in some form of matrimony. This official pairing proscribes her desire for the young gentile laborer. Dvoyre is torn between her imagined lover and her parents' desired bridegroom and can only give mute testimony to the strictures that limit her imagination and the expression and fulfillment of her desires. The story ends with Dvoyre fleeing the scene. "And when she ran off home, the words followed her: "How else could it be? The Torah is older, *we* are older" (37). The community's words chase young Dvoyre, as though demanding that she relent and accept the wisdom of the Torah by marrying her cousin. Her secret, mute desire is suppressed.

Shtok's Yiddish Feminist Aesthetic

The ambivalent endings of both "The Archbishop" and "Friedrich Schiller" are a rebuke to the tragic deaths of many female protagonists in modernist European and Yiddish fiction. Shtok's refusal to offer closure is part of her feminist critique of the vision of aesthetic modernity that impels Emma Bovary to her death. Like Flaubert, Shtok sees how prose threatens the distinction between art and life, and for Yiddish writers, between Jews and gentiles, but she does not run scared. Rather it is precisely the challenge this poses to elite male literary culture that represents the liberatory potential of her modernist aesthetic and thus returns us to the problem of her untimely death at the hands of the Yiddish literary establishment. Just as Emma threatens the authority of the male artist, Shtok's work also threatened male literary authority. Whereas Emma remains a figure of female crisis filtered through the lens of her male author, the female artist, Shtok, disappears from Yiddish literary history, dying a tragic death, forgotten and alone.

In her work on feminist aesthetics, Ewa Ziarek complicates masculinist narratives of modernism, which rely almost exclusively on male writers. Focusing on Virginia Woolf and Nella Larsen, she offers a feminist account of modernist aesthetics that is attentive to the imbrication of politics and aesthetics. Ziarek is interested in how political realities impose themselves on aesthetic work and on the artists that produce that work. She returns to early feminist debates about politics and aesthetics to offer a compelling account of aesthetic modernity, highlighting its embeddedness in experiences of political violence that include racism, sexism, and imperialism. Bridging Adorno's work, feminism, and race theory, she argues that literature "is both autonomous and a product of the social division of labor; it both reproduces and departs from capitalist relations of production."[64] Through a dialogue with Adorno, she offers a "feminist reformulation of the heteronomous autonomy of modern literature," arguing that "race and gender, in addition to capitalist modes of production, are crucial, if heteronomous categories of modern aesthetics."[65] Art emerges from these unjust social divisions and can also contest them.

In her reading of Woolf and Larsen, Ziarek identifies a feature of modernist writing that resonates with Shtok's modernist project: a melancholy acceptance of historical conditions marred by patriarchy and a coinciding revolutionary desire to change those conditions. In reading women's modernist works, Ziarek keeps in play two poles of modernist aesthetics, the melancholic and the revolutionary: "The gravitational pull of the unresolved tension between 'dumb' muteness and literary innovation, between women's transformative practice in politics and literature and the devastating impact of sexist and racist violence on women's lives and bodies."[66] Women's writing must grapple with a revolutionary vision that emerges out of a world that derides and rejects women. That is, the revolutionary emerges from the very conditions that silence women; one is not possible without the other.

Shtok's work embodies this feminist aesthetic tension between the revolutionary vision of women's potential as artists and the recognition of the social limits of that potential. Shtok focuses on women's intimate lives as the site of an aesthetic reordering that challenges the patriarchal norms of Jewish and European culture and promises new freedom for women. She envisions women transforming themselves into artists through their attention to the aesthetics of their everyday lives. In doing so, she also offers a different view of Jewish secular modernity that focuses on how women destabilize the textual norms of traditional Jewish practice, and how prose fiction not only desacralizes Jewish textuality but also authorizes women's aesthetic lives. In this, she had much in common with her Hebrew contemporary Dvora Baron, who also experimented with prose to envision women's new social role in the context of Zionist socialism. In the next chapter, we'll see how Baron's extended dialogue with Flaubert, both in her translation of *Madame Bovary* and in her prose fiction, echoes many of the aesthetic and political concerns that arose in Shtok's writing.

Chapter 3

Dvora Baron's Aesthetic Labor

Like her contemporary Fradl Shtok, Dvora Baron celebrated women's potential as artists and sought to depathologize their aesthetic desires. She did so, like Shtok, in a critical dialogue with Flaubert's *Madame Bovary*, which she translated into Hebrew in 1932. Whereas Shtok's prose never gained a foothold in Yiddish literary history, Baron is one of the few women whose works have been incorporated into the canon of pre-state Hebrew literature. Nevertheless, Baron remained apart in literary history, perceived as a woman writing about lost mythical worlds that had disappeared, a female exception to the male literary rule. Critics have overlooked her robust dialogue with Flaubert, through which she meditates on the link between domestic life and the social conditions of aesthetic labor that restrict women's literary production.[1] Moreover, they have ignored her investment in questions of labor and capital that underwrote her feminist and labor Zionist point of view. In juxtaposing Baron's and Shtok's dialogue with Flaubert and their attention to women's artistic practice, I illuminate their shared transnational feminist modernist aesthetic, which situates women's work both within and beyond their local contexts in immigrant New York circles and the labor Zionist milieu in Mandatory Palestine.

Baron turned to prose to engage with the pressing aesthetic and political demands of an emerging Jewish nationalist culture. Yet critics frequently described her prose as poetic, a term that emphasized its lyrical qualities and underplayed her formal experimentation.[2] Baron mastered her own distinct approach to free indirect discourse, representing her characters' inner lives through the intimate, if at times ironized, relationship between her narrators and their protagonists. She transgressed the aesthetic norms of Hebrew prose in the period, writing about women's intimate domestic lives primarily in the Eastern European shtetl rather than the public sphere in Palestine. In the 1930s, when the figure of the sabra, the masculinized Zionist Hebrew man, came to dominate the Hebrew literary scene, Baron continued to write impressionist portraits of women's subjective worlds. Whereas the agricultural laborer—the ideal of labor Zionism in early twentieth-century Palestine—was the typical protagonist in Hebrew literature, she attended to the work of the female artist.

Baron served as the literary editor for *Ha-poel ha-tsair*, the print organ of a political party that embraced the idea of conquering the land through agriculture "and establishing a Jewish society that lived by the sweat of its brow."[3] Yet her work veered from the agricultural realm, as well as from the discourses of masculinity that pervaded that world. She also differed from many early Hebrew women prose writers of the period, whose work shared an investment in the agricultural laborer. Instead, her writing embraced both Zionist and socialist discourses through an ethos of artistic labor and social change rooted in aesthetic work.

Most of Baron's short fiction describes the everyday lives of Jewish women in the small towns of Eastern Europe. She often wrote from the narrative point of view of a rabbi's daughter, offering sympathetic portrayals of the difficult lives of Jewish women. Her stories intersperse the interior worlds of her characters with descriptions of their everyday lives and are rich with allusions to traditional Jewish sources. She wrote not only about shtetl life but also about urban life in Palestine and Jewish exiles in Egypt under Ottoman rule.

In this chapter I examine Baron's masterful 1932 translation of Flaubert's *Madame Bovary* and the critical dialogue she sustained with the novel in her short story "Ḳeṭanot" ("Trifles") as metaliterary reflections on women's aesthetic labor. In these works, Baron shows how the practice of realism in prose fiction enables imagining other ways of life without stoking uncontrollable desires. Her protagonists' subversive longings are concrete desires for beauty. Rather than demonizing these desires, she turns her critical attention to the exploitation of women's labor in the creation of such objects, including the literary object. Baron sees parallels between women's domestic labor and the work of the woman artist, both of which were devalued by the Zionist establishment. She elevates women's domestic labors by portraying that labor in aesthetic terms and transforming it into the subject of her own art.

Locating Aesthetic Labor: Baron's Work in and out of the Modern Hebrew Canon

Dvora Baron's education and early career were shaped by the gender relations of Hebrew and Yiddish. Born in 1887 in Uzda (currently in Belarus), she was allowed to study Hebrew with her father's male students, separated by a partition. She began publishing her short stories in Hebrew in 1902 and in Yiddish in 1904, and was lionized as a Hebrew prodigy. Her career as a writer began as she traveled through several cities in Eastern Europe, seeking to gain a secular education, with her brother as chaperone. The idea of a woman studying alone was perceived as a breach of propriety. As a woman writer, Baron was especially vulnerable to this accusation. The Hebrew writer Moshe Ben Eliezer would break off an engagement with Baron purportedly because he feared that the representation of women's domestic woes in her work meant she was no longer a virgin.

Yet she succeeded in both Russian and Zionist circles. Arriving in Mariempol in 1907, she attended a Russian gymnasium and completed her studies, earning a teaching certificate.[4] She also served as a *madrichat no'ar* (counselor) for Zionist youth and gave private lessons.[5] Like many of her male contemporaries, Baron participated in Hebrew and Yiddish circles. During S. Y. Abramovitsh's 1909 visit to Vilna, he was photographed twice, once with the Yiddish writers and once with the Hebrew writers. Baron was deemed an important enough writer to be photomontaged into the Yiddish photo but not the Hebrew one, signaling that, as a woman, she was on the periphery of the Hebrew project.[6]

By the time she left Europe for Palestine in 1910, Baron had established a literary reputation as a sought-after writer in both the Hebrew and Yiddish press, with a collection of short stories in the works.[7] She also had the well wishes of a literary community that believed in her future.[8] When she arrived in Palestine, instead of working in a labor collective alongside many of her contemporaries, she took up a position at *Ha-poel ha-tsair* (The young worker), the Hebrew newspaper and organ of the Zionist socialist movement of the same name. Shortly thereafter she married the paper's editor in chief, Yosef Aharonovich, editing the literary pages until Ottoman authorities exiled them to Alexandria in 1915. Returning to Palestine in 1919, she continued to work for the newspaper until 1922, when she and her husband abruptly resigned. After 1922, she dedicated herself to her literary career, continuing to write fiction from her self-imposed seclusion. There has been enormous speculation about Baron's decision to seclude herself in her home, much of which plays into stereotypes about the fragility of women writers.[9] Rather than read her seclusion as a symptom of her pathology, I understand it as a consequence of the difficulties she experienced as a woman writer in the public sphere and an act of self-protection.

Baron's aesthetic choices stood out sharply from the socialist and Zionist norms for women, even as she shared their political commitments. To understand her unique cultural position, it is illuminating to compare her trajectory to that of Rachel Katznelson-Shazar, another highly educated literary woman of her generation. Baron and Katznelson-Shazar shared a similar upbringing and education. Born in the Russian Empire within two years of each other, they received secular educations in Russian gymnasiums and shared a passion for European literature. Both emigrated to Palestine before World War I, Katznelson in 1912, Baron in 1910. Despite their affinities for Yiddish, both writers embraced the Zionist rejection of Yiddish once in Palestine. Baron, though widely celebrated as a Yiddish writer in Eastern Europe, never wrote in Yiddish after her emigration, referring famously to her early Hebrew and Yiddish work as *smarṭuṭim* (rags).[10] Katznelson-Shazar, in her 1918 essay "Nedudei lashon" (Language insomnia), argued that Jews should reject the "mother tongue" Yiddish and embrace Hebrew as the language of Jewish revolution.[11] Roni Henig argues that Katznelson-Shazar sought an alternative path for women to enter Hebrew letters that would align with the needs of Hebrew laborers.[12] Her investment in the connection between women's labor and literature echoes Baron's.

In other ways, Baron's and Katznelson-Shazar's paths diverged in Palestine. Whereas Katznelson-Shazar was concerned with women's agricultural labor, Baron focused on women's domestic and aesthetic labors. The difference can be seen most clearly in their publishing projects from the 1930s. Baron published her Hebrew translation of Flaubert's *Madame Bovary* in 1932. Two years earlier, in 1930, Rachel Katznelson-Shazar published *Divre po'alot* (Anthology of woman workers), a collection of accounts of Zionist women pioneers during the second and third aliyah. These narratives describe key moments in the Zionist project of "conquering the land," including the founding of Kibbutz Degania and the collective farm in Sejera. In 1932 she published an expanded volume in Yiddish translation: *Vos arbeterins dertseyln: An erets yisroel bukh*, which appeared shortly thereafter in English translation as *The Plough Woman: Records of the Pioneer Woman of Palestine* (1932).[13] While the women in Katznelson-Shazar's collection dream of a new national life and execute that dream through their hard labor, both agricultural and domestic, Emma Bovary, the protagonist in Baron's translation, dreams of a better life and enacts those dreams through her adulterous desires.

Despite these differences, Katznelson-Shazar embraced Baron's writing as compatible with her own feminist and labor Zionist project. In her view, Baron was a literary conduit bringing Jewish values from the world of tradition to the national project. She writes in her 1934 review of Baron's collection *Ḳeṭanot* ("Trifles") that Baron's stories are "rooted in the thousands of thin filaments of the land of the past," and that there is nothing in them "borrowed from non-Hebrew sources."[14] Katznelson-Shazar, who was well educated in European literature, willfully ignores the European literary influences on Baron's work. Instead, she focuses on Baron's masterful and abundant of use of rabbinic and traditional sources as a means to celebrate the ways Baron's project also hews to a labor Zionist vision of the work of the Hebrew artist.[15]

Early twentieth-century Hebrew critics wrote about Baron's work in predictably biographical and psychological terms.[16] Critics recognized her artistic mastery but located her prose outside Hebrew literary history, referencing timeless mythic qualities that Dan Miron contends are more like lyric poetry than prose. "Reading Baron's stories has reminded many of the experience of reading a collection of lyric poetry," writes Miron.[17] Describing her work in this way, he minimizes her connection to the central figures of the Hebrew revival who wrote prose fiction set in the Eastern European shtetl, locating her outside the literary norm. As Wendy Zierler argues, the tendency to read her as a poet gestures not only toward her "concise, resonant style" but also to her gender, working "to downplay the element of currency, invention, and narrative ambition in Baron's work" as well as, I argue, sidestepping her choice to write prose.[18]

More recently, Sheila Jelen and Shachar Pinsker, by contrast, have integrated Baron's work into broader accounts of Hebrew literary history.[19] Arguing that Baron's writing is central to the modern Hebrew renaissance, Jelen focuses on how she both adhered to and transgressed those stylistic norms.[20] Pinsker, in contrast, reads Baron's work through a European modernist lens, describing her as "the only woman who was part of the male-dominant Hebrew modernist fiction."[21] Wendy Zierler and Orion Zakai offer feminist readings of Baron in the context of Hebrew women's writing, and both theorize her relationship to Zionism, though they take different approaches.[22] I read Baron's prose work both in the context of Hebrew nationalism and in the comparative context of a transnational modernist feminist aesthetic that she shared with Shtok and other Hebrew and Yiddish women writers.

Baron's investment in aesthetic labor distinguished her not only from her female contemporaries but also from male writers of her generation who describe Jewish men's sexual anxieties and their failure to achieve the masculine dreams they romanticize. For example, Yosef Chaim Brenner, the most prominent Hebrew writer to emigrate to pre-state Palestine during the second aliyah, between 1904 and 1914, narrates his protagonists' failure to achieve the masculine ideals of labor Zionism. Arriving in Palestine only a year earlier than Baron, his first stop was in Hadera, where he tried his hand at agricultural labor. Less than a month later he would leave in shame at his failure in the fields and take up an editorial position at *Ha-poel ha-tsair* alongside Baron.[23] Brenner's Hebrew prose described the ruptured dreams and failures of the Jewish men who traveled to Ottoman Palestine with the hopes of becoming Hebrew laborers, only to discover the impossibility of the task. His fragmented texts, which contain excerpts of fictional diaries, letters, and other documents, portray a fractured reality of male breakdown and failure. Baron's writing refigures the aesthetics of masculine anxiety that dominate the hegemonic understanding of Hebrew modernity. Unlike work by her male and female Zionist contemporaries, Baron's prose turned away from the struggles of agricultural labor and the public space of work to examine two private realms: the domestic and the artistic. In this she shared an aesthetic affinity with S. Y. Agnon (1888–1970), the Nobel prize–winning Hebrew modernist writer, with whom Baron sustained a rich literary dialogue.[24]

She achieved this in a cultural field that devalued women's labor. Despite the recognition her work received, Baron's first book-length collection appeared in 1927, when she was forty years old. This was a remarkable delay for such an author, beloved by the age of fifteen. She was stymied by the decisions of male editors, including her husband. Twice he promised to publish her collection and then failed to follow through. In the first instance, according to Nurith Govrin's account, he raised the needed funds for the endeavor but decided to use the money for "public good," writing to Brenner in 1911 that "he received the credit but used it to publish 'ha-aretz ṿeha-'avodah [Land and Labor].' "[25] Again in 1914 he raised money to publish a series of works of literary fiction but decided not to begin with Baron's book, as originally agreed. The series ended after the first book appeared, due to financial crises catalyzed by World War I. There were other failures, including rejections by European publishers. Baron's reflections on aesthetic labor are part and parcel of her own challenges as a writer in a milieu dominated by male editors and critics, who were the gatekeepers of the literary field. These were challenges she shared with Jewish women writers in both Hebrew and Yiddish.

A Worked and Working Translation: The Aesthetic Labor of Emma Bovary

Baron, like many Hebrew writers, translated widely, including works by Anton Chekhov, Jack London, and Alfred Daudet. However, her greatest legacy is the Flaubert translation that also shaped her own writing. Translating *Madame Bovary* was part of a larger cultural project to reanimate Hebrew as a Jewish national language. When Avraham Stybel founded his press in 1917 in Moscow, the same press that would later publish Baron's translation, he focused on translating European masterworks into Hebrew. In his words, "Hebrew had to prove itself worthy of entry onto the world's cultural stage by demonstrating its ability to express the ideas found in the world's 'great books.' "[26] The project of Hebrew translation in the early twentieth century was bound up with creating a new Hebrew literature. In the first decades of the twentieth century in pre-state Palestine, "translated literature was initially accorded a central status in the crystallization of original Hebrew culture, and was used to fill some of the missing functions of original literature."[27] This is what Venuti terms "translation nationalism" to describe how nationalist movements "enlist translation in the development of national languages and cultures."[28] By the late 1920s advocates of Hebrew translation began to see the project as a competitive threat to original Hebrew literature that aligned with Zionism.[29] Producing native Hebrew literature became a new national priority. It is within this shifiting context that Baron published her translation.

Baron's translation remained the definitive Hebrew version of *Madame Bovary* until the appearance of Irit Arkavi's 1991 version. An exchange between Shlomo Tsemach, who reviewed the translation for *Moznayim*, and Baron hints at tensions simmering beneath the surface of Hebrew literary culture of the period. In his critique of the translation he focused solely on

Baron's fidelity to the text. He praises the translation but challenges Baron's stamina and linguistic credentials, accusing her of taking too many liberties with the original, not from lack of skill but from "exertion and exhaustion" with the task at hand.[30] Tsemach considers translation as a form of work more suited to men. His essay echoes the sexual metaphors that historically dominate translation studies, figuring translator and translation as women unfaithful to the original male-authored text.[31] In attacking her faithfulness, Tsemach impugns her fidelity to Hebrew. Having studied agriculture in France, he viewed himself as an expert on the language and condescendingly wrote, "I know that Devorah Baron has the power to give us an improved translation of Bovary."[32]

The review infuriated Baron, and her anger is on display in line-by-line responses to Tsemach's nitpicking criticisms, which she detailed in a letter to the editor. This letter is her only published work of literary commentary, making it all the more striking. Tsemach contended that Baron mistranslated the French *potasse de lessive* as "ash water" (*me-'afar*), and should have written "potash laundry water" (*me ashlag ha-kevisah*). Baron responds, "Lessive, however, Mr. Tsemach, is ash water (*Lauge* in German), if you look at Larousse it says 'mayim me'ushlagim,' which means hot water mixed with ash and therefore there is no need for *ashlag*."[33] Baron's outrage at Tsemach's challenge to her linguistic authority is palpable in the exchange. At the very moment when Hebrew had yet to standardize these terms, Tsemach was vying for linguistic authority over the language and the female translator. Baron's actual translation practices, however, show a writer grappling with the very idea of fidelity. She performed translation as a critical practice of intertextual mediation, negotiating a range of historical, social, and artistic frames. Tsemach misses the many substantive and subtle ways in which Baron transforms Flaubert's novel because he is overly focused on her prowess as a translator and her willingness to be "faithful" to Flaubert.

Baron's translation reworks the novel for her own aesthetic and political project.[34] She elevates Emma into a woman who understands the distinction between reality and fantasy, even as she seeks to escape her reality through her fantasies. She redeems Emma from Flaubert's contempt, endowing her with greater intellectual abilities. In doing so she also theorizes the role of the female author. Similar to Shtok, Baron conceives of women's reading as a creative practice that turns the reader into an artist in her own right.

Whereas critics have read Flaubert's novel and Emma's downfall as expressions of her confusion between literature and life, Baron revises this relationship in her translation during key scenes of reading. In one passage of the novel we learn about Emma's novelistic reading practices: "Elle étudia dans Eugène Sue, des descriptions d'ameublement; elle lut dans Balzac et Georges Sand, y cherchant des assouvissements imaginaires pour ses convoitises personelles"[35] (In Eugène Sue she studied descriptions of furniture; she read Balzac and Georges Sand seeking in them imaginary satisfactions for her own desires).[36] In the Hebrew, Baron makes important modifications to the text:

> בכתבי איז'ן סי למדה לדעת את אופן סדור הרהיטים בבתים; היא קראה גם את באלזאק ואת ז'ורז' סאנד, בבקשה למצוא, לפחות בדמיון, איזה סיפוק לתשוקותיה.[37]

> In Eugene Sue's works she learned how to arrange furniture in one's home; she read Balzac and Georges Sand, wanting to find, at least in the imagination, some satisfaction for her desires.[38]

In Flaubert's rendition, Emma is seeking "imaginary satisfactions" (*assouvissements imaginaires*), even if she is not aware they are imaginary. In Baron's translation, Emma knows that she can be satisfied "only in the imagination" (*lefaḥot be-dimyon*), rather than through the material reality that surrounds her. She understands the imagination as a realm that Emma can access to satisfy her longings. Baron's Emma cannot possess the object of her desires, and yet she desires them anyway through her encounter with art. Jacques Rancière has argued that Emma embodies for Flaubert the wrong, "nonartistic" way of handling the relationship of art to life, one that spills over from the book and is "practically minded."[39] According to Rancière, "she wants to give a concrete figure to the sensations and the images. She wants to solidify them, to incarnate them in real objects and persons."[40] In effect, she wants to transform them into commodities, though Rancière does not use that term. According to Emily Apter, Flaubert writes "his way through the art of the detail into what would become Karl Marx's theory of commodity fetishism."[41] In effect, Flaubert dramatizes the commodity fetish through his practice of description. Both readings highlight Flaubert's vexed relationship to the object of both his narrative fascination and his revulsion.

Perhaps most of all, Flaubert's work ambivalently describes the machinations of capitalism as they express themselves through Emma's materialist consumption and the catastrophe that ensues from her bankruptcy. *Madame Bovary*'s convincing depiction of the circulation of capital and its deranged effects on Flaubert's protagonist appealed to female socialist thinkers. Eleanor Marx, the novel's English translator and Karl Marx's daughter, completed her English translation in 1885–86, during the period when she put on the first performance of Ibsen's *A Doll's House* in London, revised a history of the Paris Commune, and completed and published one of the most important documents of socialist feminism: "The Woman Question: From a Socialist Point of View."[42] In her essay on Marx's translation, Apter has artfully shown how Marx's English translation reflected her socialist and feminist commitments. She was "a complex figure who gained renown as a writer, an activist for anarchist and socialist causes, an anthropologist of the Yiddish language in the slums of London's East End, and a feminist."[43] Marx wrote about her translation practice in ways that paint "a portrait of the translator as literary worker, drawing on workmanly aesthetic statutes."[44] Marx, according to Apter, theorizes translation as "a kind of 'worked' textuality that stood outside the proprietary bounds of authorship; de-owned, if you will, the translation represented a 'free' form of intellectual property."[45] In a further elaboration of Marx's labor theory of translation, Apter concludes that "the work becomes something on the order of what I would call *l'œuvre œuvrée*, the worked and working text. No longer a stable object owned by a single author, it emerges as a site of translational or editorial labor."[46] Apter's description of Marx's translation captures the spirit of aesthetic labor I locate in Baron's work and in her translation of the novel. The "*œuvre œuvrée*" describes both Baron's translation and her vision of aesthetic labor as a working over of women's trifles.

Thus, whereas Flaubert demonizes Emma's relationship to mass-produced luxury items, Baron neutralizes Flaubert's contempt, conceiving of women's relationship to commodities differently. Baron opens up a space for a form of women's aesthetic experience that can be made possible by new forms of art driven by their aesthetic desires. In "Ḳeṭanot," she describes women's aesthetic labor as harnessing this desire to endow material objects with aesthetic value. The writer's task is to transform that process into the substance of art. Flaubert dramatizes how reading prompts a desire to inhabit the world of another, driving fashion and unchecked material consumption. Baron, however, envisions women's reading and their relationship to material objects as the basis for aesthetic possibility.

There is a tradition of feminist readings of *Madame Bovary* that consider Emma as an artist. Naomi Schor argues that Flaubert portrays Emma's coming of age as an author, but in a world where woman's artistic production is censured and "the apprenticeship of heroine-artist can only lead to death."[47] Ashley Hope Pérez characterizes the novel as "a portrait of female artistic failure."[48] She argues that the novel pits the male author against his inferior protagonist and that "the novel's thematic treatment of sentimental narratives—specifically as a force that destroys originality and artistic potential—is one of Flaubert's strategies for ridiculing the inferior literary company pursued by women, as exemplified by Emma."[49] In the 2006 afterword to *Flaubert: The Uses of Uncertainty*, Jonathan Culler offers a feminist avenue for rethinking Flaubert's work, noting that "the argument is clear: futility is a real value when taken as what Emma truly and essentially is, apart from circumstances, apart from action—her nature. In order for *Madame Bovary* to be that supreme formal achievement, *un livre sur rien*, Emma must be *rien*."[50] What these critics all share is the sense that Flaubert's novel pivots on the derision and annihilation of women's artistic pretensions.

In her translation and literary work, Baron takes seriously women's aesthetic labor under conditions of subjection that limit women. Her translation of *Madame Bovary* transforms Emma's acts of reading and imagination into aesthetic practices. Arza Tir Apelroit reads the translation as feminist pedagogy, describing Baron's translation as a "cure" for Flaubert's misogyny.[51] In her view, Baron's translation sought to teach women that they "should not receive myths and books as they are," and instead that "they must learn from them wisely, take from them what's worthy for their development, in order not to stop longing for a different life, without fear and worry, and to continue to study and feel things truly."[52] I read the translation not as pedagogy but as defining the work of the woman writer. Baron reworks Emma as a woman aware of the limits placed on her: she knows that her attempts at escape are in vain, but she pursues her desire for personal and aesthetic redemption to her death. Baron grants Emma's desires legitimacy by grounding them in specific acts of concrete longing. To achieve this, she removes the language of vagueness, fatigue, and confusion that swirls around Emma in the French. When, for example, Emma and Léon return from a platonic walk early in their friendship, Flaubert describes them both as unable to articulate their desires:

> Leurs yeux pourtant étaient plein d'une causerie plus sérieuse, et tandis qu'ils s'efforçaient à trouver des phrases banales, ils sentaient une même langueur les envahir tous les deux. C'était comme une murmure de l'âme, profond, continu, qui dominait celui des voix.[53]

> Yet their eyes were full of more serious speech, and while they forced themselves to find trivial phrases, they felt the same languor stealing over them both; it was like the deep, continuous murmur of the soul, dominating that of their voices.[54]

In the passage, their eyes signal serious thought they cannot express. They experience a shared languor, described as an exteriorized force that invades their words and limits their ability to act; they are drugged by feelings that are not clearly their own. In her translation, Baron removes the invading languor from the scene:

> ומבטיהם דובבו אחרת. ובעוד אשר בלשונם גמגמו ובקשו מלים של מה בכך, מלאה כמיהה אחת גדולה את נפשות שניהם. בת קול-הלב היתה זו, המית-נפש עמוקה ומתמידה, שהחרישה כל קול של דובר.[55]

> Their glances spoke otherwise. While their tongues stuttered and sought trivial words, their two souls were filled with one great longing. The echo of their hearts was the deep continuous murmur of the soul that drowned out every other voice.

In the Hebrew passage, Emma responds to Léon's desire for her. Overwhelmed by their longing for each other, they fail to speak. However, gone is the invading languor that appears throughout the novel to smother Emma's desires, her ability to act or to realize her longings. Baron uses the term *bat-ḳol* for "echo," which in the Talmud has a mystical resonance and can refer to a divine voice from the heavens. This divine voice is secularized as an expression of their desire for each other. Baron's *bat-ḳol* is an inner voice, a form of intersubjective communication that recalls Virginia Woolf's narrative technique in *Mrs. Dalloway*.[56] In this passage, Baron also departs from Flaubert's ironic formulations of Emma's lack of self-awareness, in which, as Rainer Warning has argued, "the character's thoughts are progressively distanced from her capacity to articulate them," and thus can be read ironically, as mocking Emma for what she cannot think, feel, and express.[57] In Baron's translations, Emma's and Léon's thoughts and feelings come from within. Baron grants Emma more substantive interiority and more control of expression. She tries to articulate her very real desire with her eyes, even as she mumbles her words. There is a gap between her thoughts and words, but it can be read as a lover's awkwardness rather than an encounter that lacks substance and meaning.

We can see this repeated in part 2, when Léon departs for Rouen before their affair is consummated. The French describes Emma's experience of loss as a vague confusion: "Une atmosphere noire qui flottait confusément sur l'extérieur des choses"[58] (Everything seemed shrouded in an atmosphere of bleakness that hung darkly over the outward aspect of things).[59] The confusion is Emma's and is externalized as part of the atmosphere. In Hebrew, Baron removes these lines. Instead the narrator explains:

יום המחרת היה יום אבל לאֶמה. הכל נראה לה כמעולף בערפל כה.[60]

> The next day was a day of mourning for Emma. Everything appeared to her to be surrounded in a dark fog.

Baron excises the confusion that swirls on the surface of things. Instead, she chooses a more apt expression of grief at the loss of a beloved. In the rest of the passage, Flaubert describes Emma's feeling as a dream and characterizes her desire in terms of weakness and exhaustion, "la lassitude":

> C'était cette rêverie que l'on a sur ce qui ne reviendra plus, la lassitude qui vous prend après chacque fait accompli, cette douleur enfin que vous apporte l'interruption de tout movement accoutumé, la cessation brusque d'une vibration prolongée.[61]

> Her reverie was that of things gone forever, the exhaustion that seizes you after everything is done; the pain, in short, caused by the interruption of a familiar motion, the sudden halting of a long drawn out vibration.[62]

Baron subverts this narrative in her Hebrew translation:

> הנהיה אחרי האבידה שאינה חוזרת היתה זאת, דאבון–הנפש, התוקף אותך עם כל סוף
> וגמר, הכאב, הבא בהפסק פתאום איזו תנודה נפש שהסכנת עמה–רטט מתמיד וממושך.[63]

She removes Flaubert's language of reverie and elevates the emotion, replacing the French *lassitude* with the Hebrew *da'avon ha-nefesh*, a term that appears in in Deuteronomy 28:65 as one of God's many punishments. *Da'avon nefesh* is usually translated as "lassitude," but in modern Hebrew, *da'avon* also means great sadness. Baron transforms the biblical punishment into the language of modern psychology to deepen its resonance. Baron transforms Flaubert's ironic narration of his heroine's feeling of loss into Emma's legitimate experience of pain and loss. That the object of her desire might be absurd—Léon is no great hero—is evident. But Emma still lays claim to an internal world that contains the depths of her experience. We can read her desire for Léon as a form of escape into the imagination, rather than her confusion that he might be a heroic man worthy of such desires. Emma's interior world arises in response to her encounters with fantasies sparked by reading novels and magazines. Her reading catalyzes her attempts to endow the everyday with aesthetic value, mirroring the form of aesthetic labor that Baron celebrates in her short story "Ḳeṭanot," and more broadly in her later work.

Emma Bovary in the Shtetl: Aesthetic Longing and the Trifle

In "Ḳeṭanot," Baron links women's artistic and domestic labors to the conditions of production for the objects of women's desire. "Ḳeṭanot" details the travails of a young rabbi's wife in the small town of Khimlovka. The narrator is the rabbi's wife's niece, who visits regularly in the summers from the larger town of Zhuzhikova and whose mother is described as "city-born."[64] The rabbi's wife lives with her ailing husband and domineering mother-in-law. The mother-in-law arranged the match to acquire funds to secure her sickly son a rabbinical post. She looks down on the daughter-in-law and her family for lacking religious observance and social status. The daughter-in-law views her marriage as a death sentence, her happy girlhood supplanted by her mother-in-law's brutal domestic regime. The story focuses on the rabbi's wife's travails, as well as those of Sarah Elka, an abused wife and mother of twelve daughters. Her oldest daughter, Hannah Gittel, is sent to the provincial capital to enter domestic service to support her family. There she is accused of stealing from her employer's household, arrested, and put on trial. The narrator's aunt is called to the city to testify, and her testimony exonerates Hannah Gittel. Once the trial is over, the rabbi's wife purchases a pair of embroidered slippers that she once admired in her sister-in-law's trousseau, and the story ends with her wonderment at these mass-produced objects.

Baron weaves three intricate layers into a tightly layered fabric that highlights the complex valences of what I am calling aesthetic labor to describe women's longing for material objects that they invest with aesthetic value and transform into works of art. In the first layer, the narrator describes her regular summer visits to her aunt's village home and her relationship to those memories in occasionally mournful tones. In the second layer, the narrator recounts her aunt's suffering and longing for a pair of slippers that she eyes in her sister-in-law's house. The narrator's account of her aunt yields a third narrative layer: the story of Sarah Elka—the cobbler's wife—and her daughter Hannah Gittel. Tension between the provincial women and the more sophisticated narrator, as well as a class divide between the rabbi's status as a respected authority and the working-class cobbler, run through all the layers. Moreover, these three layers—the narrator's act of remembrance and feelings of loss about the world she describes, the rabbi's wife's desire for the beautiful objects in her sister-in-law's trousseau, and the trials of the cobbler's family—mediate the relationships between women, desire, and aesthetic experience. The women desire female trifles and city delights, and they endow these longings with aesthetic force. The narrator transforms the women's relationships to these objects into the material of her art.

There are many similarities between Baron's story and Flaubert's novel. Both describe marriage plots that go awry in the provinces; in both the women long for the city. In Flaubert's novel, Emma goes for trysts with Léon in Rouen, where Monsieur Lheureux obtains the goods that he sells her on credit. For Emma, Rouen is a site of erotic discovery. For the rabbi's wife, the provincial capital represents wonder and imagination, with its modern street lamps, public parks, and shops. Both works center on unhappy marriages that include a demanding mother-in-law and fallen social status. Emma's marriage to the provincial doctor is analogous to being married to a provincial rabbi; both are functionaries who play a respected and recognized social role. Emma feels that she has married beneath herself, while the mother-in-law in Baron's story believes her son has married beneath himself. Although Emma initially hopes that marriage will save her from the boredom of her everyday life, the rabbi's wife sees marriage as a hardship from the beginning, crying out on her wedding day, "Alas, I will see no more of the world" (39, 43). The rabbi's wife is immune to Emma's romantic fantasies; she is steadfast in her sober refusal to buy into romance and instead directs her desires toward beautiful objects. Flaubert mocks Emma's pretension through his ironic narration, belittling women's aesthetic desires. As Pérez argues, "Even as Emma yearns for sensual pleasures, the narrator crafts sensory detail after sensory detail into exquisite showpieces of beauty offered to the reader—and which remain wholly inaccessible to Emma herself."[65] In contrast, Baron offers a sympathetic portrait of the rabbi's wife's suffering and her desire for beauty. If Flaubert seeks to mock a woman's aesthetic pretentions as, in Pérez's words, to attempt a "self-definition against 'feminine writing,'" then Baron imagines women as the starting point of her modernist practice.[66]

Like Flaubert, Baron dramatizes the aesthetic longings of her protagonist. However, in contradistinction to Emma's insatiable desire to consume mass-produced luxury goods, the rabbi's wife's desires are fulfilled by the purchase of a single object: a pair of embroidered slippers. The rabbi's wife looks upon these slippers as works of art. The narrator explains, "The fabric was of so delicate a texture and of such beautifully matched colors that for a moment my aunt shut her eyes, as though dazzled by a sudden strong light" (41, 46). The narrator compares the smile on her face to "the glow that tinges the edge of a cloud after the sun has set." Baron elevates the scene from desire for a fashionable object to a sublime moment of aesthetic experience. Where Flaubert links consumption of goods to erotic desires, Baron does not. In Baron's story, the possession of such beautiful objects represents the freedom of aesthetic experience and the painful realities of women's unfreedom.

Baron rejects Flaubert's demonization of Emma's deadly desires, providing an alternative vision of women's appreciation for beautiful objects as a form of artistic spectatorship. The rabbi's wife, while caught up in the beauty of the slippers, does not fall victim to Emma's romantic escapism and compulsive need for consumption. She sees only their material reality. In thinking of the slippers, the rabbi's wife recognizes that they might represent another ideal world but also refuses them meaning beyond their material presence. For example, the rabbi's wife distracts herself from her relentless domestic labor—lighting the kindling for the stove and endlessly peeling beets—by thinking of the slippers: "She was not able to see the wide world, but she imagined that all its magic was contained in those slippers, which she had seen with her own eyes and whose soft velvet she had caressed with her own hand" (42, 47). Notice how the narrator restricts the meaning of the slippers to what the rabbi's wife sees with her own eyes. The slippers embody the mysteries of the world but do not prompt her to fantasize about these mysteries. The slippers as an object of beauty suffuse her thoughts but do not prompt the vague fantasies that haunt Emma Bovary's life. The slippers' material presence is central to the story; the rabbi's wife will ride a train to the provincial city to purchase them. At the same time, she will never wear the slippers in her dusty home or on the muddy streets of the shtetl, like Hannah Gittel, who removes her new pair of "half-shoes" and walks barefoot along the muddy paths on her return home during Tishah b'Av. The slippers, secreted away as a private treasure, are objects of aesthetic appreciation like works of art stowed away for contemplation. These private spaces are a refuge from the patriarchal structures that limit women, whether the demands of Jewish tradition or the iron grip of a cruel mother-in-law. However, they are still located within the patriarchal home, secreted away in its interior—a moment's refuge but not a radical act of subversion.

Contrast the rabbi's wife's appreciation of the slippers to Emma Bovary's escapist relationship to art and literature:

> Then she recalled the heroines of the books she had read, and the lyric legion of these adulterous women began to sing in her memory with the voice of sisters that charmed her. She became herself as it were, an actual part of these lyrical imaginings; at long last, she saw herself among these lovers she had so envied, she fulfilled the love-dream of her youth.[67]

In this passage, Emma envisions herself as part of a composite scene of literary imagination and her everyday reality. Art and life blur, and Emma loses herself in fantasy. In Hebrew, however, Baron replaces "lyrical imagining" with "fictional characters" (דמויות בדויות).[68] Her translation highlights Emma's ability to discriminate between fact and fiction rather than her capacity to be seduced by the lyrical. In "Ḳeṭanot," she does not get lost in escapist fantasies. It is the materiality of the slippers that she authenticates with her own senses and that haunts her imagination. Although she is "not able to see the wider world," and therefore visualize or fantasize about it, the slippers are a metonymy of that world of art and freedom. The narrator frames the rabbi's wife's aesthetic appreciation of the slippers with her own worldlier experience; she is someone who understands the distinction between mass-produced objects and works of art. Reading both levels of the story—the aunt's relationship to the shoes and the narrator's aesthetic distance from her aunt—we can apprehend the story's relationship to the practice of prose fiction as an art form that links the material world of women to the aesthetic labor of art.

Critics have read the slippers as an escapist pleasure or, as Wendy Zierler describes them, as "a small this-worldly consolation, shared among women."[69] In their book on the dowry box in Hebrew literature, Hannah Naveh and Tsilia Abramovitz Ratner interpret the presence of the slipper in the women's orbit as part of their attempts to escape from a household regime that controls their lives by creating "moments of beauty."[70] The slippers, both beautiful and cheap, embody the rabbi's wife's longing for another world and the narrow confines through which she can reach that world. They are a small comfort, an insignificant treasure, and an object of aesthetic admiration, very much like Baron's story. Here, too, we see Baron's dialogue with Flaubert's novel, where shoes also play an important role. There are Emma's wooden clogs, her riding boots, the shoes she purchases for the ball at La Vaubyessard, and the slippers Léon buys for her. The narrator lingers on Emma's wooden soles, whose sounds attract Charles. Emma wears her boots to ride with Rodolphe and then later to sneak away and meet him in the woods. She also treasures the dainty slippers that Léon purchases, which dangle from the toes of her bare foot when she sits on his lap. Her dancing shoes retain traces of yellowy wax from the dance floor at La Vaubyessard, and the narrator explains that, like the wax, "contact with wealth had laid something over it [her heart] that could not be wiped away."[71] In Flaubert's novel, the slipper, the boot, and the satin shoe all represent Emma's aspirations and adulterous desires. In contrast, in Baron's story, shoes represent both women's oppression in the guise of the wooden clog and their aesthetic aspirations in the figure of the embroidered slipper.

Whereas Flaubert's narrator ironizes Emma's aesthetic desires, showing them to be narcissistic and superficial, Baron's narrator takes seriously the protagonist's aesthetic longing for everyday objects as an aesthetic experience that might compensate for her suffering, even as she recognizes the smallness of the desired trifle. Her attention to women's trifles and her intertextual dialogue with Flaubert serve to dramatize the limits on women's aesthetic labor under conditions of capitalism that require their subjection.

A Tale of Two Shoes: The Commodity and the Social Conditions of Women's Labor

While the rabbi's wife delights in embroidered slippers, she is ashamed of her own wooden clogs, especially when visiting her sister-in-law, whose home is decorated with luxury items that include "chinaware, an alarm clock, a lamp with a green shade on a lace doily" (41, 46). The story's focus on these two contrasting pairs of shoes is a compelling feature of its intertextual dialogue with Flaubert and a broader modernist fascination with art and adornment, with handcrafted and mass-produced goods. Shoes in the story are items of necessity and fashion, and they figure the social context of women's relationships to objects; they represent beauty, violence, and capitalist production.

We can find similar critical meditations on the relationship between femininity and capitalism in work of the interwar period. In his book on the object in Anglo-American modernism, Douglas Mao outlines the "reflexive antipathy to commodity" that underlines modernist attitudes toward the object world.[72] Yet, despite this antipathy, modernist writers were also fascinated by and drawn to objects of mass production. In her novels of the 1920s, Mao argues, Virginia Woolf seeks "to recuperate certain forms of consumption by rewriting them as artistic production," while shedding doubt on these ideas.[73] Mao reads Woolf as protraying women's desires for beautiful goods as aesthetic practice. Woolf's work also raises an important quandry: "If the achievements of a tinselly society hostess are art, does this leave the artist a figure of mere tinsel?"[74] Mao's question about Woolf's society hostess echoes Rancière's argument about the threat that Emma Bovary posed to the figure of the artist. Emma's refusal to distinguish between art and nonart challenges the very category of artist. Woolf, in contrast to Flaubert, however, celebrates the breakdown of this distinction between the male artist and the female protagonist. Woolf and Baron, I would argue, are grappling with a shared question: Are women the victims of capitalism, or do they have a distinctly productive and aesthetic relationship to the commodity and its consumption? Flaubert demonizes Emma's desire to consume as a symptom of her narrow and restricted life in the provinces and her failure to distinguish art and nonart. Baron, however, elevates her protagonist's desires in aesthetic terms, even as she ironizes her protagonist's naïveté. She envisions her protagonist's aesthetic longing as a form of productive artistic labor.

These questions about labor and art are focalized in Baron's story through shoes, which have a peculiar life as objects or "things." They are material goods that also serve as an extension of the body, a form of second skin. Scholars have focused on shoes as capturing the ambiguous border between the self and the world. Deborah Lupton looks at shoes as mass-produced objects that can be appropriated, "singularized, bearing the stamp of individuality and everyday experience," and thus lose their purely functional meaning.[75] In her book on fashion and modernity, Elizabeth Wilson argues that "dress links the biological body to the social being, and public to private. This makes it uneasy territory since it forces us to recognize that the human body is more than a biological entity."[76] In Baron's story, shoes are mass-produced goods, figures for the female body, symbols of violence, and aesthetic objects. The shoes connect women to the social realities that both restrict their freedom and ignite their imagination, and they link women to the forces of industrialization. They are like second skins, tattooed by the brutal hand of the cobbler and his hateful misogyny. In addition, they figure the porous boundary between art and everyday objects. They are necessary for life and yet not worn for their utilitarian purpose.

The wooden clogs are a source of shame and embarrassment that tie the rabbi's wife to the provincial world of the shtetl and the indignities it visits on women. The wooden clogs are also a symbol of violence and pain. The narrator recalls seeing the shriveled arm of Sarah Elka, the cobbler's wife, as her aunt inspects the "red weals left by the cobbler's hammer" (43, 49). The wooden clogs, produced by the same tools that leave these gruesome marks on the cobbler's wife, contain the brutal traces of the violence enacted on women's bodies in the village and signal the miseries of married life.[77] The rabbi's wife, a figure of moral and religious authority in town, can only agree with Sarah Elka that she has much sorrow; she cannot ease those pains. There can be no justice for the wife, who fears the devastating consequences of divorce more than the bruises on her body left by the cobbler's tools. Every year when Sarah Elka's husband demands a divorce because she only produces daughters, the rabbi intervenes to save the marriage. On the one hand, it is a measure of his kindness that he works to protect this mother from abandonment and financial ruin. On the other, it shows the moral weakness of a society that cannot protect women from abuse, only abandonment.

If the clogs—the shoes that women wear in the shtetl—signify male violence in the confines of the provinces, the slippers hold out the hope of escape from the brutality signified by the cobbler. The image of these shoes lingers in the aunt's mind, as she continues her daily drudgery of lighting the stove in the morning and peeling the beets: "Never having seen the wide world, she imagined that all its mystery and magic lay in those wondrous slippers, which she had seen with her own eyes and whose velvet softness she had fondled" (42, 47). These slippers are beautiful objects to a woman who wears her wooden boots like manacles.

Baron creates an intertextual constellation of socialist, feminist, and Jewish ideologies to highlight the reality of women's labor. In drawing our attention to the cobbler and his wooden shoes, Baron also points to the condition of the slipper's production, whose provenance is likely an urban factory employing women. The factory-made slippers recall the plight of the cobbler's daughter, Hannah Gittel, who is sent to the city to work in domestic service. Factory work and domestic service were the new urban jobs that Russian women flocked to cities to perform. In the second half of the nineteenth century, "the single largest employer of women in both cities [Moscow and Saint Petersburg] was domestic service, and it absorbed more and more women as time went on."[78] Between 1864 and 1890, the number of women in domestic service rose from 55,307 to 87,777, reaching a third of all working women in Saint Petersburg.[79] Domestic service was widely recognized as degrading work: "Domestic servants were deprived of a private life; they were permitted neither visitors, including legal husbands, nor holidays," and they were excluded from minimal labor protection.[80] In Eastern European Jewish culture, domestic service was particularly reviled, and women often traveled far from home to avoid the shame.[81] The preferred servants came from the provinces without any education because they were unlikely to complain about terrible working conditions. To work in service or in the factory was what stood between women and prostitution, but these jobs were also marked by economic and sexual exploitation.

Hannah Gittel embodies this historical trend as a young woman sent off to the city for service. She enjoys the economic fruits of her new urban employment, returning home with a fashionable pair of heeled shoes that she must take off to walk through the muddy streets of the shtetl. She regales the narrator's aunt with tales from the city, describing the fake mole her employer applies to her face to look fashionable, the public parks and fountains, and all the delights and possibilities the city offers. Her tales of the city objects seduce the rabbi's wife with the promise of the world. The slippers contain the traces of Hannah Gittel's domestic exploitation, her wrongful accusation, as well as delight in city life.

Moreover, working in the city opens up new forms of social freedom for Hannah Gittel. The city appears to her like a dream, even as it also the location of her exploited labor. One evening, when she returns to her family in the village, she steals away to visit the rabbi's wife, waiting outside her home to make sure the dreaded mother-in-law is asleep. They both perceive the nighttime walk as a transgression shared between two women. Leaving the domestic confines of home, they speak privately on a bench, far from the Jewish space of the town, near the priest's house. This is the space of women's freedom, notably on the border between Jews and Christians. Although Baron's story doesn't address social intercourse between Jews and Christians, her dialogue with European literature recalls the concerns raised in the early twentieth century about women's affinity for secular European literature as a form of conversion.[82] In this moment, the liminal space between Jewish and gentile is the space of female comraderies and art. Tamar Hess notes that in the Hebrew literature of the period, women meet on benches whereas men meet in train cars: in the train car, men pass by the world, but on a bench, women sit still, watching the world pass by them.[83] Sitting on the bench, in this case, they delight in the sounds of piano music that emanate from the nearby count's estate. Hannah Gittel speaks of the piano at her mistress's home, describing with delight the staircase and an enclosed garden. She tells about the street lamps that illuminate the night, and public parks with vendors and amusement rides. When she sneaks back into her home in the early morning, she whispers to herself, "Just like a dream" (49, 56). The urban life that Hannah Gittel treasures reverberates in the rabbi's wife's mind as a modest fantasy, a world of wonders she longs to see. On this very night, there will be a theft at her mistress's house, and her fateful visit with the rabbi's wife will become the alibi that exonerates her. This episode highlights the tension between the dream of the city and the labor conditions that make that dream, between the sounds of the piano and the reality of who gets to play that piano. Moreover, it highlights the contradictions of capitalism as a source of both possibility and oppression for women.

Hannah Gittel is a feminist and socialist double of Emma. Emma Bovary experiences desire unleashed by the rising circulation of mass-produced goods and fueled by her consumption on credit of Monsieur Lheureux's fashionable wares. For example, Emma attempts to soothe her sorrow after Léon departs for Rouen by making grand purchases to mourn the sacrifice she made in not declaring her desire for him. The narrator describes her response contemptuously: "A woman who had required of herself such great sacrifice could surely be permitted to indulge her whims."[84] These whims include a long list of purchases to beautify herself and her surroundings: a Gothic prie-dieu, lemons for bleaching her fingernails, a blue cashmere dress, and a scarf. Similarly, Hannah Gittel purchases bleaching cream and high-heeled shoes with her new salary. These luxuries are the accoutrements of modern urban femininity. Her exploited domestic labor produces the conditions for this new commodified project of beauty. Once Hannah Gittel is imprisoned, she will lose her bleached complexion and revert to the body of a provincial Jewish woman. In Flaubert's novel, Emma becomes like the fashionable goods she purchases—an exchangeable commodity that quickly becomes out of date. By contrast, Hannah Gittel is the victim of social forces that exploit her labor and shape her femininity. Emma's debt and not her adultery ultimately leads to her downfall, as creditors plot to repossess her property and she commits suicide. In contrast, Hannah Gittel's downfall occurs because of an economic system that forces her into domestic service and leaves her vulnerable to exploitation. At the end of Flaubert's novel, Emma takes her own life, annihilating her femininity and desires. We know less about Hannah Gittel's fate. Released from prison, she walks through the city with the rabbi's wife, but does not join her on the train back to the village. Her options are few: domestic service, factory work, or prostitution. Wendy Zierler reads the story in a more positive light, noting that rabbi's wife returns home on Shabbat Nahamu and testifies during the days of repentance; she argues that "the transcendent notion of prayer and divine judgment is displaced by the experience of an individual woman testifying on behalf of another woman in an actual court of law."[85] Zierler draws attention to the ways Baron mobilizes allusions to amplify the plight of her female protagonists.

Intimacy, Irony, and the Work of Observation

In "Ḳeṭanot," as in many of Baron's stories, the first-person narrator slips into and out of the third person. Over her career, Baron developed a complex narrative perspective in which participant narrators move in and out of stories and report events and narratives beyond what they could possibly witness or know. Baron's narrative style relies on a dialectic of intimacy and distance, recasting Flaubertian irony into a more generous portrayal of women's suffering. Sheila Jelen describes these narrators' affective relationship to the stories as "sympathy or compassion" that "is rendered from an uncomfortable distance."[86] I argue that her narratorial distance mirrors the structure of aesthetic labor that governs Baron's writing. Baron's narrators elevate women's domestic experiences by aestheticizing them from a distance.

We can see this form of mediated labor in "Ḳeṭanot" by looking at the narrator's relationship to her aunt's aesthetic desire. The narrator describes the rabbis's wife's reaction to the slippers as an encounter with the sublime. These everyday slippers fill her aunt with awe: "The fabric was of so delicate a texture and of such beautifully-matched colors that for a moment my aunt shut her eyes, as though dazzled by a sudden strong light" (41, 46). The narrator describes her aunt's encounter with the slippers as a spectator experiencing a work of art, while reminding the reader that these are, in fact, "ordinary, flat slippers." The irony is in the gap between the aunt's awe of the slippers and the narrator's awareness of their commonness. The niece looks on sympathetically at her aunt's provincial appreciation of these objects but also draws attention to her provincialism. She informs the reader that the slippers were purchased in the provincial capital for five rubles and five kopeks; they are ordinary, mass-produced goods available at reasonable prices. The low price does not diminish the aunt's sense of their beauty. She puts her hands in them and walks them across the table; her eyes wide with pleasure contain "the faint human sadness in them that the poets tell us always overwhelms us at the sight of beauty" (41, 46). As the narrator describes watching her aunt absorbed in a pair of cheap slippers, the aesthetic object she observes is not the slippers but her aunt's authentic encounter with them: "The smile of wonder still remained on the face of our visitor, like the glow that tinges the edge of a cloud after the sun has set" (42, 47). This multilayered perspective—the niece observing the aunt, who is observing the slippers—draws attention to a layered form of aestheticization. The aunt's longing for the slippers becomes a form of aesthetic experience that can be ironically mobilized in the creation of Baron's own writing practice.

Baron enlists Flaubertian irony to feminist ends, drawing the reader into her complexly layered prose. In the last lines, the narrator answers an imagined reader's skepticism: "'Big deal,' you say, 'a pair of slippers.' But after all of our wandering and searching, who among us can boast of having returned with a greater possession?" (55, 65). What are we to make of the address to an implied reader and the excess of fulfillment in the story? The story celebrates the smallness of her dreams in the pair of beautiful embroidered slippers, a desire so easily satisfied through the consumption of a single mass-produced good. This celebration also includes the reader, whom the narrator addresses in the second-person plural. Both author and implied reader recognize the smallness of the item; it is a trifle. The narrator, however, tries to convince the sophisticated reader that the item is in fact "a great possession" (*rekhush gadol*), emphasizing its significance in the language of size: *gadol* is the opposite of *ḳaṭan* or *ḳeṭanot*, a trifle. The term *rekhush gadol* is also an allusion to Genesis 15:14. In this biblical passage, God tells Abraham that his offspring will be oppressed for four hundred years, and then God will free them and reward them with *rekhush gadol*, or great wealth, as compensation for their suffering. Just as in the biblical text, then, the "great possession" in Baron's story could be translated as "a compensation for suffering," and thus the ending can be read as a potential liberation of the rabbi's wife from her oppression. These slippers are indeed no trifle.

Whereas Flaubert's narrator ironizes Emma's aesthetic desires, showing them to be narcissistic and superficial, Baron's narrator takes seriously the protagonist's aesthetic longing for everyday objects as compensation for her suffering, even as she recognizes the smallness of the desired trifle. Baron structures the story around the ironic gap between her implied readers and the women she depicts. Even as she recognizes the subjective significance of the slipper for the rabbi's wife, she does so by addressing an educated readership whom she knows would never see the item as *gadol*. This ironic gap is intended to mobilize compassion and pity, not contempt and derision. Baron recasts the desire for embroidered shoes as a desire for beauty that, even when realized, cannot protect the rabbi's wife from the brutality that surrounds her, even if the language hints at some redemptive ending. This is the feminist aesthetic potential that Ziarek describes, born out of violence, and it becomes Baron's modernist feminist aesthetic.

In her 1939 story "Mah she-hayah" ("What Has Been"), Baron describes a practice of observation and reading that similarly reworks the objects of domestic life. Just as in "Ḳeṭanot," the story's participant narrator is a rabbi's daughter recalling events she observed in her childhood. She tells the story of Mina, a young girl despised by her mother and protected by a loving father who becomes ill. The family is forced to leave their home in the city and move to the narrator's village. This narrator bears witness to Mina's coming of age. The story pivots on the narrator's affective relationship to Mina's storytelling. Before Mina and her family arrived, the narrator heard stories about them, but these stories seemed remote to her, as if shrouded in fog. In contrast, when the narrator meets Mina and hears her story directly from her, she feels the following:

> They felt close to me so *clear and concrete* [barurim u-muḥashim] that I began to form a close attachment to them: when she spoke about her father, I pitied him for his failing health and helplessness; and when she mentioned her young brother, Ephraim, or her sister, Batia, I was filled with a surge of tenderness as though I were in the presence of something pure and delicate.[87]

Mina's storytelling brings her family into clear focus like a photograph, drawing the narrator's sympathy and attachment. The adjective *muḥashim* also implies that Mina not only offers a clear image of her family, but also conjures their embodied presence. They are not only seen but felt. The narrator reflects on this transformation as central to her own coming of age as a writer: "It was much later that I learned the good narrator does not labor his subject and encumber it with explanations" and instead "merely shines his torch on it" (128, 80). The narrator describes a three-dimensional mimesis. She does not "labor" her subjects but only illuminates them; she does not transform, shape, or otherwise aestheticize them. In the story, Baron appears to erase the artistry of the writer. Just as in "Ḳeṭanot," the narrator sees authentic experience as already aesthetic.

Baron develops a narrative technique that relies on a tension between objectivity and subjectivity that is also central to free indirect discourse, but is based on relations of intimacy and not contempt. The story's narrator famously describes herself as "the negative plate that remains alone after the photographed subject has been lost" (127, 79). The negative plate is not the photograph, not the mimetic object, but as Jelen notes, "it is something in between, a kind of medium or mediator."[88] The narrator mediates between the present and the lost past, and between herself and the protagonists whose thoughts and feelings she represents.

Like Baron's narrator in "Ḳeṭanot," the narrator in this story also observes the more naive protagonist's experience of the aesthetic. Mina reads and, in reading, transforms art into everyday life:

> The "characters" [*Ha-nefashot ha-po'alot*] in the book she read came to life before her; she came to know them intimately, she shared their joys and sorrows, but above all, she felt a kinship for the downtrodden and the wretched, who aroused in her not only deep sympathy, but also a kind of wonder. It was as if she were looking into a magic mirror where she saw, next to her own image, many others that were uncannily similar: the same plain face, the same softly echoing sighs, the same taste to the tears they shed in secret. (90, 135–36)

Baron places *Ha-nefashot ha-po'alot*, the literary term, in quotation marks, highlighting the tension between the literary and the authentic; these are the dramatis personae in the literary sense, but they are also real and experienced as concrete beings. Mina reads and forms an intimacy with the literary characters, sharing "their joys and sorrows," as if "looking into a magic mirror" that reflects both her image and theirs; she enters their world and they hers. The narrator first tries to teach Mina to read Hebrew, but there are no works that resonate with Mina's life experience in Hebrew, a critique of the failure of Hebrew literature to capture women's experience and speak to someone like Mina. She then teaches her to read in Yiddish, describing the Yiddish books as "no great works," a familiar trope of Hebrew literature. Yet the narrator characterizes the books Mina reads as kaleidoscopes; through them, "the world opened up before her" (90, 135–36). She who has always been looked down upon "was now enabled to penetrate the lives of others without being under observation." These descriptions of her reading sound quite a bit like writing: observing the lives of others without being observed. She responds and "patterned her actions and behaviors" on the characters within them (91, 136). Mina is a reader, like Emma, who merges literature and life, but not as an escapist act. Instead, she reads as an act of identification: it does not prompt Mina's demise but rather secures her happiness. Reading for her is a form of *l'œuvre œuvrée*. Mina conjures the stories and works them into her life, just as her life surely shapes them. She does not interact with them as art, divorced from life, but rather brings them to life.

Reading Baron in dialogue with Flaubert and the material conditions of women's oppression offers us a different lens on the intersections between Hebrew prose and Jewish cultural modernity. Although Baron's work integrates traditional sources with modern European literary intertexts like her male contemporaries, she is less interested in the break with the Jewish textual tradition's crisis of faith between fathers and son. Instead, she highlights the entrance of women into the aesthetic and theorizes the aesthetic as a form of labor. Baron articulates the challenges of the female Hebrew artist at a time when the Jewish sexual-linguistic system was breaking down and becoming reoriented.[89] She develops a feminist labor aesthetic that can be read in dialogue with her Yiddish modernist contemporary Fradl Shtok and with modernist writers like Virginia Woolf, who were invested in similar questions about imagining how women's aesthetic experiences could be harnessed for modernist art.

Part 2

New Languages for New Collectivities

The Role of Literature in Cultural Identity

Chapter 4

The Minority Literature Question

Literature and Political and Cultural Belonging in the Interwar Period

In his 1951 essay "New Horizons in Jewish History," the preeminent Jewish historian Salo Baron grapples with how to categorize the Jews, asking whether Jews fall under "the accepted general categories of nationality, religion or race."[1] He answers by offering the hypothetical example of three Kiev-born brothers living in New York, Kiev, and Tel Aviv, presumably after the First World War. According to Baron, the New Yorker would be considered "a member of the Jewish 'faith,'" the Kiev brother "would be classified by law as a member of a recognized national minority," and the Tel Aviv brother would be "a national of Israel."[2] No longer Jewish residents of the Russian Empire, these brothers are divided by oceans and new national identities that shape the different ways their lives would unfold. The brother in Tel Aviv would become a citizen of a new Jewish state, the one in America would maintain a confessional difference as Jewish citizen of the United States, and the Kiev brother would ultimately become a Soviet citizen. Baron's imagined fraternal family highlights how new forms of Jewish collective identity emerged out of the collapse of empires and the throes of competing nationalisms across Europe and its colonial outposts in the twentieth century.

During the first half of the twentieth century, the breadth of Jewish linguistic, national, religious, and artistic affiliations went far beyond the formal categories outlined by Baron, however. These kaleidoscopic identities were not only produced by the formal mechanisms of the state but also internally generated, fragile, flexible, and interconnected. Jews participated in a range of international and transnational political movements and cultural institutions that crossed national borders, colliding and overlapping with one another. As Jewish men and women sought to establish and transform their own commitments and communities, they did so in the confines of their homes through their romantic and marital choices, in cafés and lecture halls where they espoused new political and artistic affiliations, and in the hallways of educational institutions where they embraced new ideas and ways of thinking. Not all defined themselves along Jewish axes; some committed themselves to international political causes, to non-Jewish cultural movements, and to other forms of personal, political, and artistic identification.

Salo Baron's anecdote about the three brothers overlooks the complexities of Jewish cultural life that shaped new identities and elides the central questions of this book: How did women experience and engage with changes in Jewish political belonging? What did it mean for them to be minorities in the post–World War I political order? More fundamentally, how did Jewish women engage these transformations of Jewish cultural modernity? Baron chooses not to imagine the sisters who would have wrestled with and negotiated new state-mandated identities as well as other competing forms of identification. The sister who remained in Soviet Kiev would have acquired new rights as a woman: to marry and divorce at will, to access an abortion, and to attend university. The sister in New York in the same period would have a harder time securing a divorce or an abortion and faced restricted access to certain professions. The sister in Mandatory Palestine would confront the sexism of male-dominated Zionist institutions, marginalized by the leadership as she sought to gain a foothold of power. Women responded to these new circumstances by rethinking the boundaries of Jewish communal life and the future of Jewish culture. Some, like Puah Rakovsky and Esther Frumkin, played visible political leadership roles, while others remained less visible, often sidelined by male colleagues or erased from the historical record by historians. Some, including the women writers in this book, took up their pens and began writing modern Hebrew and Yiddish prose fiction as part of a larger project of Jewish and minority self-definition. Through their literary experimentation, they theorized the relationship between state-mandated identities and new cultural possibilities. Their writing served as a laboratory for thinking about alternative modes of community and possible futures that embraced Jewish difference without hewing to ethnonationalist divisions. Tracing their projects in different locations, much as Baron seeks to do with male writers, deprovincializes women's writing. As Cristanne Miller observes, a comparative approach to writing modernist women's literary history "shifts the locus of modernist studies from the individual as such" and demands that the "local be understood in relation to gender and in comparison with other locations."[3] A transnational approach undoes the provincializing of women's contributions and challenges precisely the sort of male-centered narrative forwarded by Baron.

At the end of the nineteenth century and in the first decades of the twentieth, Hebrew and Yiddish literatures played an integral role in reimagining Jewish collectivity in the wake of imperial decline and rising nationalist sentiment. Benjamin Harshav has aptly named this process of cultural and national revival the "Modern Jewish Revolution."[4] The early twentieth century offered a dizzying array of possibilities for new forms of Jewishness that revolved around Jewish experience rather than Jewish law. Cultural and political activists in Eastern Europe seized on language as an essential tool for forging new collective communal and political loyalties. The choice of writing in Yiddish or Hebrew was entangled with politics. Jewish socialists and diaspora nationalists who sought to preserve Jewish cultural autonomy in Europe relied primarily on Yiddish, whereas many who embraced territorial nationalism and envisioned a Jewish national future outside of Europe chose Hebrew. Hindsight has oversimplified these divisions: while some believed in the project of a robust Hebrew culture in Europe, others felt that Yiddish should be the language of a new territorial nationalism. Literature played a central role in this process, as Robert Alter argues regarding Hebrew: "The act of writing in Hebrew was not just an aesthetic pursuit, but a programmatic renegotiation of the terms of Jewish collective identity."[5] The same could be said for Yiddish. In this period of cultural revolution, writers clearly grasped how the representation of reality could shape new grounds for a Jewish future.

These decades represent a moment when writers and readers were keenly aware of the political valence of the aesthetic. Scholars of Eastern European Jewish literature and culture have long argued that the rise of Hebrew- and Yiddish-language cultural arts and the emergence of realism in prose fiction were intimately connected with emerging forms of Jewish national consciousness.[6] In the early twentieth century, as Europe was torn apart by revolution and war, Jewish activists responded by creating Hebrew and Yiddish schools, theater troupes, and literary journals, as well as founding PEN clubs in both languages, all with the intent of rethinking Jewish society in Europe. Barry Trachtenberg shows, for example, how the failed 1905 revolution in Russia catalyzed modern Jewish cultural movements: "With political avenues blocked, they increasingly focused their attention on the cultural aspects of their newly identified nation, in particular by developing its Yiddish and Hebrew creative and scholarly forms."[7] In looking at both Hebrew and Yiddish literary fermentation between the tumultuous revolutionary years of 1917 and 1920, Kenneth Moss describes Hebrew and Yiddish writers in Russia as "culturists" who "were almost by definition cultural nationalists (whether left or liberal, autonomist or Zionist) in that they saw their bid for Jewish culture in service to a secular Jewish 'nation' in the making."[8] In doing so they also modeled themselves on European literary and cultural norms, seeing their embrace of European genres as proof of their worthiness as a nation. Literature represented a linguistic leap of faith and an act of political imagination meant to secure a new future in Jewish languages. Jewish writers intuitively understood the ways that the aesthetic was political. Hebrew and Yiddish literature in Europe emerged from the struggles of marginalized communities to redefine and articulate a future for the language and culture of a Jewish political and cultural minority.

The writers I analyze in this section came of age in the former Austro-Hungarian and Russian empires and witnessed the emergence of Jewish national expression in Palestine, an outpost of the crumbling British Empire, and in new European states, where they were subject to the upheavals of national and minority identity in the wake of World War I and the Paris Peace Conference of 1919 and 1920. As James Loeffler insightfully observes, the Paris Peace Conference produced both the Minorities Treaties, which "extend[ed] linguistic, cultural, and other group rights to national minorities living in the belt of post-imperial states," and the Mandate System, which divided the former Ottoman Empire and German colonial empire into territorial mandates, including British Palestine, that were to be ruled "magnanimously" by the European victors of World War I.[9] Both the nation-state of Poland and Mandatory Palestine emerged from this new postwar order; both were products of the forces that gave rise to two seemingly contradictory but simultaneous modes of Jewish national expression: minority cultural autonomy and majority self-rule. The writers I discuss in this section came of age or lived in Poland, the Soviet Union, and pre-state Palestine, where the definition of minority culture was being radically rethought and, in the case of Palestine, reconceptualized in majoritarian terms.

In Poland, Loeffler illuminates, the very notion of the concept of national minority was formed by Jews who sought to envision a form of territorial nationalism that could encompass both a territorial state and the existence of a diasporic minority. That diaspora nationalism "came to dominate the entire spectrum of Jewish politics by the beginning of the twentieth century" in Poland, where the legacies of the Habsburg Empire shaped politics, is not a surprise.[10] Poland played an important role as a Jewish cultural center, with its competing diaspora nationalisms.

Meanwhile, Zionist activists in Mandatory Palestine sought to establish a nation-state with Jews as the national majority. As Deborah Bernstein explains, "The Zionist enterprise was, in essence, an enterprise of social change, an attempt at transforming the Jewish people from a persecuted minority in the diaspora to a sovereign majority in the old-new Jewish homeland."[11] The leading figures on the Zionist left, however, sought to refashion a nativist Hebrew culture in Palestine, asserting the rights of Jews to the territory against the claims of the established Arab community there. Anita Shapira has used the term "defensive ethos" to describe the ideology that allowed the Zionist left to pretend that "the Zionist project was not one of conquest, but rather of settlement" and to repress "the basic facts of the existing confrontation between Jews and Arabs," including the idea that Palestinian Arab nationalism was also a movement of national liberation and self-determination.[12] Although Zionism in the 1920s and 1930s was dominated by labor parties that embraced socialist ideology, its adherents primarily aimed to inculcate Jewish nationalist principles.

In the 1920s, the Soviet Union attempted to define new parameters of minority ethnic and national identity as it confronted the diverse multiethnic nationalist loyalties within its borders. In contrast to Zionism, Soviet authorities sought to inculcate the values of socialism and weaken minority nationalist identifications. Rejecting both assimilation and extranational cultural autonomy as solutions to the national minority problem, Lenin and Stalin embraced a policy of limited autonomy for national minorities, including Jews.[13] The Soviet policy of *korenizatsiia* (nativization) established national minority cultural institutions, such as schools, cultural organizations, and newspapers, in various minority languages. The Soviet Union went so far as to create an autonomous Jewish region, Birobidzhan, in 1928.

Part and parcel of this new paradigm of national identity were new political rights for women. The 1920s saw the emancipation of women in Poland and the Soviet Union. Moreover, in 1926 in Palestine, women were granted the right to vote within the autonomous Jewish community. Even as women obtained their hard-fought suffrage and won equality under the law, they faced barriers to their political and economic independence. For example, Jewish women who immigrated as pioneers to Palestine, dreaming of entering an "egalitarian workers' society," were "unable to overcome the marginal position to which they were relegated by a movement in which the priorities did not include economic parity for women."[14] These contradictions were not unique to Palestine. The 1921 constitution of the Republic of Poland guaranteed women equal rights, but in practice the constitution did not provide "a complete and consistent liquidation of legal limitations discriminating against women, most obvious within civil law."[15] Conservative factions in Poland, including in the Polish Jewish community, restricted women's rights. In Polish Zionist circles, the figure of the new Hebrew woman "was to be healthy both in body and spirit, and her fundamental role was to bear children and raise them according to Zionist national tradition."[16] The 1918 Soviet Code on Marriage, the Family, and Guardianship radically upended traditional marriage practices that restricted women, introducing civil marriage as well as divorce on demand, and eliminating illegitimacy.[17] However, in the 1930s Stalin introduced a new code eliminating abortion and encouraging women to embrace motherhood.

In the interwar period, women celebrated new social, economic, and political opportunities and yet also suffered from the ways these new nation-states instrumentalized their bodies and labor as part of a larger project of nation building. Their attention to minority experience was shaped by the tensions between the new possibilities afforded to women and the gendered constraints of reality.

The interwar period was a time of new sexual freedoms for men and women. Dagmar Herzog argues that World War I "offered numerous opportunities for new sexual pleasures, experiences, and relationships—often including the transgression of boundaries of nation, color, sexual orientation, and class."[18] This was a period when the transnational sex-reform movement flourished, which aimed to "rethink the entire complex of issues relating to marriage, reproduction, gender relations, and the very idea of what sex was and could be."[19] It was also a moment of heightened sexual regulation, and saw the rise of fascism and the backlash that ensued against women's newfound sexual freedoms.

Scholarship on nationalism, politics, and literature in this transformative period has focused predominantly on male writers and thinkers. Yet Jewish women writers energetically portrayed and theorized these large-scale social transformations of the twentieth century and the new identity constellations they inspired. Their voices captured messy and politically charged questions about what Jewishness meant, at times in more radical ways than their male counterparts. These writers proved willing to embrace non-Jewish cultural forms and to call into question the orthodoxies that had determined the boundaries of Jewish and non-Jewish culture. They achieved this in their prose through their aesthetic innovations and willingness to revise and even discard the borders between Jewish and non-Jewish cultural forms. As women and minorities, they understood the fragility of the state as a guarantor of their rights.

As the following chapters show, Leah Goldberg, Elisheva Bikhovsky, and Debora Vogel grappled with the explosive potential of Jewish languages for nationalist and cosmopolitan modes of Jewish identity. All three writers posed political and aesthetic questions about the social role of art in creating community and the role of woman as artist. They conceived of Jewish minority experience as including women and offered their own feminist takes on what Jewish culture and new forms of Jewish collective identity should look like.

Goldberg and Bikhovsky both emigrated from Eastern Europe to Palestine, Goldberg from Lithuania and Bikhovsky from the Soviet Union. Goldberg embraced Hebrew and Zionism, envisioning both as refuges for the humanist ideals that Europe could not sustain. Upon arrival she was embraced by the Zionist establishment. Her literary work, however, also countered prevailing aesthetic and political norms, challenging Zionism's national divisiveness and ethnic chauvinism. Probing the Orientalist frameworks underwriting the revival of modern Hebrew, her novel asks what role women can play in envisioning a new Hebrew culture outside of European Orientalism.

Bikhovsky arrived in Palestine with her Zionist husband Shimon Bikhovsky, hoping to find common cause with the struggle for Jewish national self-determination. For Bikhovsky, a non-Jewish Russian author who adopted a language and culture that was not her own, Hebrew and Palestine offered a cosmopolitan alternative to Soviet politics. Moreover, Bikhovsky saw in Zionism a liberation movement that recalled her own Irish roots and the Irish resistance struggle against British rule. In many ways, Bikhovsky's novel *Simṭa'ot* (Alleyways) set the stage for Goldberg's novel *Avedot* (Losses), particularly its attention to women's Hebrew culture as a catalyst for a new modernist Hebrew poetics. Both works try to imagine forms of attachment to Hebrew that are neither Orientalist nor chauvinistically nationalist through the lens of their female protagonists. Both dramatize these concerns through their representations of intimate relationships between Jews and non-Jews. If both works imagine alternatives to the dominant nationalist and minority cultural model, they also portray the failure of these alternatives, highlighting the precarity of a diasporic and woman-authored modernist Hebrew culture.

In contrast to Bikhovsky and Goldberg, Debora Vogel embraced a diasporic Yiddish culture, choosing to remain in her beloved Galicia. Born into a Hebraist family and educated in German, she adopted Yiddish as her Jewish literary language. Living in Poland, Vogel held onto the Habsburgian ideal of Galicia, with its historical model of "nonnational" belonging in a region where Jewish diaspora nationalism eclipsed territorial nationalism.[20] In her writing, she envisioned Yiddish as a minority national language in the context of a multiethnic and multilingual community. Refusing to leave Galicia, she perished at the hands of the Nazis in 1942. Like Goldberg, she sought nonchauvinist forms of Jewish culture, and like Bikhovsky, she embraced a minority language for her modernist expression.

All of the women writers in this section adopted a language that was not their mother tongue, finding in that language an expression for their political commitments. Goldberg studied Hebrew in a modern Jewish school and then pursued her doctorate in Oriental studies at the University of Bonn. Vogel, by contrast, chose Yiddish in interwar Galicia, a language that situated her outside the Polish center. Having grown up in a Polish-speaking family of Hebraists and participating in a Zionist youth movement, Vogel found Yiddish to be an expression of her commitment to diasporic Jewish culture in Galicia. Bikhovsky, a non-Jewish writer, chose Hebrew as an expression of her attachment to minority nationalism. She began her career as a Russian poet and then adopted Hebrew as her literary language, without imagining herself as Jewish. For Bikhovsky, Hebrew signaled her rejection of Russian literary culture. She ultimately left behind the Soviet Union to find a new life in Mandatory Palestine. There she stood out as a minority figure, a non-Jewish writer whose embrace of the language signaled the future cosmopolitan potential of Hebrew as an international literary language. In choosing their languages, all three writers imagined and created new forms of cultural and political affiliation that were at odds with their parents and their mother tongues.

These authors explored these new affiliations in prose narratives that focus on the details of women's everyday lives and their romantic attachments. As Haiyan Lee articulates in her work on the history of love in modern Chinese literature, "Discourses of sentiment are not merely representations or expressions of inner emotions, but articulatory practices that participate in (re)defining the social order and (re)producing forms of self and sociality."[21] Lee illuminates the centrality of love to the project of modernity, both in producing the modern experience of interiority and making possible new forms of nationalist attachment. "The modern subject is first and foremost a sentimental subject," she asserts.[22] Lee shows how an imported romanticist discourse on love helped reorient ideas of identity and collectivity around individual romantic desires in China, displacing kinship as the cornerstone of personal identity in ways that produced new forms of national community. All three writers shared the keen perception that intimate relationships and interior experience were sites of social and political transformation and a means to reorient Jewish society and envision new forms of sociability. Both Goldberg and Bikhovsky explore intimate relationships between Jews and non-Jews to theorize new forms of national and minority identity. Vogel's montages sought to harness women's everyday lives toward creating a new minority aesthetic that could imagine expansive and radically equalizing forms of collectivity, Jewish or otherwise. Their heightened investment in interiority came from their awareness of the limits of political transformation that failed to penetrate into the intimate regions of peoples' lives and thus left untouched the gendered norms that governed and limited women's horizons.

Multicultural, metropolitan European cities provide the settings for their literary works, which describe Jewish and non-Jewish experiences in Jewish languages. Each author returns Jews to the center of these vibrant cultures while drawing upon Jewish experiences to rearticulate understandings of modernity and political transformation. Bikhovsky's Moscow, Goldberg's Berlin, and Vogel's unnamed Polish metropolis were sites to explore the political, social, and economic crises of the interwar period. Goldberg dramatizes the rise of Nazism; Vogel, the economic crises and social unrest of 1930s Poland; and Bikhovsky, the Bolshevik transformation of Moscow in the 1920s. Through their analyses of life in these metropolitan centers at the heart of new political experiments, the authors wrestle with questions about the place of Jews in Europe and the political meaning of minority identity. Choosing to set their novels in Europe, Bikhovsky and Goldberg veered from the aesthetic norms of Hebrew literature of the period, which turned its attention toward the creation of a new Hebrew life in Palestine. Similarly, Vogel departed from the aesthetic norms of Yiddish women's writing, and of Yiddish modernist prose, as she turned to montage and the chronicle to envision a new Yiddish literature.

Europe presented models of national and minority identity different from those being formulated in Palestine. Goldberg's work explored tensions about the place of Jewish culture in Europe. What future, she asked, would Hebrew have as it became the language of a national culture in Palestine? What did its European legacy mean for that future? Bikhovsky, by contrast, tried to envision a cosmopolitan Hebrew worldview through the eyes of a non-Jewish woman by looking to European Hebrew culture as a potential model. Vogel put faith in a national minority model, a multiethnic legacy of the Habsburg Empire. For Bikhovsky and Goldberg, setting their works in Europe also meant averting their gaze from ethnonational conflicts taking place in their new homes in Mandatory Palestine. Both women explore

Jewish minority identity at the very moment when Zionism was seeking to consolidate a majority Jewish nation-state. Neither author addresses this tension directly in their literary work. However, we can see in their writing moments of contestation to the project of consolidating Jewish national and territorial identity.

Set against the backdrop of revolutionary ideological programs and rising nationalism, all three understood their literary projects as responding to urgent questions of political and cultural belonging in the interwar moment. They saw literature as offering the promise of new modes of identification and as a place of robust cultural experimentation. None of these women found that Jewish nationalism alone offered a simple answer to the dizzying transformations overtaking Europe and the world in the early twentieth century. All of them offered feminist accounts that probed the ways various national formations—both Jewish and non-Jewish—sought to instrumentalize women's bodies and their creative work. For all three authors, modern Hebrew and Yiddish literatures offered potentially radical new ways to transform the gendered social order. They embraced different expressions of minority nationalism as they grappled with the explosive potential of Jewish languages for a modernist and cosmopolitan expression of identity and belonging.

Chapter 5

Leah Goldberg's Orientalist Bind

Leah Goldberg's *Avedot* (Losses) narrates the travails of Elhanan Yehuda Kron, a Hebrew poet and Russian Jewish emigrant to Palestine who travels to Berlin in 1932 to research the Islamic origins of Jewish mysticism. During his time in Berlin, Kron completes what he deems a poetic masterpiece, a Hebrew poem cycle titled "Briḥat Elohim" (God's escape), which he transcribes in pseudo thirteenth-century Hebrew script on antique parchment from Palestine. He initially dedicates the poems to his wife, Lily, but after they separate, he struggles to find a new dedicatee. Just after completing the poems, Kron misplaces them while attending a lecture at the Oriental Institute in Berlin. At the end of the novel, following the burning of the Reichstag and the Nazi rise to power, Kron is reunited with his poems, which two Nazi sympathizers have published in a well-respected Orientalist journal as evidence of early Jewish anti-Christian sentiment in Germany. Kron's Hebrew poem cycle becomes the Orientalist object par excellence. Kron responds by returning to Mandatory Palestine and declaring himself "an Oriental," a decision that signals the fallen dream of a Hebrew culture in Europe.

Through Kron's appropriated poetry, Goldberg theorizes troubling affinities between Orientalism and the secular revival of Hebrew as a literary language in Europe; both his poetry and the Orientalist enterprise separate Hebrew poetics from its sacred Jewish sources and their authoritative Jewish interpreters. The Nazi appropriation of his poetry magnifies and enflames the dangers of such separation. To move beyond this double bind, the novel envisions a modern secular Hebrew distinct from Orientalism, by turning to modern women readers whose entrance into the world of Hebrew letters disrupts the Orientalist project. Kron addresses his poems to the women in his life, both Jewish and non-Jewish. These women have not abandoned a traditional world of Jewish text to embrace the secular ideal of a modern Hebrew culture and a Jewish national state. In Goldberg's novel an Orientalist secular Hebrew can only come into being through a radical revisioning of the gendered order of Jewish textuality and the recognition of shared ties among Judaism, Christianity, and Islam. In this way, Goldberg also interrogates her own relationship to modern Hebrew and its connections to Orientalism and the gendered politics of Jewish textuality.

Celebrated as a poet, Goldberg also was a critically acclaimed critic, scholar, playwright, and novelist. Born in Königsberg in 1911, Goldberg spent her childhood in Kovno's Russian-speaking milieu. Her family fled to Russia during World War I but returned in 1918. Upon their return, her parents elected to send her to a Russian-language Jewish school; however, just after Goldberg enrolled, the language of instruction was switched to Hebrew.[1] Unable to speak either Yiddish or Hebrew, she felt alienated from the student body, whose native language was predominantly Yiddish.[2] And yet she embraced her Hebrew studies, becoming a devotee of modern Hebrew poetry and later of Hebrew prose fiction.[3] She chose to pursue higher education in Germany, which had a more developed scholarly history in her field. She began her studies in 1931, first in Berlin and then in Bonn, where she enrolled in a doctoral program in Semitic studies as part of the Oriental Institute at the University of Bonn. In 1933, in the wake of the Nazi seizure of power, she was forced to return to Kovno and began teaching in a small Hebrew school in the provinces, where she completed her first collection of poems, *Ṭaba'ot 'ashan* (Smoke rings). These poems blend depictions of the Lithuanian landscape of her childhood, the Christian iconography that surrounded her, and allusions to the work of European artists.[4] They introduce many of the themes about European Jewish culture and gender and textuality that Goldberg develops in *Avedot*.

In 1935 Goldberg immigrated to Mandatory Palestine, where she became a prominent member of the Moderna, a group of Hebrew modernist poets that included Avraham Shlonsky and Nathan Alterman. Goldberg quickly established herself as an important intellectual and cultural figure of her generation, teaching courses at Hebrew University and founding its Department of Comparative Literature. Goldberg began writing *Avedot* in 1936, just as she completed the final requirements for her doctorate. Goldberg's novel distills many of the themes of her poetry but through extended attention to her protagonists' inner worlds and with a greater emphasis on the historical events of her day. She never published *Avedot*, shelving the manuscript for good in 1939. Two years later she would begin writing a semiautobiographical novel, *Ṿe-hu ha-or*, also set in the 1930s against the backdrop of Hitler's rise to power.[5] That novel, completed in 1946, grapples with the place of women in both Hebrew and European culture from the perspective of a young female student of Orientalism in Kaunas, Lithuania.[6]

Like her male poet protagonist, Goldberg wrestled with her distance from Eastern Europe's Yiddish-speaking cultural world and her estranged position in Western Europe. As a Jewish woman, Goldberg could study Hebrew only in the secular institutions that her novel calls into question: the Hebrew gymnasium in Kovno and the German university. As a student of Orientalism, she was drawn to medieval Jewish religious texts, but as a woman, she could study these texts only in secular, non-Jewish contexts. A modernist poet born in Europe whose first languages were Russian and German, she was highly educated in classical and modern European literature. She embraced European humanism at the very moment when the humanist project was imploding under the weight of Nazism. Moreover, she had to locate herself as a woman writer in literary traditions—both Jewish and non-Jewish—that devalued and at times excluded women. In *Avedot* she experiments with creative forms of address that jump between the medieval past and an unknown future, between Jews and non-Jews, and men and women. She moves elliptically between these traditions to locate a place for women in Hebrew and a place for Hebrew as a minority language in Europe, beyond the confines of a patriarchal textual tradition and an Orientalist European worldview.

Hebrew beyond Orientalism

The fate of Kron's poetry illuminates a crisis within secular Hebrew culture in twentieth-century Europe. Could a generation of Hebrew writers who embraced European literary culture find a home within that culture? Could a European-inflected Hebrew literature embrace a secularism that was not subject to or representative of European Orientalism? Asking whether a writer of secular Hebrew texts could ever be more than an object of European Orientalist fascination or a participant in that discourse, Goldberg anticipates contemporary theoretical debates that developed in the wake of Edward Said's *Orientalism*, which link Orientalism and secularism to the larger project of Christian European imperialism. Building on Said's arguments, Gil Anidjar argues that the secular is a Christian formation, contending that Christianity "reincarnated itself as secular,"[7] a perspective that Vincent Pecora terms "secularization as transference."[8] These discussions have reshaped the field of European Jewish history by drawing attention to the role Orientalism played in the development of secular Jewish identity. Scholars of Jewish history have linked the emergence of secular Jewish culture to German Orientalism, which Said's work does not address.[9] As Jonathan Hess has demonstrated, debates in Germany about the emancipation of the Jews were predicated on the view that Jews were Orientals, who either could or could not be successfully Occidentalized, with both sides buttressing their arguments through an Orientalist discourse that justified "the internal colonization" of the Jewish minority population in Germany.[10] Amnon Raz-Krakotzkin has likewise traced the history of modern Jewish studies and secular Jewish nationhood to the shared ties among European Orientalism and Christian Hebraism, the study of Hebrew, and postbiblical Jewish literature.[11] In his view, eighteenth-century Orientalist discourse that established the borders of European identity through the visage of a Jewish Other was internalized by Jews and then deployed in the twentieth century to create a secular, national

Jewish culture.[12] He extends this observation to the Zionist project to argue that Jewish emancipation was predicated on Jewish acceptance of a Christian view of history: "Just as Christianity criticized Judaism as a historical anachronism, so did Zionism criticize the Jews in exile as having been left behind by history."[13] Zionism, in short, sought to transform Jews from Orientals into Occidentals by embracing a Christian messianic vision of the Jewish return to the land of Israel. Here Raz-Krakotzkin identifies a central anachronism within the Zionist narrative: the acceptance of the Christian view of Jews' ahistorical existence. Although Raz-Krakotzkin's argument does not extend to secular Hebrew literature, it raises some troubling questions about the place of Hebrew in European culture. If Hebrew nationalism and Orientalism represent two sides of the same coin, where do we locate the modern Hebrew writer or reader? If we view secular Jewish culture and Zionism as extensions of a European Christian worldview, where does that leave the creation of a secular Hebrew literature? Finally, where do women fit into this narrative of Jewish self-Orientalization? How did they disrupt the new masculine secular Hebrew cultural norm rooted in this Orientalist worldview?

Goldberg's awareness of the tensions between Orientalism and modern Hebrew emerged from her studies in Bonn. Yfaat Weiss has established that Goldberg's participation in the Oriental seminar in 1932 brought her into contact with the world of Indian and Sanskrit studies and contends that "in her writing of the 1930s [Goldberg] 'borrowed' the colonial experience of her Asian friends and through it discussed, in an indirect and mediated manner, her experience as a Jewess."[14] In her view, Goldberg's prose fiction critiques the exotification of the "Far East" and, by extension, the Orientalization of Jews. Weiss reads Goldberg, then, as a sympathetic Jewish Orientalist who employed Orientalist studies as part of an "inward-looking" project of Jewish identity formation.[15] I argue, however, that Goldberg's novel displays a deeply skeptical relationship to Orientalism that prompts her to question the possibility of a European Hebrew literature. She experienced firsthand the invisibility of the Hebraist, European-Jewish intellectual in larger projects of European modernity. Her skepticism also arose from the flaws embedded in the German vision of world literature. Premised upon the geopolitics of national literatures, this model could not encompass minority, nonnational writers, thus erasing "the internal difference represented by the Jew, the foreigner who belongs within Europe and speaks Europe's own language (or, specifically, speaks German and does not require translation)."[16]

Goldberg embraced her role as a public intellectual who sought to translate contemporary political and aesthetic developments for a Hebrew-reading public in Palestine. Although her voice has not been integrated into Jewish intellectual history, her contributions to interwar Hebrew culture offer critical reflections on the ethics and future of the Hebrew and European humanist projects. During her years of study in Germany, Goldberg had a front row seat to the turbulent forces that stood poised to destroy Jewish life on European soil, and she distilled this experience in her essays and prose fiction from the 1930s and 1940s.[17] In her writing, Goldberg identified the nexus between European humanism and Hebrew culture in light of the rise of Nazism. She envisioned a Hebrew literature that could take up the tradition of humanism that had been abandoned in the name of fascism. In her 1938 essay "Le-'or ha-raḥamim" (To the light of mercy), she argues that for Hebrew literature to achieve the greatness of Russian literature, for example, it must transform itself by embracing an ethos of *raḥamim* (mercy) toward its fictional characters. In contrast to *ḥemlah* (pity), which she contends dominates Hebrew literature, *raḥamim* has the capacity to transform the ugly into the beautiful; as such, it is a marker of great European writers (for instance, Tolstoy and Dostoevsky). Its absence in Hebrew literature "narrows our world and sentences us to a literary ghetto."[18] In an interesting twist, she contends that Hebrew writers need only look to their own tradition, to Hasidic writing, which already contains this "hidden light of mercy." As Natasha Gordinsky argues, Goldberg viewed her essay as an explanation of Hebrew literature's role in a "state of emergency," when humanist values were under threat.[19] But the essay is also a plea for Hebrew literature to escape the ghetto of Jewish culture, to become more cosmopolitan and European. Even as Goldberg looked toward Europe with suspicion and anger, she would not abandon its great writers, whom she felt Jews needed to emulate, not through imitation but rather by returning to Jewish traditions.

In her 1945 essay "Eropah shelakhem" (Your Europe), Goldberg reflects more critically on the legacy of European humanism for Jewish culture. She likens her generation's quest for secular learning to the intellectual aspirations of the eighteenth-century adherents of the Jewish Enlightenment: "We were naive and foolish, like Solomon Maimon in his day. Like people of the Enlightenment, we young people left 'the margins' to drink from the fountain of knowledge. An affinity for the enlightened world was in our blood, a legacy from the blood of the *maskilim* [Jewish adherents of the Enlightenment]."[20] In turning to Maimon as a symbol for her generation, Goldberg points to the vexed legacy of the Jewish Enlightenment in Germany; he is naive and foolish in his hopes of achieving enlightenment. For "Maimon was both spectacularly successful at entering the highest reaches of European discourse and self-consciously unsuccessful at doing so as anything but an odd and exotic Jew."[21] Writing in 1944, Hannah Arendt argues that although Jewish emancipation should have been "an admission of Jews as Jews to the ranks of humanity," it resembled "a permit to ape the Gentiles or an opportunity to play the parvenu."[22] If European learning signified expanded intellectual vistas to Jewish youth in the eighteenth century, the acceptance of Jews within this secular realm was conditional on their willingness to transform themselves into acceptable subjects of a secular state. As Goldberg asks, "What was Europe to us?—Dante, Giotto, and Michelangelo, Goethe, and Flaubert, and Mozart, and Stendhal, Verlaine, and Rilke and Rodin, Cezanne,

Stravinsky and James Joyce . . . names, names, names, different in their meanings and values, contradicting each other, so many, and it is possible to add: Plato, Spinoza, and Bergson. Is this the point? Did we have to read, to see, to know all of them, to understand them completely, to value them?"[23] Her list of writers and artists, some of whom were also Jewish, is a monument to secular European culture from antiquity to modernity. Yet Goldberg calls into question the idea of a shared Enlightenment legacy. These names don't represent a unified tradition to her any longer, but instead signal a morass of contradictory ideas and values. Reflecting on the history of Jewish acculturation in Europe from the Jewish enlightenment to the Nazi extermination, Goldberg can neither reject European culture outright nor embrace that culture as her own: "'Your Europe,' 'their Europe' it would seem is not 'our Europe,'—despite the fact that we were hers, very much hers."[24] We may have belonged to Europe, but she no longer belongs to us, Goldberg explains.

The fate of Kron's poetry illuminates a crisis within secular Hebrew culture in twentieth-century Europe. Could a generation of Hebrew writers who embraced European literary culture find a home within that culture? Could a European-inflected Hebrew literature embrace a secularism that was not subject to or representative of European Orientalism? Goldberg poses these questions through Kron's search for connections to a medieval past where Jewish and Islamic traditions meet. Kron writes his poetic masterpiece in pseudo thirteenth-century Hebrew block script on antique parchment from Palestine. These pseudo-medieval poems, narrating the Passion of Christ, are far removed from mid-twentieth-century Hebrew intellectual life in Europe.

Playing with literary-historical temporality, Goldberg draws attention to the challenges Hebrew literature history poses to women, who until the twentieth century were often excluded from public textual study and formal education. Goldberg's own literary authority rests on her mastery of European and traditional Hebrew sources. In an essay on queer temporality, Carolyn Dinshaw asks, "What does it feel like to experience a 'totally different form of time'? To live asynchronously? To be out of time? And what will allow us to analyze these feelings, these experiences?"[25] To answer these questions, she proposes a queer historical methodology "that reckons in the most expansive way possible with how people exist in time, with what it feels like to be a body in time, or in multiple times, or out of time" (109). In their recent work, Zohar Weiman-Kelman identifies locations in Goldberg's poetic corpus where Goldberg "resists the forward-looking gaze, creating her own queer history,"[26] allied with what Carolyn Dinshaw has identified as a queer temporal aesthetics. In *Avedot*, Kron experiments with moving between temporalities, writing his poetry in medieval-style Hebrew with block letters on antique parchment. His research in medieval Hebrew and Arabic texts enables him to play with temporality, and the experiment is so successful that "it was hard for Kron to believe that he had written them with his own hands."[27] He looks at the words from "a distance, like the reader of a foreign text (the strange letters, thirteenth-century script, were like a screen between him and the poem)." He is divided from the words by the centuries he fabricated, as though separated from a thirteenth-century past he briefly inhabited. Kron attempts to transport himself to this historical past and its mystical poetic tradition. Through his quasi-mystical poetry, he strives to escape the contradictions of secularism and evade a modern Hebrew-reading public. Reaching back to the thirteenth century, Kron escapes Hebrew secularism and its uncomfortable relationship to German Orientalism, and looks back to a golden age when Jews, Muslims, and Christians coexisted in relative harmony.

Moving between twentieth-century Europe and thirteenth-century Christian, Jewish, and Islamic relations, Goldberg diverts our attention from the intense conflict taking place in her home in Mandatory Palestine. The years when Goldberg composed the novel overlapped with the Arab Revolt (1936–39), which sparked conflict between Zionists and Arab nationalists, who were vying for the creation of their own independent states, with each side advancing competing national claims. Goldberg does not attend to these conflicts directly in her writing. Instead, Goldberg's novel displaces contemporary political tensions onto a medieval past, but in doing so, she subverts the divisions between Jews and Muslims, and by extension between Jews and Arabs. If Kron can locate the Islamic origins of Jewish beliefs, he can find a way to disrupt the developing national binary of Arab and Jew.

Kron is a poet and a scholar, and travels to Europe from Palestine, where he had immigrated years earlier, to research the thirteenth-century influences of Sufism on the Zohar. His project recalls the work of Jewish Orientalists, including Abraham Geiger, Ignaz Goldziher, and Heinrich Graetz, who also employed the scholarly tools of Orientalism to study Islam. Rather than tracing the Jewish origins of Islam (like Geiger, for example), Kron traces the Islamic origins of Jewish mysticism, analyzing Sufi influences on Jewish mysticism and focusing on the Zohar, a founding text of Kabbalah written in the thirteenth century by Moses de Leon and attributed by de Leon to the second-century rabbi Simeon ben Yohai. The Zohar, like Kron's poem cycle, is a work of pseudoepigraphy, published in the thirteenth century as a work discovered from the second century. Gershom Scholem defended the Zohar against accusations of forgery, describing it "as a legitimate category of religious literature of the highest moral order."[28] As David Biale elucidates, in Scholem's view "the pseudoepigrapher identifies himself with a former age because he believes in the eternal significance of his message."[29] Kron creates thirteenth-century poems, similarly, not as forgeries but as authentic expressions of a truth that he locates in the medieval period. By writing his poems in a thirteenth-century script, Kron grants them spiritual authority, as if they were written by another hand or resulted from a divine or mystical—and not necessarily Jewish—experience. Kron, like Goldberg, pushes the boundaries of Jewish culture to envision its Islamic origins and consider its shared history.

Kron's fascination with medieval Jewish mysticism draws attention to the place of women in Jewish tradition. The Zohar, written in the thirteenth century, invested sexual relationships between husbands and wives with divine power: sexuality was "to be divested of its purely physical aspect and endowed with transcendent spirituality."[30] What distinguished the Kabbalah from other sacred writings was its embrace of a divine feminine aspect. David Biale observes, "The Kabbalists' interest in incorporating a female dimension into its image of God resembles in many ways the contemporaneous new cult of the Virgin Mary as a part of the Christian pantheon. But as opposed to medieval Christian mysticism, which involved both men and women, the Kabbalah was exclusively a movement of men."[31] There is no place within Jewish mysticism for women except as wives. We can see that in turning to the Zohar, Kron embraces an all-male intellectual space invested in women's spirituality and their bodies but not their intellectual and artistic agency. Yet these poems are addressed to the women he loves. In effect, Kron cannot step outside the gendered hierarchy of traditional Jewish textual culture or the masculinist ethos of modern Zionism, even when he tries to do so. In contrast to Kron, the novel wants to envision that possible alternative in a female readership.

Returning to the medieval past, Kron spurns the Orientalist impulses of modern secular Hebrew and its rejection of its ties to Islam. But his recourse to a mystical spiritualism resonates with a resurgent European interest in mysticism, even as Kron puts them to different ends. In the late nineteenth and early twentieth centuries, "it was fashionable to ascribe this seemingly inexorable decline of Europe to the ruthless hegemony of reason, and its superficial, mechanistic view of reality, that began with the enlightenment and the triumph of the bourgeois."[32] Popular fascination with Orientalism and the religions of the East blossomed in Western Europe. However, this second Oriental renaissance sought to exclude "Jews from Aryan Christianity" and perceived Judaism as "legalistic and soulless."[33] Among Western European Jews, this spurred interest in Oriental forms of Jewish religious practice, including Eastern European Jewish mysticism.[34] Martin Buber, for example, sought to rehabilitate the Orientalized figure of the Eastern European Jew as a source of spiritual wisdom by embracing Hasidism. Gershom Scholem was also drawn to Jewish mysticism, which he sought to rescue from the contemptuous gaze of the Jewish Enlightenment and return to a central place in Jewish history.[35]

Kron's research on the ties between Jewish and Islamic mysticism is a generative project that sparks his creative process. He uncovers links between Jewish and Islamic mysticism, including a manuscript by Al-Qushayri that connects "Qushayri, Al-Ghazali, and Ibn al-Arabi to the Zohar, the Sabbateans and finally to Hasidism" (153). This enables him to trace connections between Islamic *shirat mistorin* (esoteric poetry) and the Bal Shem Tov by way of Plotinus. Establishing these dizzying links affects him powerfully: "His research overtakes him, his whole being, just as writing poems overtakes him sometimes. Foreign thoughts violate him. This was not drunkenness. This was the pleasure of the mind plunging, sinking into the drunkenness of others" (154). In the past, his research made him feel inadequate as a writer and thinker, propelling thoughts of self-doubt: "Why can I understand all of this and yet I can't create like this? Why can I think and feel like this, but when I touch the paper, in contact with its direct expression, my ideas lose half their significance?" (153). Suddenly, making these connections elevates him and his writing:

> However, in his work that same summer on the collection of brilliant slips of the tongue and slips of the pen in simple legends whose greatness lay in the purity of their innocence, a purity which gave even time a moral definition, he found that in the illusions that by chance excelled the written text, in the dream world identified with the world of ideas, everything was different. Among the Muslims and Jews from the hills of Italy, from the kingdom of the Sultan, and from the small far flung shtetls of Ukraine and Galicia, there were different heights and a different renown. Here thought and its attire, thought and its flesh—inarticulate and incomplete expression notwithstanding—had to unite, never to be separated. They could not achieve eminence on their own, but he, Kron, was able to arrive at these heights only thanks to the push they gave him. It sometimes seemed to him that he breathed a completely different air, mountain air. And nevertheless he didn't feel cold. (154)

Reading these simple legends from traditions both Jewish and Muslim, he is inebriated with the pleasures of writing and creating that come from losing oneself in ideas. Linking Jewish and Muslim expression in these multiple locations and temporalities by way of the unconscious or unintended words of great thinkers and writers, he finds a "dream world of ideas" and illusions that propel his reading. Even the air he breathes is no longer the same. These texts disrupt everyday life and animate his sense of intellectual importance, changing his own experience of reality. The world of text is part of the world, and this shapes his experience.

Of course, the fantasy of returning to a mythic past resonates with Orientalist projects, but here Kron is also resisting the ideologies behind the differentiation of Judaism, Islam, and even Christianity. In effect, Kron feels that he is an anachronism, out of time and place, and this sensation inspires him to embrace eighteenth-century Hasidism, particularly the Bal Shem Tov, even as he shuns contemporary adherents of Hasidism, declaring his alienation from his fellow Jews. The narrator explains, "And even today when he draws from Hasidism's traditions and infinite sources, it sometimes seems to him that he is closer to Rav Nakhman from Bratslav and the Bal Shem Tov, than to all his people who are living today" (173). Born to an assimilated Russian family, Kron is alienated from the Eastern European Jewish masses, from the Russian Jewish immigrants in traditional clothing he sees in Berlin's Jewish quarter, even as he feels a spiritual connection to the Jewish textual world. Kron does not simply seek to embrace the spirituality of the Jewish past; he wants to enter that past completely. He seeks to evade the Orientalist machinations of his contemporaries and return to the historical moment when Jewish mysticism was not imbricated with European Orientalism. But, there is no possibility of such a return, and the impulse is inevitably bound up with Orientalism.

Goldberg's novel links medieival Jewish and Islamic mysticism to secular European literary culture and Christian humanism. Goldberg views Hebrew as a refuge for humanism because in the Weimar era, "the defense of humanistic institutions and ideals had become bound up with right-wing politics."[36] In effect, Goldberg wants to rescue European humanism from Europe. And for this too, she returns to the thirteenth century, to Dante's *Divine Comedy*. A cheap bust of Dante smiles atop Kron's bookshelf in Berlin. In a scene in the novel, Kron lies on his bed staring at rays of sunlight that remind him of the soles of the feet of a woman who once lay on his bed. The narrator then describes how "the statue of Dante smiled on top of the bookcase, green from rust. 'Why does every educated German display Dante's head for all to see?' 'Why this brilliant Florentine?' He remembered how the village servant, Hedwig, would use a wet cloth to wipe the rusted face of the great Italian and claim: 'I even have to wipe the face of this dog!' " (112). In this moment, Goldberg draws the narrator's and then Kron's attention to the statue, in a mix of third-person narration and with the use of free indirect discourse. The passage links Dante to Antonia, and to his childhood. It then pivots from the third person to Kron's first-person monologue, an imagined dialogue between himself and Dante:

> Do you remember how I once got lost in the alleyways of your birthplace, the enchanted rain of the beginning of May, not far from the gold Arno, and I searched for your house among the houses that resembled each other and didn't find you. I sought you out, but I could not find you, my spiritual guide [*mori ve-rabi*] who is greater and wiser than me, I sought you also among the lines of those who rhyme in the Hebrew language and who loudly proclaim the Hebrew renaissance, and I didn't find you. But what are you doing here in the room of Mistress Ernestina-Ana, with her musical name, who will come soon to ask for the rent for this room in which we found refuge from the cold and rain, and not from loneliness? What are you doing here? What am I doing here? In my father's study, in Bobruisk, hanging on the wall next to each other were Alexander Herzen and Doctor Herzl. I, with the poet inside of me, was always certain that

> he chose the two of them because of the mysterious element of unity, alliteration, and Nina would simply say: two old men. On the whole, their presence was justified by Father's liberal tendency, for example, that he participated in his youth in the first congress. But you, my esteemed friend, and you have no justification. Despite that . . . I must get up. (112)

The narrative structure of this passage, which repeats throughout the novel, blurs temporal and spatial boundaries to link Kron to a diasporic historical past that meanders from the Sultanate to the streets of Florence. This particular interior monologue works through a process of association, linking Kron's memory of a cleaning woman to his search for Dante's home in the rainy streets of Florence and to the portraits of two important Russian and Jewish political figures, Herzen and Herzl, one a socialist and the other a Zionist. This jumble of male figures is comically remarked upon by Kron's sister as a group of "old men." There are no women on the walls to celebrate. Whereas Kron's father chooses men who reflect his political commitments, Dante's presence in his landlady's building represents an unreflexive decorative impulse, a marker of his landlady's social class. Kron's Renaissance humanism is foreign to 1930s Berlin. However, Kron identifies with Dante, as an exiled poet without a living audience. Kron addresses Dante, referencing Song of Songs 5:6, in which the beloved rises up to meet her lover, her hands dripping with myrrh, only to find him gone: "I sought you but I could not find you." The spiritual and erotic allusion locates the Christian poet as a divine object of the female lover, here figured as Kron. Dante becomes the object of Kron's erotic investments, a substitute for the woman whose feet he initially thinks of while lying down in his room. In referring to Dante, Kron employs the stock Hebrew honorific for a rabbi, *mori ye-rabi* (my teacher and my master). Just as Virgil was Dante's guide, so too is Dante Kron's guide. However, Dante does not guide Kron to the world of the Hebrew renaissance, nor does he bridge the gap between a Hebrew poetic tradition and a Christian humanist one. Instead, Kron finds Dante's statue in a room in Berlin, where Kron muses, "We both found refuge from the cold and the rain, but we did not find refuge from loneliness" (112). In this passage Dante is a fellow immigrant-writer seeking refuge in Berlin—a modern Jewish exile on the bookshelf.

Dante was a providential figure for exilic Jewish intellectuals and thinkers in the twentieth century, including Osip Mandelstam, Erich Auerbach, and Goldberg, both because of his experience of exile and his formative place in the European humanist tradition. Goldberg wrote extensively on Dante, identifying with him as a poet in exile, a man writing about the historical brink, and writing in the vernacular.[37] Erich Auerbach referred to him as Dante, poet of the secular world, and in his major work, *Mimesis*, credits Dante with the creation of secular realism.[38] Unlike Erich Auerbach, however, Goldberg, in her essay "'Al ha-ḳomediyah ha-elohit'" (On the *Divine Comedy*), identifies Muslim and Jewish influences on Dante's Christian contemplation of Hell, including the work of Ibn al-'Arabi, the same poet and philosopher that Kron links to the Zohar.[39] Goldberg situates Dante in the world of the Orient via the Andalusian universe of thirteenth-century Islam. This meeting point between Dante's *Divine Comedy* and the Zohar—the former a document of European humanism and the latter a document of European Orientalism and Jewish mysticism—presents Kron with the possibility to escape an Orientalist paradigm that would see these traditions as separate.

Goldberg's complex engagement with Dante's Christian and Islamic influences departs from the Hebrew nationalist project, even as she was part of its institutions. This might explain the ambivalent reception of Goldberg's prose fiction and the derogatory label "evropeiskaia sabra" (European sabra) that was leveled against her in the 1930s by the Hebrew critic Moshe Beilinson.[40] Dina Berdichevsky argues that Goldberg's relationship to European literatures and languages "transgressed contemporary norms," whereby "foreign influences are to be assimilated through a careful process of harmonization that effaced all traces of foreignness."[41] Berdichevsky views Goldberg's project of world literature in nonuniversalist terms, describing it as a practice that "does not bridge gaps, but rather constantly measures distances."[42] These distances are never to be resolved but rather open up unrecoverable worlds to the reader. Both Maya Barzilai and Natasha Gordinsky have highlighted Goldberg's intertextual dialogue with the history of Hebrew and European literatures in *Avedot*, including Micah Yosef Lebensohn's nineteenth-century Hebrew poetry about Berlin; Vladimir Nabokov's novel *The Gift*, about a Russian emigre poet in Berlin; Dostoevsky's oeuvre; the work of the Hebrew modernist Gnessin; and of course Dante.[43] Kron refracts Goldberg's intellectual project to rescue world literature and humanism from the grip of European Orientalism and ultimately Nazism, to envision a European literary tradition that does not assume the superiority of Christianity and, subsequently, does not instrumentalize Judaism and Islam.

Goldberg also distills these concerns through Kron's personal relationships with male colleagues, including his former professor, Ivan Yulevitch, a Jewish convert to the Russian Orthodox Church, and Ivan Yulevitch's estranged nephew, Shimshon Berson, an observant Jew. These two men, one a convert and the other an observant Jew, prompt Kron to rethink his social position in Europe and his relationship to his Jewish origins. Although Ivan Yulevitch was born to a traditional Jewish family in Homel, a town in Russia that was briefly a center of modern Hebrew literature, he renounced Judaism, embraced the Jewish Enlightenment, and traveled to Switzerland to study philosophy. Ivan Yulevitch tells Kron that one summer, while traveling in Tuscany, he encountered a monk whose erotic relationship to Catholicism led him to a new appreciation of Christian art, particularly the figure of the Madonna, and then to convert to Russian Orthodoxy. Through Christianity he can express his spirituality and passion for European art, including works by Italian painters such as Carlo Crivelli. Although Yulevitch proclaims that he has not "betrayed" Judaism through his conversion, Kron's feelings about this conversion are left unspoken (212). In contrast, Yulevitch's nephew, Shimshon Berson, claims that all of Jewish culture is to be found in "our religion"; as a result, all Jews should observe Jewish practices whether or not they believe in God. Whereas Yulevitch overidentifies with Christian art to the detriment of his Jewish faith, Berson embraces Jewish faith as a mode of Jewish national expression and culture. Kron rejects both options. He desires neither to convert nor to observe, but rather to find, through his relationship to Dante and Jewish and Islamic mysticism, a secular Jewish alternative that is neither Christian nor connected to Jewish orthodoxy. This desire recalls Goldberg's own relationship to Dante and to Hebrew traditions.

Women, Literary Address, and Goldberg's Modernist Project

Toward the end of the novel, Kron travels from Berlin to the Harz Mountains during Christmas to visit his non-Jewish love interest, Antonia—a young student of Orientalism—and her family. Along with another friend, Kron and Antonia take a long hike in the snowy mountains, where they come across a stunning all-glass restaurant catering to mountain-climbing tourists. Kron is absorbed by the vision of this ice palace until he is disrupted by the arrival of Albina Seidman, a young Jewish-German actress he befriended years ago in Palestine. She is there to divorce her husband, who has discovered an affinity for Nazi racial mythology and suddenly views his wife as a stain on his racial purity. His contempt for her racial origins transforms her from a German actress to a Jewess. Albina is agnostic about her Jewish heritage: "Perhaps I'm a Jewess," she tells Kron (226). Weeks later, Albina, a rising star of the German stage, loses her position in the theater because of her origins. Alone in Berlin without a husband or a source of income, she contemplates emigrating to Palestine and comes to Kron for advice. Kron strongly discourages her because of "the language"; she cannot speak Hebrew and therefore will not have a place on the stage in pre-state Palestine (287). Albina is under the weight of a Jewish identity that she feels is not her own. Although she is a peripheral character in the novel, she is also the only female artist in the novel, but one who cannot read or speak Hebrew. The remaining female characters—including the tragic Ada Weiss (an educated reader of modern Hebrew literature), who commits suicide; Kron's ex-wife, Lily; and his non-Jewish love interest, Antonia—are portrayed as the potential audience for Kron's Hebrew poetry. The novel not only questions whether the non-Hebrew-speaking Albina has a future in Palestine, but also whether there is any future for women in Hebrew. Moving between male and female perspectives along the hallways of European Orientalist institutions, the all-male spaces of traditional Jewish piety, and the private drawing rooms of non-Jewish Christians, Goldberg struggles to envision the role of women in transforming modern Hebrew into a secular literary language.

Through these women and their male doubles, the novel offers a metaliterary reflection on the problem of literary address. Kron conceptualizes his poetry as private words that will never be read by any audience except for his beloved. Initially, he writes his poem cycle for his wife, Lily, as a "personal, divine book" that he does not want to become a "sacrifice for an audience or to the publishers" (39). His poetic ruse falls apart when Lily leaves him for another man, and the poems lose their intended addressee to become "a love letter" addressed to no one (39). This idea of private address governs the novel and Goldberg's secular relationship to Hebrew, expressed in the tension between poetry and prose, whereby poetry in the novel is private, "divine," and anachronistic, and prose is the opposite: public and secular, resulting in a modernist poetics of estrangement and fragmentation.

In her 1937 novel, *Mikhtavim me-nesi'ah medumah* (Letters from an imaginary journey), written at the same time as the unpublished *Avedot*, Goldberg explores a similar thematics of private address. *Mikhtavim* is an epistolary novel composed of letters by the protagonist Ruth addressed to her beloved, Emanuel. Ruth's letters describe an imaginary journey through Europe on the verge of war, but they are never meant to be sent to their addressee, Emanuel. In the preface, Goldberg describes the novel as an "intimate correspondence" and insists that Ruth writes love letters "not in order to burn them afterward in the oven" but for a "literary purpose."[44] The epistolary frame creates two audiences: the diegetic audience is Emmanuel, who will never read the letters, and the extradiegetic audience is the book's reader. This unintended epistolary reader is, of course, the novel's intended addressee, an audience that guarantees its literariness. Both of Goldberg's works theorize the idea that the literariness of prose depends on the impersonal relationship between the reader and the text. Moreover, they both stage the dynamic tensions between male and female readers and writers. In these works, Goldberg underscores how the public and anonymous address of prose conceals a deeper, private relationship between men and women. Kron's search for a female audience is also Goldberg's search for a female readership to rescue Hebrew for the future.

Both novels dramatize intimate relationships between men and women as metaphors for the relationship between authors and their audiences. In *Mikhtavim*, Goldberg plays with the gender fluidity of authorial identity, imagining a female poet describing herself in the masculine. In *Avedot* she gives voice to the figure of a male poet. In her reading of *Mikhtavim*, Tamar Hess argues that Goldberg, playing on the epistolary novel's historical connection to women, arouses feminine expectations in her reader, only to overturn them. Ruth is the one traveling (even if only in her imagination), while Emanuel is left behind. Adopting this imaginary masculine subject position in the correspondence "enables Ruth to create and see herself as a 'poet' (and not necessarily as abandoned and weeping). She is transformed from victim to artist."[45] In her letters, moreover, Ruth describes herself as a *meshorer* (poet, masc.) and not "'almah ha-kotevet shirim" (a young woman who writes poems; 95). She's writing as a woman in masculine form to a male addressee who will never receive her words. Even as the novel appears to imagine a female author speaking to a male reader, it precludes the intended male addressee because Ruth never sends her letters. The female-authored text will never reach the object of its desire, a male reader. Instead, her female protagonist imagines herself in the guise of a male poet and, in doing so, invokes another audience: women. In *Avedot* Goldberg takes a different tack, giving voice to a male poet who fails to reach his female audience. Like Ruth, Kron writes his poetry not to be published, but rather as a form of private address that never finds its proper addressee. *Avedot* focuses on this misalignment between author and reader as its core principle.

Addressing a private female audience in the guise of thirteenth-century Hebrew, Kron attempts to elide the politics of secular Hebrew. His poems address the women in his life: his ex-wife Lily, his non-Jewish, German lover Antonia, and a Jewish émigré to Berlin named Ada. Written on antique parchment, his poems appear like medieval objects, they stretch back to the thirteenth century and yet they also reach forward to the twentieth century. In *Avedot*, Goldberg seeks to envision a secular literary culture that engages a community of women readers whose exclusion from the world of traditional Jewish texts might enable them to imagine and create a secular Hebrew culture outside of an Orientalist gaze. Yet the novel also points to the dangerous misalignment between the intended and actual readers of these texts. When Kron's poem cycle falls into the wrong hands, the public literary sphere proves to be a very dangerous space for his poetry.

Despite his desire to find a private female addressee for his poetry, the poems index a very different audience—that is, the most likely contemporary readers of medieval Hebrew manuscripts: Orientalist scholars. Thus, in his desire to escape the world of secular Hebrew culture and its public institutions—publishing houses, critics, and modern readers—he ends up writing "divine" poems that reach a more dangerous audience, ensuring that they will be exploited by Nazi Orientalists.

Kron's lost poetic masterpiece depicts a Christian narrative of the Passion of Christ. This purloined poem at the novel's center contains the key to Goldberg's conception of the relationship of women to Hebrew prose and of Hebrew to Christian and European literary traditions. Although only a snippet of the last poem in the cycle appears in the novel, the narrator explains that the entire poem tells the story of "an old and frail God who, on the night of Jesus's death, sees Mary Magdalene surrendering herself to Judas Iscariot for the price of a drop of blood from the crucified one; of a God who created man's heart with all its urges and did not leave himself a single desire" (40). In these poems, Kron imagines Mary Magdalene in a sexual relationship with the man who betrayed Jesus and juxtaposes this narrative of seduction and betrayal to an aging God who lacks all desire to fulfill the Second Coming. The only lines of the poem included in the novel describe a cold divinity: "For it is cold, it is very cold, the infinite coldness of God, and he knows" (40). Reflecting on these poems, Kron identifies not with the central male actors of the story, Jesus and Judas, but with Mary Magdalene. He declares, "I will create these poems like a whore, God's whore. Prostitute!" (40). Giddon Ticotsky argues that the poem represents Kron's love for a non-Jewish German woman (Antonia) "in light of the New Testament" and contends that both Kron and his non-Jewish love interest are Judas figures, betraying each other and their cultures.[46] However, I argue that Kron identifies with Mary Magdalene, thus imagining himself in a Christian narrative. In these Hebrew poems about Jesus, Kron writes as a woman (i.e., as Mary Magdalene) and for women (Lily and Antonia), and in doing so, personalizes and secularizes a Christian narrative of desire, appropriating Christian tradition in Hebrew for a sexualized secular poetics that aligns with a feminist countertradition.

Jewish modernist writers and artists in the first half of the twentieth century were drawn to images of Jesus and other Christian figures. Marc Chagall, Sholem Asch, Moshe Leyb Halpern, Uri Tsvi Grinberg, Yosef Klauzner, and Aharon Kabak depicted Jesus in their work, identifying with him as a Jewish symbol of martyrdom, rebellion, and even Jewish nationalism. Matthew Hoffman argues that in portraying Jesus, Jewish writers were breaking from traditional Jewish sources and turning to a figure of universal interest, yet one who also retained, at least for Jewish writers, some Jewish particularism. This process was an "integral part of creating a new and distinctive secular Jewish culture."[47] This was not the case for Hebrew writers in British Mandatory Palestine in the 1920s and 1930s, who instead "adopted the figure of Jesus, not as part of an external and apologetic discourse, or as a mediator between Judaism and Christianity, but rather in the context of the new national identity, as a model for the desired New Jew."[48] In Palestine, male Jewish writers turned to Jesus as a powerful symbol for new forms of collective Jewish male identity with which to justify their presence in the land.

In contrast to this masculinist and nationalist appropriation of Jesus, modernist Jewish women writers turned to the Virgin Mary and Mary Magdalene as figures for their own modernist projects. Feminist scholars have offered insightful readings of this countertradition in the writing of Goldberg and the Yiddish poet Anna Margolin. Barbara Mann reads both women writers' engagement with Mary as "a symbolic intervention, denoting the presence of women poets within a male dominated field," part of the poets' attempts to carve a place for women in Hebrew and Yiddish literary culture.[49] Weiman-Kelman argues that unlike their male poet counterparts, Goldberg and Margolin do not "reclaim" Jesus because, she surmises, "as women Judaism itself was not theirs to claim."[50] Instead, the poets distance themselves from both Christian and Jewish tradition, while using their exclusion from Judaism "as enabling freedom of movement and cross identifications."[51] In *Avedot* Goldberg envisions a male poet adopting this countertradition as part of his erotic identification with a female reading audience. She draws on Christian tradition and her own poetic corpus to envision Kron as a double for Magdalene, blurring the boundaries between gender and religious identity. The male poet turns to the female tradition within Christianity to rupture the boundaries between Jew and gentile, as between men and women.

The orchestration of the erotic gender confusion in Kron's poem recalls Goldberg's poetic rendering of Mary Magdalene in her 1931 poem "Ḥalom na'arah" (The dream of a young girl), which appeared in her 1935 collection *Ṭaba'ot 'ashan* (Rings of smoke). In the poem, Goldberg describes Carlo Crivelli's fifteenth-century painting *Saint Mary Magdalene*, depicting a beautiful young woman offering a golden goblet to Jesus. In the first stanza, the poet imagines herself in the place of Jesus seduced by the beautiful Magdalene in an act of imaginative substitution. In the second stanza, the poet transforms herself into her ex-lover, who is drawn to the golden-haired Renaissance visage in Crivelli's painting. The poem describes Goldberg's experience examining Christian art as a spectator in Berlin's Kaiser Friedrich Museum. She enlists iconic images from the New Testament, displacing them from their Christian theological context to produce a personal narrative of erotic desire and rejection. At the same time, she imagines herself within the aesthetic world of Christian Europe, if only to be erased by its image. Goldberg's poem sidesteps the theological significance of the painting, focusing on its erotic dimension instead.

In *Avedot*, Goldberg seeks to envision a secular literary culture that engages a community of women readers whose exclusion from the world of traditional Jewish texts might enable them to imagine and create a secular Hebrew culture beyond the pale of both a Christian and Orientalist worldview. The novel hinges on the gendered cultural history of Hebrew reading practices, as well as the disruptions various readers pose to those practices. Goldberg reminds us that modes of reading and interpretation are historically contingent and culturally specific—that whatever the address of a given text, there is always more than one reader. As Kron negotiates these various reading audiences, he has no control over the ultimate fate of his poetry; this is his nightmare. Moreover, this anxiety also haunts Goldberg's prose oeuvre, as she envisions an erotically charged relationship between an author and her audience that must be suppressed to transform her work into literary prose.

Kron imagines his Hebrew poem cycle addressing four possible readers: (1) observant Eastern European and Hebrew-literate Jewish men, who were unlikely to read modern Hebrew poetry about Jesus, Judas, and Mary Magdalene; (2) Orientalist scholars, the most likely modern readers of medieval texts; (3) secular Hebrew readers in Europe or Palestine; and (4) the women to whom he dedicates the poems, Lily and Antonia. Kron is vexed by his potential male readership, which calls into question his relationship to secular Hebrew culture, Jewish piety, and Orientalism. Although he turns to women, they too remain an imperfect audience. In imagining these various readers for Kron's cycle, Goldberg negotiates her own unstable position as both writer and reader of secular European literature, traditional Hebrew texts, and modern Hebrew literature.

Goldberg stages Kron's encounter first with traditional Jewish male readers when he travels to Berlin's Jewish quarter to procure a rare Hebrew manuscript for his research. Surrounded by the city's Eastern European Jewish immigrants, Kron confronts his secular alienation from the masses of Eastern European Jews who cling to their Jewish observance. Despite his interest in Jewish mysticism, Kron does not observe Jewish law, and yet Kron also recognizes his Jewish alienation from his secular Orientalist colleagues.

Kron's experience of the Jewish quarter catalyzes a crisis of personal identity that also represents a metaliterary problem of finding and defining an audience for secular Hebrew writing in Europe. Arriving on the Jewish neighborhood's central thoroughfare, Grenadierstrasse, Kron is assaulted by the Eastern European Jewish "faces that surround him on all sides" (174). He averts his eyes from these disembodied faces, which he derisively refers to as "Haim'im" (Chaims or Himeys) or "Yankl'im" (Yankls) and later "Kasrilevkans" (residents of Sholem Aleichem's fictional town, Kasrilevke; 174). Kron's relationship to the Jewish quarter recalls the pathos expressed by German Jewish writers like Josef Roth in his 1929 description of the Grenadierstrasse, "The Wailing Wall," or Alfred Döblin in his 1926 account of Eastern European Jews in *Reise in Polen* (*Journey to Poland*). Unlike the narrative perspectives of these assimilated German Jews, Goldberg's novel avoids ethnographic descriptions of Jewish difference. Furthermore, *Avedot* does not romanticize their religious observance; instead Kron looks upon these *Ostjuden* (a derisive term for Eastern European Jews) with contempt. They are Orientalized Eastern European Jews, the backward, lazy remnants of a Jewish past that Kron rejects. Although he embraces early Hasidic writings, he feels no affinity to actual adherents of Hasidism.

Despite Kron's disgust, he still acknowledges his personal connection to a male Yiddish-speaking Eastern European Jewry. He recalls growing up in a Russian-speaking assimilated Jewish household in Bobroisk, "on a quiet, beautiful street surrounded by gardens among Gentile homes" (174). Although his family lived among non-Jews, their friends "were half-assimilated Jews—Russian style." In their Russian-speaking home, Yiddish had not disappeared but was relegated to the realm of humor. One generation removed from the Jewish shtetl, Kron recalls that the "the scent of the shtetl, the scent of the Jewish street, arrived in their house only with the visits of his grandmother and grandfather." He thinks of his father in a train car with a non-Jewish Russian doctor, reading the liberal Russian paper and thinking about Dostoevsky. He even imagines the Russian doctor musing to himself that the Jews "are not such a bad element" of Russian society, a vision that recalls Sholem Aleichem's description of assimilated Jews who ride in second-class train cars, attempting to hide a Jewishness that is still visible on their bodies (175). This all-male assimilated world collapses with the onset of the Russian Revolution: his father dies, and the family falls apart.

As a Hebrew writer, Kron must sustain a connection to the male Jewish masses; however, as a "half-assimilated" Jew, he remains distant from them: "Perhaps it was the fault of literature that he, a Hebrew poet, had not learned to this day to love these filthy streets, these narrow alleyways, with a true love" (175). Kron marvels at his educated male Jewish friends, who as natives of the Pale of Settlement and "prisoners of the *beit midrash* [Jewish house of study]," can feel a deep attachment to the Jewish masses. These male friends and acquaintances respond enthusiastically to Jewish folk culture and the nationalist movements that rely on that folk culture. For Kron to do so, however, he would "feel in the depths of his soul that he was dishonest"; indeed, he senses that something "was fake here, something not compatible with the essence of his soul" (175). On the one hand, Kron blames Mendele and Sholem Aleichem for their failure to nourish his attachment to Jewish folk culture. On the other, Kron suspects that as an assimilated Russian Jew who did not experience the *beit midrash* or the shtetl, he cannot understand this literature.

Confronted with his disgust for these largely male Jewish masses, his thoughts turn to another possible audience for his Hebrew writing: his Orientalist colleagues, including his mentor, Professor Brake; Antonia; and Wang, a Chinese student. He asks himself, "Aren't you closer in your soul, in your spirit, in your interior world and all its structures, a thousand times closer to Professor Brake, Antonia, and to the Chinese Wang, than to all these people walking on this street?" (176). Kron reserves a special place for Wang, whom he recognizes as a fellow Asian, asking Antonia one evening, "Aren't I also Asian?" (80). However, their bond is primarily based on a shared scholarly investment in Semitic texts and their outsider status in a racialized Europe. These non-Jewish characters thus represent a possible audience for his Hebrew poetry.

Despite his declared affinity to his fellow scholars, Kron cannot fully disavow his connection to the Jews on the street, which distinguishes him from his non-Jewish colleagues. If anyone were to harm one of these "Haims or Yankels," Kron muses, "you would cry foul, you would scream and weep loudly, you and not Professor Brake" (176). Furthermore, Kron is at times fearful that Antonia will one day "blame him and the remainder of his people" and join up with the antisemites of the day (150). This is his bond with the Jewish street; their victimhood is his own. And it is their victimization that defines his Jewish difference.

Trapped between two potential audiences, one Jewish and the other Orientalist, Kron rejects them both, and yet he cannot escape from either. "Aren't you sure," Kron asks himself, "that everything you write, if we forget the question of language, of course, is nearer and dearer to every Gentile with your same education and your same outlook, than to any single one of these people of yours?" (176). If he did not write in Hebrew, then the audience for his poetry would be primarily Gentile readers. There is no possibility, however, of forgetting the question of language, for it underlines his Orientalist project and poetics. The Hebrew language also delimits a specific audience. Is Kron suggesting that his poetry is European or universal, save for the fact that it is written in Hebrew? In part, he seeks to elide Hebrew nationalism by imagining a medieval, thirteenth-century poetics, escaping from Orientalist dynamics into a medieval past.

Kron does not find a home among his fellow Hebrew writers from Palestine either. Instead he feels distant from the Hebrew literary world he left behind to study in Berlin. In one scene in the novel, Kron encounters a group of friends from Palestine, including a fellow Hebrew poet, in a café on the Kurfürstendamm, and "he began to yearn for them, those who understand Hebrew and read his poems" (90). But once he sits among these modern Hebrew speakers in Berlin, "it suddenly seemed to him that all of these people speak an old language covered with rust. This was not his language" (90). Kron even surmises that the medieval Hebrew poet Ibn Gabirol or the modernist prose writer Uri Nissan Gnessin would feel the same suffocation sitting with these modern Jews. Kron attempts to transcend the everyday world of modern Hebrew through his attachment to a Hebrew poetics that is mystical and medieval. His poetics strive to move beyond the confines of both Orientalism and secular Zionism. Kron imagines an alternative secularism rooted in a female readership, turning to women readers to envision the future of Hebrew culture. Hebrew women writers, however, are nowhere to be seen in the novel, even though the author is one. Their absence is a product of the masculine Hebrew world that Kron inhabits. Yet there were Hebrew women poets writing in the 1930s, including Goldberg and Bikhovsky. Goldberg, however, excludes them from her novelistic universe. Instead, she approaches Orientalist Hebrew as a crisis of masculinity that awaits its rescue at the hands of women.

Kron forges intimate relationships with two of his ideal women readers. He dedicates his poem first to Lily and then Antonia, yet the most devoted reader of his poetry is Ada Weiss, an Eastern European Jewish immigrant in Berlin whom he never meets in person. Weiss represents an ideal secular reader for his poetry; as a Jewish woman, she has no connection to a Jewish textual tradition that excludes her, and her bookshelves, like Kron's, are filled with European volumes. During the 1930s, Goldberg wrote a number of *reshimot* (a genre of impressionist essays, sometimes translated as "notes") under the pseudonym Ada Grant, and many of these essays were presented as Ada Grant's literary diary.[52] Goldberg gestures to her literary alter ego to grapple with her place in Hebrew literature as a Hebrew reader and writer.

She also enters into a rich tradition of self-reflexive, metaliterary writing that includes Sholem Aleichem and S. Y. Abramovitsh, who wrote under pseudonyms and playfully navigated the boundaries of their various personal identities and pseudonyms.[53]

Still, Lily, Antonia, and Ada are a problematic community of readers. Antonia is a student of Orientalism whose knowledge of Hebrew is restricted to the Hebrew alphabet. Although she cannot quite read Kron's poetry, she does read his Jewish body, transforming him into a Hebrew text. One morning when Antonia is left alone in his apartment, she browses his bookshelves, which are filled with Russian, German, Italian, English, Arabic, and Hebrew books and newspapers. She thinks to herself, "Foreign books, and a foreign man. I will never learn to read him" (138). Attempting to read Hebrew, Antonia stumbles over the Hebrew word *yalḳuṭ* (anthology):

> She read the gilded letters on the black binding of one Hebrew book. It came out strange: "yalḳuṭ." She read it again. She thought she must be mistaken with the letters. The 22 letters of the alef-bet passed through her memory. She read again, and again it came out: "yalḳuṭ." What could be the meaning of this word? Perhaps a name? Maybe the name of an old man, of an old Jewish man with a long beard. And long sidelocks. Perhaps this was the name of Kron's grandfather. She described to herself this old grandfather wandering down a very long avenue outside the city and in his wrinkled hand is a young Elhanan's small palm. If only she could approach this old Jewish man and simply say to him: "Mr. Yalḳuṭ, it is so terrible for me." It was terribly difficult for her. (139–40)

Antonia reads Kron's Jewish body in Hebrew words whose meaning eludes her, transforming Kron's modern secular scholarship into the image of his grandfather, a shtetl Jew who studies canonical texts in the *beit midrash* and not the hallowed halls of academia. Despite all the other books on Kron's shelf, and the statue of Dante on top of his bookshelf (which Antonia describes as "idiotic"), she can locate him only in the foreign Hebrew letters on his books. Moreover, she is drawn more to this elderly Jewish man than to Kron, and it is to the former that she turns for comfort and advice. Antonia's longing for Kron's Jewish grandfather is a rejection of Kron's secular cosmopolitanism in favor of an authentic Jewishness that she locates in his grandfather's visage. She is ultimately a failed audience for his poetry, a woman who cannot read Hebrew and cannot separate him from the Eastern European Jewish men who wander the Grenadierstrasse. Goldberg considered titling the novel "Muḳdash le-Anṭoniyah" (Dedicated to Antonia), referencing the one woman in the novel who cannot read Kron's poetry, a title that emphasizes their relationship as central to the novel.

In contrast to Antonia, Ada is a mirror image of Kron: a secular European Jewish woman with cosmopolitan reading habits and a love of Hebrew. Kron never meets Ada in person, but he learns about her on a visit to the bookseller in the Jewish quarter, where he is surprised to see a photograph of himself cut from a Hebrew newspaper and pasted onto the wall. This newspaper clipping belonged to Ada, who lived with the bookseller's family until she committed suicide. Among the German, Romanian and Hebrew titles on the bookshelves in her rented room, Kron spies an anthology that contains his long poem and an issue of a Hebrew journal that includes his poetry. Kron also discovers that Ada's Hebrew diary contains numerous references to him and his poetry, including one in which Ada writes, "Kron would understand this. I read his poems again. I am still sorry that I never succeeded in meeting him. I don't believe that this man is less than his poems. If I were a poet, I would write only like this. He is the only one who knows everything about me, and all those similar to me" (188). Frightened by Ada's declarations of affection, Kron declines to read the rest of her diary, thus ensuring that Ada's secret Hebrew writing will not find a public. Her diary is the only female-authored work of Hebrew represented in the novel, and it is destroyed by Kron. Kron then takes a photograph of Ada, which he carries in his wallet. If Ada represents Kron's (and perhaps Goldberg's) ideal reader—a secular European Jewish woman who is literate in Hebrew—it is surely significant that Ada commits suicide out of personal and cultural despair, foreshadowing the violence to come and providing an ominous gesture toward the future of European Hebrew culture. Moreover, in failing to preserve her diary, Kron fails to preserve a woman-authored document of European Hebrew. Here too, Goldberg captures the erasure of women's Hebrew literary voices, in the figure of the diary that Kron will toss away.

Despite Kron's idealization of women readers, he never succeeds in addressing any of them. In a surrealist dream sequence in the novel, Kron imagines himself watching a film about his life projected onto a movie screen. In the dream, Ada boards a train and then calls out to him to catch the next train. Kron does so only to see two different trains pass by—one with Lily aboard and the other with Antonia. He shouts out to the women and then suddenly realizes that he is sitting alone in a detached car—metaphorically, himself (Kron's Hebrew name also means train car)—as this female readership spins out of control. The dream also connects to the novel's Christian narrative: as Maya Barzilai argues, the figure of the detached train car stuck on the track "symbolizes the Jew's inability to escape the Christian narrative that perpetuates him as the victim or forerunner."[54] In his dream, being the Jew is imbricated with his erotic and literary failures but also with his failure to escape an Orientalizing gaze that threatens to turn him into a Christian allegory.

Ultimately, Kron's lost poem cycle finds an audience—albeit a completely unintended one—when two Nazi-sympathizing Orientalist scholars, Dr. Karl Bach and Fadei Kruchko, steal the manuscript and publish it in a respectable academic journal as an example of thirteenth-century medieval Jewish anti-Christian sentiment. In their analysis, the poem is a religious "psalm" that describes with "Jewish chutzpah" the "sacred figures of Christianity" (307). They read the poet's universalist strivings as evidence of Jewish particularism. Kron reacts ambivalently to the publication of the poem. On the one hand, he is relieved to be reunited with his lost manuscript. On the other hand, his poetry is being exploited to stir up anger against the Jews. He is in an impossible situation. If he declares that Bach and his colleague are liars, he will have to claim the poem as his own. And if the faculty at the university believe him, he will then be claiming authorship of a poem that has now been declared anti-Christian, putting both himself and his fellow Jewish immigrants in Berlin at risk. The only possible solution, he realizes, is to depart Europe and return to Palestine: "He, an Oriental, Yehuda Elhanan Kron, will not remain here as an objective observer of this foreign tragicomedy: he is a participant, albeit a reluctant one. Perhaps this is good. He is the Jew, the Jew in everyone, despite his uprootedness, and his is the Jewish fate; in every country he takes one of its beatings—he wanders and wanders. And his eyes are always directed toward the *hamsin*—and maybe he will arrive there" (308–9). Kron finally identifies not as a European but as an Oriental, a wandering diasporic Jew without a home, not unlike the Eastern European Jews he held in contempt on the Grenadierstrasse. Although he views his poems, in part, as complicit in the tragicomedy that is the Nazi rise to power or as emerging from the very culture that produced the Nazis, he also views them as his best work—albeit the work of an exotic Eastern Jew who embraces an Oriental identity.[55] Kron's view of himself as an Oriental is decidedly European in sharing the Christian Orientalist perspective that Jews are irascible Orientals. In this Eastern guise he transforms himself into the visage of his poetry, a lost Hebrew manuscript whose audience remains the secular and the Christian. At the end of the novel, on the eve of his departure from Europe, Kron becomes a text fleeing his unwanted audience. But as Natasha Gordinsky notes, in returning to Palestine, Kron (and by extension Goldberg) does not succeed in connecting his Russian, German, and Hebrew literature worlds.[56] Moreover, he does not imagine their connection to the Arab community that shares his refuge.

If he cannot rescue his poetry, however, he does rescue an old acquaintance, another peripheral female character, Elizavet, marrying her so she can emigrate to Palestine. Elizavet is a progressive schoolteacher who embraced modern German culture and entered into an open, "modern" relationship with a fellow teacher. When her German lover embraces his Aryan identity and joins the Nazi Party, Elizavet, like Kron and Albina, finds herself expunged from her ties to Germany and German culture. Although she and Kron had once been set up by a mutual friend to rescue them from their non-Jewish love affairs, the two do not find common ground. Now they both must flee Germany for their lives. Unlike Kron, Elizavet knows no Hebrew.

Her journey is an escape, not a return. Their marriage of convenience has no erotic overtones; there is no desire between them, only shared refuge. In effect, they are mirror images, two young secular Jews, reduced by the Nazi state to an essentialized identity they eschew. Elizavet's only connection to Palestine is as a Nazi refugee, and Kron sees his return as a retreat into an Orientalist narrative that would expel the Jews from Europe.

Departing Europe, Kron contemplates to whom he should dedicate these poems: "Lily did not want them. Certainly, Ada would have wanted them, but he never knew her, and these poems did not come from her" (314). He reflects that they "contain this country and its love, its hate, and its betrayal, and his longings for another love—one that is here, a red flame above a pale forehead . . . his betrayal." As a result, Kron chooses to dedicate the poems to Antonia, who represents the world that he is escaping, a woman who views him as an Oriental Other. He wonders whether Antonia will ever read the poems, and whether she too will don a brown shirt and join the Nazis.

Goldberg concludes her novel with Brake's suicide, Ivan Yulevitch's death, and a newspaper report that Lily has been murdered by Nazi youth. The title Goldberg once considered—"Mukḳdash le-Anṭoniyah"—suggests that she viewed the novel as dedicated to the European world that consumed and expelled its Jewish population. Kron cannot excise himself from the secular European view of the Eastern Jew. Instead, he transforms himself into an unrepentant Oriental, whose most willing readers are composed of antisemitic Nazi scholars. At the end of the novel, Kron's seemingly nationalistic gesture to return to Palestine transforms him into the allegorical figure of the wandering Jew: "He is the Jew, the Jew in everyone, despite his uprootedness, and his is the Jewish fate; in every country he takes one of its beatings—he wanders and wanders" (308).

This vexed ending helps explain why Goldberg decided not to publish the novel. Whether Antonia did or did not become a brownshirt, Germany had descended into darkness. Whatever aesthetic questions Goldberg began to ask in the novel, the atrocities committed during World War II extinguished them. Goldberg's unfinished novel, however, offers a view of the pressures that Hebrew writers faced in the first half of the twentieth century as they struggled to situate themselves within both a European literary tradition and an emerging Jewish national tradition. Framing these struggles in terms of competing reading publics, Goldberg highlights the centrality of women to the secularization of Hebrew reading practices, even if she cannot resolve her own conflicted relationship to Orientalism. The novel finds no clear way forward for a Hebrew woman writer whose only access to Hebrew is dependent on the language's secularization. Yet she illuminates how central questions of gender and textuality are to our understanding of Orientalism, secularism, and Hebrew modernism.

Chapter 6

Elisheva Bikhovsky's Minority Cosmopolitanism

Elisheva Bikhovsky was for a time in the 1920s one of the most successful and celebrated Hebrew poets in Palestine. Born Elizaveta Zhirkova in Ryazan in 1888 to a Christian family, she was raised in Russia by her maternal aunt, who identified as British. She was drawn to Jewish culture at a young age, identifying with the Jewish minority struggle for cultural and national autonomy. Like many of the modernist women writers I have written about, she was most recognized and celebrated as a poet. Her first Hebrew collection of poems, *Kos ḳeṭanah* (Small cup; 1926), had the distinction of being the first book of poetry published by a woman in Mandatory Palestine. In 1925, the year that she and her husband departed the Soviet Union for a new life in Palestine, she began composing her modernist novel *Simṭa'ot* (Alleyways), the first published by a woman in Palestine. Elisheva's identity as a non-Jewish woman shaped her reception in Hebrew literature: critics dubbed her "Ruth from the Volga," referencing the biblical Ruth who willingly adopted the faith of her mother-in-law, Naomi.[1] The Hebrew literary community embraced her enthusiastically, then later reviled her as an outsider to the Zionist enterprise. In many ways, she represented the ideal Zionist subject, with no attachments to a diasporic Jewish past or traditional Jewish textuality, and thus she was also in a position to secularize and internationalize Hebrew. With Hebrew, Bikhovsky embraced the minority language of an emerging ethnic nationalism that was not her own. She introduced a modernist poetics of simplicity that was widely recognized and celebrated, but her novelistic attention to the political and social questions regarding minority nationalism and female authorship have received little critical attention.

Bikhovsky's prose explores alienation and minoritization as generative processes that propel a modernist Hebrew poetics beyond ethnonationalism. In the early twentieth century, writing in Hebrew was not necessarily synonymous with Jewish territorial nationalism. Rather, it was an expression of a Jewish cultural minority identity. In *Simṭa'ot* she highlights the tensions and misalignments between identity and authorship, exploring intimate relationships among Jews and non-Jews, and between Hebrew and Russian literature. As Dana Olmert has pointed out, a central theme of the novel is “the reciprocal desire among the Jewish and non-Jewish characters.”[2] Through these relationships, the novel questions the meaning and substance of national literature and imagines the transformative project of a minority nationalist literary culture from the perspective of woman artists.

Simṭa'ot is set amid the bohemian milieu of Hebrew and Russian literary culture in 1920s Moscow. In the novel Bikhovsky portrays Soviet Hebrew as a minority language that had been attacked by the forces of revolution and was withering in the absence of official national recognition (in contrast to Yiddish), without any sustainable literary community. If the novel does not imagine a dynamic Hebrew culture, it also depicts a less than vibrant Russian literary milieu composed of self-interested writers dreaming of immigrating to Western Europe. The novel is set in the Soviet Union in the shadow of war communism and the beginning of the New Economic Program (NEP). Ideological fatigue runs through the narrative; the characters have little optimism regarding the revolutionary promises of international socialism, the Soviet avant-garde, or the Zionist project. Literary discussions and debates are overshadowed by the interpersonal dramas of the various writers and artists in the novel, and these tensions dominate the narrative.

There are two central protagonists in the novel: Ludmilla Vivyen, an established Russian poet, and Daniel Royter, a Hebrew writer who attempts to gain acceptance in Russian literary circles. The novel meditates on the conflict between minority and nationalist literary cultures through the various unconsummated erotic relationships between Jews and non-Jews, including Ludmilla's and Daniel's. Neither can overcome their ethnic and national differences to embrace the other. These failed relationships highlight the tensions and interrelations between two different linguistic, cultural, and national systems: Soviet national minority policy and Jewish national culture in Palestine. Neither is presented as ideal; rather, the novel attempts to situate Hebrew at the interstices of Soviet and Zionist ideologies and imagines it as a language of minority cosmopolitanism in the hands of a non-Jewish woman. The novel articulates an ambivalent Zionism, voiced by a non-Jewish woman.

Notably, between 1929 and 1938, when few women published Hebrew novels, several women writers in Palestine composed novels set in the Soviet Union.[3] The Soviet Union offered the perfect stage for women writers to describe the rise of the secular Jewish subject who splits from the traditional authority of the Jewish family and works to form a political community, embracing the new freedoms promised by the revolution. The revolution brought about large-scale changes for the Jewish community in Russia. The Soviet state officially recognized a Jewish national minority. This minority national identity was a Soviet alternative to the Zionist goal of building a majority Jewish state in Palestine. Women writers observed and celebrated the radical reorganization of family and domestic life and this reshaping of national minority culture. One of the first priorities of the Soviet government was the 1918 Code on Marriage, the Family, and Guardianship, which abolished religious marriage, legalized civil marriage, eliminated illegitimacy, and made divorce available on demand to anyone without a partner's consent.[4] The code legalized marriage across religious and ethnic divides. Indeed, three novels published in pre-state Palestine and set in the Soviet Union—*Simṭa'ot*, Sarah Gluzman's *El ḥa-gevul* (To the border), and Miriam Bernstein-Cohen's *Mefisto* (Mephisto)—portray romantic relationships between Jews and non-Jews. In both Bikhovsky's and Bernstein-Cohen's novels, intimate relationships serve as a laboratory for the new social practices of revolution and as a metaphor for the intimate mixing of Jewish and non-Jewish literary cultures.

Both the socialist and Zionist movements shared in the project of radically reorganizing the axes of identification that governed the modern subject and everyday life. Many Jewish immigrants to Palestine in the early twentieth century arrived from Russia, and brought with them Russian revolutionary ideas that then influenced the Jewish labor movement in Palestine.[5] Moreover, similar sexual and domestic experiments were under way during the second and third aliyah in Palestine, for example in the communal living arrangements of the kibbutz.[6] Zionism revolutionized Jewish domestic life; however, just as in the Soviet Union, the movement never fully embraced women's equality.[7] The labor movement welcomed women's participation in the labor force but never resolved the inequalities inherent in the apportionment of domestic labor. Without addressing women's unpaid labor or childcare demands, the labor movement failed to achieve equality for women. These women writers turned to the Soviet Union to answer pressing questions in their domestic milieu in Palestine. The Soviet Union offered a promising stage for conceptualizing a woman-authored cosmopolitan Hebrew. It also offered distance from the conflict brewing between Zionists and Arab nationalists in Palestine, and the vexed question of how Jewish national awakening affected the Arab nationalist struggle for national self-determination.

In Search of a Cosmopolitan Hebrew

Bikhovsky's personal story and her literary career figure the contradictory impulses of Hebrew modernist writing of the period: the twin poles of aesthetic universalism and ethnic national particularism. As a young woman, she was drawn to the minority cultural struggle that Zionism represented. She studied both Hebrew and Yiddish in her twenties, translating from both languages into Russian.[8] Her earliest original Hebrew poems appeared in 1922 in *Ha-tekufah* (The Era), a premier publication of the project of Hebrew revival. She married the prominent publisher and Zionist cultural activist Shimon Bikhovsky in 1922. In a letter written in 1923, she describes her affinity for Hebrew as her literary language even though she does not identify as Jewish or as "completely Russian."[9] Bikhovsky saw parallels between the struggles of her Irish ancestors under British rule and the Jews under Russian rule, explaining that if she were to translate the Irish poet Thomas Moore (1779–1852) into Hebrew, it would read like a "shirei Zion" (lyrical poems of longing for Zion or the Land of Israel). She writes that from her earliest memories, she "always felt a fondness for any nation, particularly to smaller nations that are persecuted and oppressed."[10] She was not burdened by the textual norms of diasporic Judaism and its attachment to traditional texts, nor did she have any religious attachment to Hebrew. As Miryam Segal explains, "Her foreignness reinforced her femininity by detaching her completely from the traditional Jewish learning and textuality that were associated with the Diaspora."[11] Like Leah Goldberg, Bikhovsky easily established herself in Hebrew cultural circles and became a household name in Hebrew letters. Her success paved the way for other women poets, including Rachel Bluwstein, Bat Miriam, Esther Raab, and later Leah Goldberg. She revolutionized Hebrew poetry, breaking down the boundaries between spoken and literary Hebrew, a feat Dan Miron refers to as "one of the principal innovations of that generation."[12]

Hebrew writers adored this non-Jewish woman whose embrace of Hebrew and the Jewish people signaled to many the success of the Zionist cultural project. When she immigrated to pre-state Palestine, she was feted as a Ruth-like figure who proved that Hebrew could transcend Jewish provincialism and enter the world literary stage as a language of high culture and avant-garde poetics. Yet by the 1930s and 1940s she became little more than a forgotten cultural curiosity living in a strange land on the brink of war, suffering from extreme poverty and loneliness. Critics turned against her work, asserting that as a convert to Hebrew, she lacked a rooted connection to the language; that she had no access to its hidden depths; and that her poetry was superficial.[13] In a letter in English dated December 6, 1947, addressed to Major General Fitzroy Maclean, MP Head of the Special Refugee Commission in England, she petitioned to be granted refugee status to reside in Great Britain, explaining that she had "positively no vital interest in the life of the Jewish community of Palestine where I have had my residence for the last 20 years: no property or business of any kind, no family or other intimate relations, no regular professional work, and no part whatsoever in the manifold activities of the Jewish population here."[14] At the end of her life, she turned against the Hebrew nationalist project that had animated her poetics, disavowing her relationship to Jewish culture and even to Hebrew. Her cosmopolitan embrace of Hebrew failed, unable to thrive in the context of an ethnic nationalist movement that excluded her. The cultural opening that she envisioned in her prose of the 1920s was foreclosed by the 1940s.

It was in prose and not poetry that Bikhovsky grappled with the pressing aesthetic and political questions for her: the possibility of a non-Jewish, cosmopolitan Hebrew. Prose offered a stage for her to imagine how her characters grappled with the everyday demands of their lives and the larger historical pressures that shaped these demands. *Simṭa'ot* examines the intersections between the broader social movements of the twentieth century and the everyday lives of artists and intellectuals, refracting the larger political dimensions of national identity through the intimacy of romantic connections between Jews and non-Jews. Although her poetry steered clear of these political and social concerns, her prose became an avenue of literary self-reflection on these questions. Focusing on protagonists who are poets, the novel gives narrative form to the everyday romantic and economic struggles of artists and writers, both Jewish and non-Jewish. Moreover, in bringing Russian poetry into a novel written in Hebrew, Bikhovsky conceives of her own writing as a form of translation. Several of the poets in the novel translate from Hebrew into Russian, drawing attention to the practice of translation. Bikhovsky's novel actually performs a reverse operation, translating her protagaonists' Russian-speaking milieu into Hebrew.

Writing a Hebrew novel set in a decidedly non-Hebrew-speaking milieu, Bikhovsky indexes the language politics underlying Soviet and Zionist Jewish national and minority culture and draws attention to both languages. The Soviet Union created national minority cultural institutions in Yiddish with the goal of eliminating Jewish national identifications, though it had the unintended consequence of nurturing those minority-language cultures.[15] By contrast, the Zionist movement created Hebrew national institutions with the aim of establishing a new Hebrew national culture. In the late 1920s, as Bikhovsky was writing in Hebrew in Palestine, Hebrew no longer remained a cultural option in Russia. The Soviet Union formally recognized Yiddish as the official minority Jewish language. Hebrew was not outiawed in the Soviet Union in the early 1920s, but it was associated with Zionism and severely restricted. The Evsektsiia, the party's Jewish section, which was responsible for administering the Jewish national minority, "urged the persecution of Zionists" and censured Hebrew.[16] Zionism, and by extension Hebrew culture, existed in a liminal position in the early 1920s.[17]

Yet Bikhovsky's project is not elegiac. She doesn't mourn the loss of Hebrew. Instead she appropriates the language for her own aesthetic project: to envision a cosmopolitan literary culture divorced from nationalism and ethnic chauvinism.

In the novel, Bikhovsky portrays Hebrew as a minority language within the Soviet context at a moment when Jews are seeking to nationalize the language in Palestine. The novel transplants the language politics of Jewish life in pre-state Palestine to the Soviet Union in the 1920s. Yiddish in the Soviet Union refracts the status of Hebrew in Palestine; both functioned as the sanctioned languages of Jewish nationalism. In contrast to Hebrew in Palestine, the novel's Soviet milieu marginalizes Hebrew as the language of a beleaguered minority without official national status. Bikhovsky explores the idea of a non-state-based minority language that is not tied to a territory or sanctioned national community, unlike the Zionist vision of Hebrew in Palestine.

Although for many, Yiddish represented the possibility of a transnational minority idiom, in Bikhovsky's novel, that language is Hebrew.

The Possibilities and Limits of Minority Language

Simta'ot is replete with expressions of pathos for a language that cannot find a footing in Soviet Russia. The Hebrew writers in Bikhovsky's novel openly reflect on Hebrew's decline. Daniel, the central Hebrew writer in the novel, has not written a word of Hebrew in the past year. Buried in his desk is a Hebrew story that he began working on two years earlier. It contains "the treasures of his soul."[18] Despite its importance to Daniel, he cannot bring himself to complete the story, although toward the end of the novel he briefly tries. Bertha Segal, Daniel's friend from prerevolutionary Hebrew circles, is a victim of postrevolutionary despair: she is poor, hungry, and ailing, ironically foreshadowing Bikhovsky's fate. A brief conversation between her and Daniel at a literary lecture illuminates the state of Hebrew at that moment in Russia. Daniel confides in his old friend Bertha that "it is hard to work when you don't feel that the surroundings demand it, you don't see the reader before you" (25). Bertha is so traumatized by the historical tumult of the revolution and the ensuing repression of Hebrew that she declares, "Who thinks of these things now?" and claims that she has "almost forgotten" the language (25). Later in the novel, when Ludmilla discusses Daniel's Hebrew writing with him, she notes that his "stories must have a very narrow circle of readers" (156). Daniel responds, "They have absolutely no readers. My readers were only a few friends and acquaintances that have dispersed in recent years, and I have no connection with them now." Even Daniel's own wife does not read Hebrew. This is a surprise to Ludmilla, who, ignorant of the traditional norms that prevented women from studying Hebrew, cannot fathom that Daniel's wife is unable or unwilling to read his work.

Daniel serves as the living intersection of Hebrew literary culture and Russian literature in the Soviet Union. He longs to develop connections between Russian and Hebrew, integrating Hebrew into Russian cultural circles and institutions. At the beginning of the novel, Daniel tries to establish a small association of Hebrew writers within the larger Russian literary association. He views this as an alternative to the extant Yiddish writers' union. He meets with a drunken writer and official of the Russian association named Mitroponov, who has promised to help. Mitroponov is ambivalent about the idea. The Russian official drunkenly suggests that they begin modestly with a Hebrew writers' studio and that later a smaller Hebrew association could affiliate with the general organization. Whereas Daniel sees Hebrew as part of Russian literary culture, Mitroponov pushes Hebrew into a literary ghetto. Sensing Daniel's disappointment, he opines, "What do you think? I personally love the Jews . . . an interesting people . . . you probably think: Goy. The goy always has a worm in his soul, a worm of ancient anti-Jewish hatred. He doesn't know if they will suddenly turn on him, yelling *Zhid!*! But it's not like that—my friend, I understand" (20). Mitroponov pronounces himself a friend of the Jews, despite his decidedly unfriendly attitude. He imagines himself penetrating Daniel's mind as he hazards a guess at Daniel's thoughts. His "you probably think" is followed by Daniel's imagined response, expressed in third-person free indirect discourse. Rather than giving voice to Daniel's thoughts, however, Mitroponov gives voice to his own prejudices, describing the chauvinist perspective that pretends to understand the challenges confronting a Jewish writer. In fact, Daniel isn't worried that Mitroponov will yell "*zhid*" [a derogatory epithet for a Jew]; he's worried that he won't embrace Hebrew as a legitimate literary language. He's looking for an advocate, not a friend. Instead, Mitroponov projects a mirror image of his own anti-Jewish sentiments onto Daniel, where all he can see is a "*zhid*." Then he offers false comfort, trying to reassure Daniel that he would never throw an antisemitic epithet at him. In this strange moment of failed Russian-Hebrew literary relations, Mitroponov cannot imagine the actual thoughts in Daniel's mind or transcend his own prejudices toward the Jews. Instead he sees a reflection of his own fears mirrored back at him. The scene highlights Mitroponov's failure to imagine Daniel's internal world. Through Mitroponov, Bikhovsky offers a metonymy of her own literary practices, wondering if by embracing Hebrew, a Jewish minority language, she might cross the borders between Jews and non-Jews that Mitroponov fails to cross.

In contrast to Daniel's aspiration to address a Russian audience, Daniel's childhood friend, Yosef Shmulevsky, fully embraces a modernist Jewish aesthetic practice that might flourish when directed at a Jewish audience. As an artist and theater director, Yosef has returned to Moscow with his wife and daughter to manage the musical department of a new Jewish theatrical studio. Although Yosef and his wife are filled with hope about his future after suffering years of poverty and homelessness, Daniel is skeptical of the project. Yosef produces one avant-garde musical performance that Daniel attends. He is stunned by the "gymnastics, jumping, and dancing, and all the noisiness and multicolor of the grotesque that appeared before him" (264). He deeply admires the avant-garde mix of folk music and contemporary dance, whose rhythms and sounds recall "echoes of the voice that captured his and Yosef's hearts in those distant years when they would walk at night through the shtetl and sing the songs and tunes that they collected around them" (264). Yosef's Jewish art speaks most strongly to a cultural insider, since it gives voice to the Jewish sounds of the pre-Soviet past. Yosef fights to continue as an artist speaking to the Jewish cultural world, but it is a fight he loses. When Daniel visits him and his wife Rivka, he learns that Yosef has not been paid, that the family is being evicted from the apartment provided by the theater, and that Rivka has lost her temporary job. At the end of the novel, Yosef figures Jewish cultural despair, signaling the failure of Yiddish-language art in

Moscow. As Daniel speaks to Rivka about the revolution's failure to sustain Jewish culture, resulting in their dire fate, he contemplates his future position as a Soviet bureaucrat. To succeed in the Soviet Union, it appears, is to give up the project of Jewish art.

Although the absence of an audience or a circle of literary interlocutors signals the death knell of Hebrew literary culture for Daniel and Yosef, to Ludmilla Hebrew represents creative potential as a language detached from a specific ethnic or national audience. Although, unlike Bikhvosky, Ludmilla ultimately rejects Hebrew, Bikhovsky expressed similar sentiments about the creative potential of a denationalized Hebrew. In a letter to the modernist Hebrew writer Gershon Shofman, she fantasized about moving to London and writing Hebrew literature that addresses no one: "You and me together in London or some other place, working on Hebrew literature and answerable to no one."[19] In her correspondence, Bikhovsky envisions a literary project that requires the anonymity of a major metropolitan city, London, Paris, and even Moscow. Like Kron in Goldberg's novel, and Bikhovsky herself, Ludmilla fetishizes the idea of poetry without an audience—in this case, a private address to no one. Hebrew appeals to her because it appears to address no one, and thus has the potential to become a modernist language of radical estrangement at a time of creative malaise. At the end of the novel, Ludmilla decides to leave for Paris, a city where she hopes to remake herself by reuniting with an old lover. Instead of becoming a cosmopolitan Hebrew writer, she chooses to become a refugee Russian writer in Paris.

Ludmilla's cosmopolitan aspirations are deeply connected to her view of Daniel as a denationalized Jew who writes in a language that in her mind is without an audience or national community. She expresses the desire to learn the language when her lover Karavtsov derides Daniel as a Zionist. Threatened by Daniel, he refers to him as "the last romantic," a term he heard from Ludmilla's friend Mitroponov. Both Mitroponov and Karavtsov refer to Daniel's Zionism as a form of romanticism. Ludmilla, by contrast, exoticizes his cultural alienation and marginalization, comparing Daniel to Peter Schlemihl, the eponymous character of the popular nineteenth-century novel by Adelbert von Chamisso. She explains to Karavstov, "Do you know what he reminds me of sometimes? The story of Peter Schlemihl. . . . I don't remember it exactly, but you surely know it: the story of a man who loses his shadow . . . he's just like that. He moves here among us like someone who is searching for something, but doesn't know where to look for it" (71). By referring to Daniel as Peter Schlemihl, Ludmilla views him through the lens of allegory, a figure for Jewish exile as envisioned through the eyes of Christian Europe. In the novel, Peter Schlemihl sells his soul to the devil and wanders the earth without a shadow, chased from everywhere that he seeks a home. The figure of the wandering Jew has its origins in medieval Christian anti-Jewish thought but was reclaimed by modernist Jewish writers in the early twentieth century, including S. Y. Agnon, Dovid Bergelson, and Dvora Baron, as a symbol of

Jewish modernist displacement.[20] In her discussion of Jewish appropriations of the wandering Jew, Galit Hasan-Rokem argues that the "Wandering Jew is a multivalent sign in Jewish culture. In every instance of its use it seems to be a sign for a number of unresolved oppositions between centre and periphery, between history and redemption, nationhood and universality."[21] Moreover, she stresses that these Jewish appropriations tend to take on an allegorical rather than narrative form.

Ludmilla turns to this anti-Jewish historical trope, reclaimed through Jewish modernist sources, as a figure for Daniel's literary language and her own Hebrew modernist project. Whereas Ludmilla embraces the Jew as a cosmopolitan figure, her lover looks upon Daniel with antisemitic disgust. He derides Daniel as a Zionist afflicted with eternal Jewish romanticism: "The romanticism of the people for generations, chased and oppressed, and dreaming of reviving their nation and of returning to their ancient heroism. Have you not heard such things? Do you have the romantic imagination to be attracted to him, if only the man who carried them were interesting in himself?" (70). Here and elsewhere, Karavtsov fixates on Daniel's Jewishness as synonymous with Zionism, which he views as a hopelessly romantic movement bordering on the absurd. Karavstov continually asks Daniel why he hasn't moved to Palestine, as though there were no place in the Soviet Union for a Jewish-identified writer. Karavtsov rejects Ludmilla's idealized cosmopolitan vision of Daniel, reducing him instead to a figure of Zionism. Such accusations of Jewish nationalism were dangerous in Soviet times, and Karavtsov wields them as a veiled threat. These two contrasting affective reactions to Daniel represent two different relationships to Hebrew: the first, an Orientalized, philosemitic embrace of Hebrew as a diasporic Jewish language, and the second, an antisemitic stance toward Hebrew as a language of Jewish nationalism. Bikhovsky's novel documents these two views of Hebrew and attempts to move beyond them to locate another possible relationship to Hebrew that is neither Jewish nor instrumentalizing. She strives to open up a space within Hebrew that is capacious enough to include a non-Jewish woman. But Ludmilla's indifference toward Hebrew also clouds that vision. Just as easily as Ludmilla adopts Hebrew, she chooses to abandon the project. It is precisely her privileged relationship to minority culture that undermines her cosmopolitan visions.

Daniel, however, is by no means a Zionist or a homeless wanderer. Unlike the non-Jewish Russian writers and artists, he has no desire to leave Moscow. At the end of the novel, he receives a government sinecure that guarantees his livelihood in the Soviet capital. Yet Ludmilla embraces him as the figure for an unmoored diasporic Hebrew language; he represents her fantasy of cosmopolitan culture in the figure of the Jew. Moreover, she reinterprets this iconic figure as her own, hoping that if she studies Hebrew she might become the wandering Jew in the guise of the non-Jewish woman. In effect she becomes the *telushah* (uprooted, fem.), the uprooted and alienated female intellectual who heads into self-imposed exile.[22] The creative force of the *talush* (uprooted, masc.) in Hebrew writing was his displacement from the traditional norms of Jewish culture and his longing to embrace the European cultural world that awaits him. Bikhovsky's novel transfers this potential from the Jewish male to the non-Jewish woman and artist who enlists the cultural dislocation that had been the marker of Jewishness into her own poetic and personal project. In this way, she employs Jewish modernist strategies; she turns to the wandering Jew to grapple with the tensions between minority and majority cultures. She attempts to liberate Hebrew and herself simultaneously, to engage the language as her own and, by extension, to free herself from the restricting bonds of identity.

In contrast to Daniel, non-Jewish women represent a degree of cultural malleability that is not available to male characters. Ludmilla's younger protégé, Nina Berg, turns to Ludmilla and asks, "Is it true that your mother was a gypsy?" Ludmilla answers, "No, she was Russian, but she was born in the Orient," where her father was a consul (17). Nina explains that she is asking "because . . . I thought: it sometimes seems to me that you have no roots, that you have no connection to this world, no race so to speak" (17–18). Ludmilla deflects the comment and changes the subject, but the exchange between the two is telling. Ludmilla is not Jewish, but when Nina imagines her a rootless gypsy, she characterizes her in quasi-Jewish terms. She appears not to be Russian and not to have ties to any land. She is ethnically marked and without a home. A similar exchange takes place between Daniel and Nina. Daniel asks her if she's Russian because her name sounds German and she associates herself with many young Jewish artists. She replies, "Perhaps you wanted to ask me if I am Jewish? Unfortunately, no!" (29). She then goes on to describe herself as a mix of different ethnicities: Swiss, German—anything but Jewish. Whereas Daniel's identity is ethnically and linguistically fixed in the novel, Nina's and Ludmilla's are ambiguous. Why are these two women ethnically unfixed, in contradistinction to the Jewish men in their lives? Bikhovsky locates them outside the dominant masculine ideologies of the day. For her, they represent flexible forms of attachment that are not restricted to race and birth, and they can import these freedoms into a minority language. We can see a similar phenomenon in Bernstein-Cohen's 1938 novel, *Mefisto*, in which the protagonist, Tamar, abandons her Jewish husband and falls in love with a gentile. The novel celebrates her transgressive love as a force that can transcend the narrow ties of family, religion, and race, an ideology that trumps both ethnic nationalism and revolutionary socialism. In Bikhovsky's novel, however, it is non-Jewish women, who through their attempted romantic attachments with Jewish men, embrace a Jewish aesthetic that becomes a catalyst for a secularized cosmopolitan poetics.

Even as desire propels women's transgressive, creative potential, their artistic lives are still proscribed by the male-dominated literary world. One evening, Karavstov asks Daniel what he thinks of this new type, "the literary woman" (65). Unable to answer, Karavtsov describes the plight of a new generation of women writers: "It's hard to live in Moscow in these times, to support yourself and organize your affairs, without a home or a family, and with all this to be a 'poetess'—he emphasized this last word with something of irony" (65). As Olmert notes, both men agree that such women are doomed to "weaken their souls and their bodies in moving from man to man," a sentiment that conceals their very real fears of such talented and powerful women.[23] Karavtsov embodies the ways revolutionary ideologies cannot always transform prejudice. Notably, the new woman writer that Karavtsov describes and mocks is a "poetess," not a novelist. He cannot imagine such a strange creature. Ludmilla, however briefly, considers writing a novel. She is fascinated by Nina's eventful romantic life as a student in the dorms. Nina, keenly aware of Ludmilla's fascination, asks her whether she wants "to try her powers at writing prose" and use her friend's life as the material for her novel. Ludmilla demurs (97). Toward the end of the novel, Nina asks Ludmilla again if she's still interested in writing a novel about Nina's romantic adventures. Nina offers Ludmilla a bundle of her notebooks neatly tied with a string, but Ludmilla declines. Ludmilla's refusal to write the novel and Nina's choice not to write and publish her own story mean that they will end up in the hands of a male writer to whom Nina has also offered the manuscript. Nina does not imagine herself as capable of transforming the personal into the aesthetic. Bikhovsky is the novelist who will transform both Ludmilla's and Nina's lives into the subject of prose and become that new creature, the female novelist—and in Hebrew, no less.

By turning to Hebrew, Ludmilla attempts to satisfy some unnamed longing through the marker of an outcast Jewish culture. In doing so, she seeks a new artistic subjectivity for herself that is outside the Russian cultural tradition she rejects, but she also risks instrumentalizing a minority culture that is not her own. Ethnic and racial appropriation characterize twentieth-century European modernist art, whether images of tribal masks, imitations of dialect, or the translation and rewriting of ritual incantations and songs.[24] Bikhovsky's novel meditates on the two sides of such appropriation: cultural revitalization and cultural theft. If Ludmilla embraces the idea of the wandering Jew, she also imposes this trope on Daniel, reducing him to a stereotype without artistic agency. In doing so she draws attention to Bikhovsky's own aesthetic role as an outsider to Hebrew who introduces a modernist secular poetics that distances the language from its ethnic or national attachments.

The novel conceives of a form of minority cosmopolitanism in which writers adopt a minority perspective to transform themselves into cosmopolitans. There is something troubling about this paradigm, which enables a privileged writer to adopt a minority identity without necessarily giving up the protected status of the majority. The novel also draws attention to the troubling nature of such an identification. In the novel, Ludmilla's project fails because it relies on her exotification and allegorization of Daniel. Through

Ludmilla, however, Bikhovsky offers a critical reflection on the boundaries of minority identity and the risks at stake in adopting a minority language. Ultimately, Ludmilla does not pursue Hebrew, turning her back on the language. Ludmilla's failure reflects the ambivalence toward Zionism at the heart of Bikhovsky's larger Hebrew project. It is as though Bikhovsky perceived the impossibility of the cosmopolitan nonnational Hebrew she sought to create.

The novel raises questions that resonate with late twentieth-century and early twenty-first-century discourses on cosmopolitanism. Critics such as Paul Rabinow, James Clifford, Arjun Appadurai, and Bruce Robbins have theorized a new cosmopolitanism that looks beyond elite intellectuals and is self-reflexively critical of Hegelian abstract universalism. This new cosmopolitanism allows for multiple and overlapping affiliations, no longer envisioning that one must give up all ties to embrace the whole of humanity.[25] However, these scholars also identify a conflict between cosmopolitanism and nationalist minority discourse.[26] Bruce Robbins questions whether the multiple affiliations of diasporic communities actually produce new sentiments that transcend ethnic or national chauvinism or instead reinforce those sentiments.[27] In envisioning the potential for new forms of minority cosmopolitanism, Susan Koshy defines an explicitly minority cosmopolitanism through the "translocal affiliations" of minority communities that produce cosmopolitan forms of identification that register "the disruptions and asymmetries of intercultural encounter while sustaining an openness to its transformative possibilities."[28] In a similar vein, Shu-mei Shih and Françoise Lionnet introduce the term "minor transnationalism" to critique discussions of transnationalism and globalization that ignore the specificity of minority experiences. They contend that "minority and diasporic peoples, even under duress, develop cultural practices and networks of communication that exceed the parameters of these theories."[29] Bikhovsky's novel questions the tensions between minority affiliation and cosmopolitanism. The novel attempts to overcome these tensions by imagining an outsider embracing a minority national position not her own. Bikhovsky employs a minority language to produce new forms of literary expression unbeholden to chauvinistic ideologies—a radical move in Hebrew in the late 1920s, when the literary establishment was shoring up a national literary and cultural identity founded on the emergence of a new ethnonational identity.

Cosmopolitanism has its own complex history in relationship to both Jews and the Soviet Union. Although historically in Europe, the term had been associated with universalism, in the Soviet Union it took on new meanings. By the 1930s, according to Katerina Clark, Soviet authorities viewed cosmopolitanism as anathema to their internationalist ideology, and cosmopolitanism became a bad word "identified with certain ethnic groups only," and in the 1940s primarily with Jews.[30] But as Clark shows, cosmopolitanism persisted as a Soviet ideal, bound up with both Soviet ideas of internationalism and patriotism, and driven by "a desire to interact with the cultures and intellectuals of the outside world."[31] Cosmopolitanism in Russia and later in the Soviet Union undergoes a series of ideological transformations; however, despite Soviet hostility to the term "cosmopolitanism," the concept never disappears as an ideal, and Bikhovsky's novel captures this Soviet potentiality.

Ludmilla and Daniel: Minority Identity and the Future of Hebrew

Bikhovsky's prose, like that of Leah Goldberg and other women writers in Mandatory Palestine, was dismissed or overlooked because of her interest in her female protagonists' personal and romantic lives, which were viewed as superficial distractions from the important political concerns of the moment. And yet critics from a range of literary traditions, including British and Chinese, have argued that novels focused on women's desires do so to grapple with and even augment large-scale social transformations.[32] Hebrew literature was similarly invested in the transformations of sentimental and erotic norms, and women engaged these questions from different angles than their male counterparts. Where early twentieth-century male Hebrew writers portrayed male desire for non-Jewish women as the catalyst for their protagonists' internal psychic crises, Jewish women writers used these relationships to theorize questions about women and the future of Hebrew secularism.

In *Simṭa'ot*, the failed romances between Jews and non-Jews refract the shifting relationships among language, nationality, and minority identity. These romantic relationships, which center on translation, must be read as part of a larger cultural shift, and their failures point to the pitfalls of such transformations for women. These romantic failures differ from the account of literary modernity and women's desire offered, for example, by Haiyan Lee, in which free love in the literature of the May Fourth Movement in China is fervently embraced and realized. Bikhovsky's novel expresses a more ambivalent attitude to the power of individual desire to enact social change and bridge languages.

Ludmilla and Daniel represent two forms of minority thinking. Ludmilla internalizes the tropes of Jewish cultural difference to transcend her Russian identity and adopt a minority subject position. Daniel remains committed to a Jewish cultural identity at the cost of his acceptance into Ludmilla's bohemian cultural circle. Although each relies on the other to secure these identities, they must also maintain their distance. Ludmilla invites Daniel to take a walk with her in a convent cemetery. As they wander along the Russian Orthodox graveyard, she draws attention to Daniel's Jewishness in the Christian space. The Soviet eradication of religion in the public sphere cannot erase these distinctions in the realm of intimate relationships, where these prejudices, imprinted over the course of a lifetime, still hold power. During the walk, Daniel finally makes an advance, kissing Ludmilla's shoulder and her lips. She barely responds. Daniel reflects on how little satisfaction he takes in this physical encounter: "As before she remained aloof and serene, and her restfulness, so pure and undecipherable, bothered him. She is a foreign text in a foreign tongue" (162). He looks toward her and asks, "Am I entirely alien to you, forever?" She responds, "If I were not alien to you, what would you do with me?" (162–63). This is the height of their romantic encounter, a shared kiss that proves unsatisfying, a sign of desire without love—and an unanswered question. That they are alien to each other drives their desire and prevents its consummation. Ludmilla does not so much want to be with Daniel as to transform herself by embracing what she imagines defines his secular Jewish identity: placelessness and wandering. To achieve this aesthetic fantasy, she cannot allow herself to see him as he really is, a Soviet Jew tied to his home and to Hebrew. Meanwhile, Daniel cannot cross the religious or ethnic divide between them because his secular commitment to Hebrew is a rejection of the very trope of the wandering Jew that Ludmilla imposes on him. The novel questions her fetishization of Daniel's difference, highlighting its connection to Karavtsov's antisemitic views.

Daniel, in contrast, seeks a place for Hebrew in the Soviet Jewish project, without being essentialized as "the Jew." Unlike Ludmilla, who freely pursues other identities, Daniel's identity is fixed by those around him. A scene at the Yiddish writers' cafeteria emblematizes this tension. With his wife preparing for her exams, Daniel decides to ease her burden by eating at a members-only cafeteria established to support Yiddish culture. In the past, he ate there regularly to sustain his connection to the Jewish literary and cultural world. Of late he dreads entering the cafeteria, fearing that "he appeared to others as a foreign face [*panim zarim*] out of place, like an uninvited guest" (193). He fears that by trying to integrate into Russian literary circles as a Hebrew writer, he is losing credibility as a Jewish writer. After a Hebrew lesson with Ludmilla, he eats lunch there and runs into a dreaded acquaintance whom he refers to as the "small critic." The two exchange pleasantries; however, once Daniel announces that he is no longer writing in Hebrew, the critic accuses him of trying to become part of "the Christians" (*ha-notsrim*) and "their 'great' literature" (197). He asks, "What do you hope to gain from this?" (197). The critic distinguishes between Jewish and Russian literature, not along linguistic lines but along religious ones, according to a binary paradigm of us and them. By referring to the Russians as "Christians," he emphasizes that Russian is a language for non-Jews alone, and thus to write in Russian is a form of cultural conversion. Daniel responds angrily, outraged at this challenge to his private choice to surround himself with "goyim" (197). Here Daniel chooses the more familiar and colloquial term, "goyim," over *notsri*. "Goy" is a biblical Hebrew term meaning "nation" that returned to modern Hebrew via Yiddish, where it was a derogatory term for a non-Jew. Daniel activates a feeling of cultural difference by using the decidedly Jewish conceptual term "goyim," which enforces an us-and-them binary. The goyim, according to these terms, are by definition a community you cannot gain access to as a Jew. By using the term, Daniel asserts his connection to the Jewish world that the critic believes he has abandoned, but does so in similarly binary terms.

Daniel wants to enter into non-Jewish literary culture, without seeing that culture as entirely other. He fails at the project. Other Jewish writers in the novel view his choice of Russian as form of cultural betrayal, as though his entrance into secular European literary culture represents a form of conversion. This plot twist reflects contemporary critical discussions of secularism by Raz-Krakotizkin and Anidjar.[33] Daniel doesn't want to become Christian; rather he wants to locate Jewish literature within the Soviet literary world and perhaps to write in Russian. In the 1920s, however, language, not religion, defined modern nationhood in an officially atheist state. The Soviet Yiddish intelligentsia embraced the idea that "Yiddish marked Jews as a distinct ethnic group—or, in the language of the Soviet Union, a distinct nationality."[34] Daniel, in contrast, is a Hebrew writer who chooses a language not endorsed by the Evsektsiia (Jewish section of the Communist Party). Although he writes in Hebrew, he does so without territorial nationalist objectives. Rather, he embraces Hebrew as a language of Soviet national expression that could be part of the larger Soviet/Russian literary culture. In this way he is a mirror image of Ludmilla. Like Ludmilla, Daniel turns to Russian to imagine new forms of belonging. When the critic accuses him of cultural betrayal for traveling in Russian literary circles, Daniel's rejoinder is to compare the critic's accusatory questioning about why he spends time among "the goyim" to that of his non-Jewish acquaintances who ask, "Why don't you travel to Palestine?" (198). These are the sentiments that Karavtsov, Ludmilla's antisemitic lover, expresses when he assumes that Daniel is a Zionist. Both views are essentializing and suffocating. Daniel is in an impossible situation. Either he adopts a Jewish language in opposition to Russian and remains a minority national in the Soviet Union or he embraces Hebrew and emigrates to Palestine, where Hebrew belongs. Daniel wants the freedom to move among Russian and Jewish circles, and like Ludmilla he wants to write literature outside an ethnonationalist literary paradigm. Yet he is also aware of the impossibility of his own utopian dream. In a moment of self-criticism he thinks to himself, "'Yes, Daniel Royter,' here you are, 'pushed aside by the goyim,' and the devil knows what you are looking for there! The goyim are expressly not eagerly pursuing you just like these Jews . . . but to what end? In another two weeks you will begin your new sinecure—that it seems is the important thing, you will be a citizen, according to the law, and everything will go according to its place" (201). So long as Daniel remains tied to Hebrew he continues to be associated with an ethnonationalism that he rejects. At the same time, if he tries to become part of Russian literature, he will always be perceived by the Russian literary establishment as an outsider Jew trying to push his way inside. He seeks to escape this bind by becoming part of the Soviet apparatus, where he will be a citizen and servant of the state. As a writer, he cannot become part of Russian literature; he will always remain a Jew. However, as a Soviet citizen he is the equal of all other citizens. Ludmilla, by contrast, adopts Hebrew as the expression of an ambivalent cosmopolitanism, one that might free her from a stagnating Russian literary culture. Through her perspective the novel imagines Hebrew outside its diasporic world of decay but never locates its revival in Palestine. Yet the subtext of the Hebrew novel, completed and published in Palestine, is that the creation of a Hebrew state might transform Hebrew into an international language, like French or German, which could become a language of international and cosmopolitan literary culture. This did not bear out in Bikhovsky's own life; Bikhovsky remained a non-Jewish outsider to Hebrew literary culture in Palestine and later Israel, just as Daniel could not escape being a Jewish outsider to Russian literature.

Translation and Desire

Ludmilla and Daniel's unrequited and ambivalent relationship mirrors the relationship between Bertha Segal, a Hebrew and Russian poet, and Edward Vitinsky, a Russian poet and friend of Ludmilla's. Ludmilla and Daniel weakly desire each other, and Edward's passion toward Bertha only arises after her death. In both cases the Jewish partner serves as a mediator between Hebrew and Russian. Edward turns to Bertha to help him translate the Hebrew psalms into Russian, a task he cannot undertake without her because he knows no Hebrew. Bertha bridges both languages. She gives Edward access to the Hebrew original through her Russian translations. Bertha plays a historically Jewish role. European Jews regularly served as translators between Hebrew and European languages, for example between German and Hebrew.[35] The novel transforms these two relationships into a broader meditation on the possibilities of cultural and literary translation though romantic desire. It also offers a critique of the Soviet project of subsuming minority literatures into Russian-language Soviet culture.

Like Ludmilla, Vitinsky, the non-Jewish poet, is similarly attracted to Hebrew culture, in this case biblical Hebrew. He is drawn not only to the psalms but also to Bertha, the woman he enlists to help him with the project. He desires Bertha, who, unlike Daniel, exhibits a cultural flexibility similar to Ludmilla's. Before the revolution, Bertha was part of a thriving Hebrew and Russian cultural and literary scene. She published an important collection of poems that Daniel describes as "filled with restrained tenderness, about secret love, about an expansive Slavic soul and its hidden Slavic bravery" (296). The narrator never explicitly states whether the collection is in Hebrew or Russian; we know that she wrote in both languages and that she publicly recited poems in Russian. This linguistic ambiguity situates Bertha at the interstices between Russian and Hebrew. Perhaps Elisheva imagines Bertha as a Russian literary precursor who succeeds in publishing a collection of poems in Hebrew in the 1910s.

Before her death, Bertha was secretly working with Edward on a translation of the Psalms. He translates from the Hebrew, preserving "the unique qualities and meter of the original" (127). Bertha's role is to read aloud in Hebrew so that Edward can perceive the rhythm of the original and capture it in Russian. Bikhovsky's description of Edward's translation project resonates with the discourse surrounding translation among German Jewish intellectuals in the 1920s and 1930s. In his famous essay on translation, Walter Benjamin argues that translation "serves the purpose of expressing the innermost relationship of languages" and explains that "the task of the translator consists in finding the particular intention toward the target language which produces in that language the echo of that original."[36] Vitinsky seeks echoes of the original Hebrew in his Russian translation. Moreover, his fascination with retaining the sounds of Hebrew mirrors Martin Buber and Franz Rosenzweig's project of biblical translation, which began in the 1920s. The two German Jewish critics developed a translation method to allow the original Hebrew to speak through German. Buber and Rosenzweig's translation met with controversy. Siegfried Kracauer, for example, famously critiqued the translation as "Wagnerian," seeing it as an archaized and, by extension, de-Judaized German that was meant to estrange the reader from the language.[37] Naomi Seidman argues that Buber and Rosenzweig's translation presses a "turn away from Yiddish."[38] According to Seidman, their translation was meant to expose the gap between German and Jewish cultures; it relied on their "anti-colonial insistence on foreignizing and Hebraizing German" at the expense of Yiddish.[39] These discussions highlight the complex politics of translation and linguistic difference within national contexts. Just as Buber and Rosenzweig seek a de-Judaized German, so too does Bikhovsky's novel imagine a de-Judaized Hebrew. In contrast to Buber and Rosenzweig, Vitinsky translates for a non-Jewish Russian audience, from a language he cannot read, hoping to use Bertha to connect to a mystical core at the center of Hebrew that is legible to non-Jews. The anxieties regarding translation are in inverse relation to the German-Jewish case; the non-Jewish Russian turns to the Jewish text to become closer to its origins for non-Jewish ends. Vitinsky wants to internalize a mystical Jewish spirit in his Russian world and transform that spirit into Russian, divorcing it from its Jewish roots and, by extension, secularizing that spirit through translation into Russian for non-Jewish audiences. If Vitinsky Hebraicizes via translation, Bikhovsky performs a reverse operation. Her novel translates her protagonists' Russian language speech into Hebrew, potentially Russifying Hebrew. The novel hovers around this idea of translation as a means to break language apart from its native speakers and envision its cosmopolitan future at the hands of others. If the Soviets envisioned universalizing Russian, Bikhovsky envisions a cosmopolitan Hebrew.

For Vitinsky translation is also an intimate project that draws him close to Bertha. At first, he denies any romantic interest. Echoing Ludmilla's sentiment toward Daniel, he tells Ludmilla that "she is one of the least interesting women I've seen in my life" (127). Ludmilla senses something behind his denial. She explains to him, "Contained within this young woman is a sort of hidden flame, a kind of tragic beauty—a profound sadness peeks through her very Hebraic eyes" (128). Bertha's Jewishness appeals to Ludmilla, but she can only see her as the prototypical Jewess, with Jewish features and sad eyes. Bertha recalls Ada from Goldberg's novel, a young woman absorbed in a Hebrew cultural world that has disappeared around her. However, in contrast to Ada, Bertha is an author. After Bertha's death, Vitinsky proclaims to Ludmilla, "And now she has departed and taken everything with her, her doleful power, her hidden flame, and the secret of her desiring eyes. Her eyes, and the secret of her face which I will never see again, and that I would have been able to see if I had stayed with her" (311). He describes her as the quintessential "Jewess." She is a source of literary and romantic fascination only after her tragic death, when she can be transformed from an individual to an abstract concept. There is no possibility for a Jewish woman writer in the Soviet literary universe described by Bikhovsky—she is a double victim of antisemitism and sexism. Bertha dies tragically of hunger, but it is Edward who descends into a profound psychic crisis. Her absence ends his translation project and disconnects him from his ties to Hebrew. Bertha becomes a living embodiment of Hebrew for Vitinsky, a sacred light from the Jewish past. Her death extinguishes not only the dialogue between the poets but also the living flame of the Hebrew language.

Edward and Bertha's relationship to translation is an inversion of Bikhovsky's literary practices. Whereas they attempt to bring the essence of Hebrew into their Russian translation for a Russian audience, Bikhovsky's Hebrew novel translates an entirely Russian-speaking milieu into Hebrew, bringing Russian into Hebrew for a Jewish audience. This tension between the Hebrew and Russian languages recalls an earlier generation of Hebrew writers who confronted the challenge of describing everyday life and vernacular conversations that were taking place in Russian, Yiddish, or another language into Hebrew, which was rarely used in everyday life. Hebrew writers relied on the narrative technique that Ben Tran terms "literary dubbing" to describe narratives in "which the language that the reader encounters on the page is not the same language that the character thinks and speaks."[40] Tran investigates dubbing in the context of Anglophone postcolonial literature, arguing that while "literature in this mode may nod to cultural exchange and understanding, this form of translation potentially negates such liberal sympathies."[41] In Tran's account, the danger of dubbing occurs when it operates so smoothly that the fictional source language disappears and linguistic power relations are smoothed over. Yosef Haim Brenner, for example, resisted this narrative transparency, exposing what he saw as the linguistic hypocrisy of Hebrew realism by foregrounding his characters' failed Hebrew speech and emphasizing that even in Palestine, Hebrew was not the language of daily life.[42] For Brenner, this was a critique of Zionist discourse. Bikhovsky, writing from Palestine, in a more robust Hebrew literary center than Brenner, gestures to this linguistic gap to different ends. Rather than exposing an ideologically motivated linguistic illusion, she enlists Hebrew to describe a world that is at best indifferent to the language. This decaying Hebrew milieu appeals to Ludmilla, holding out the potential of a nonnational language for poetry. Daniel's relationship to Hebrew is not Zionist. He tells a colleague, "To the Land of Israel—of course, obviously, I would never go there" (198). Bikhovsky's novel draws attention to the failure of Hebrew-Russian relations even as her novel is written in fluid Hebrew and does not draw attention to its acts of what I've termed elsewhere "fictional translation."[43] Instead, her point is to show how Hebrew can be capacious enough to narrate non-Jewish and nonnational contexts.

In contrast to Bikhovsky's project of portraying a Russian literary milieu in Hebrew, Edward and Bertha attempt to produce a Hebrew literature in Russian translation. They want Russian to express the sounds and spirit of the Hebrew original. However, their project ends in tragedy, with Bertha's untimely death and Edward's mental breakdown. Bertha's death catalyzes Vitinsky's longing for her and for the Hebrew literary culture she represents. At her funeral, Daniel encounters two young scholars with whom Bertha participated in a society for the study of Russian, one of whom studies ancient Russian church iconography. They remind him of Bertha's first collection of poetry, published over ten years earlier, before the revolution, which was filled with "modest poems that both reveal and do not reveal, filled with a restrained softness about a secretive love for the broad 'Slavic' soul and the hidden 'Slavic' courage that recall the broad evenings and quiet flowing rivers" (296). Daniel thinks to himself that he's happy to meet the Slavic soul who so enchanted Bertha, the "Hebrew poet." There is an ambiguity here about the language of Bertha's collection: is she writing in Hebrew, publishing a collection of Hebrew poetry in Russia that precedes Bikhovsky's? What is clear is that Bertha represents an aesthetic and romantic blending of Hebrew and Russian. Yet when Daniel finally gets close enough to the young man to overhear his conversation, he is troubled to discover that he is not even speaking about Bertha. Her love for Russian embodied in this Russian intellectual is unrequited.

Uncertain Cosmopolitan Futures

Both Ludmilla and Edward turn to Hebrew as a gesture of self-transformation and literary revitalization that differs from the Zionist project. How are we to understand Ludmilla and Edward's Orientalized views of Hebrew and their instrumentalization of Jewish minority culture? Ludmilla appropriates the figure of the Jewish wanderer for her own modernist project of self-minoritization, while turning her back on Daniel and modern Jewish culture. Edward's relationship to Hebrew catalyzes his descent into mental illness and his Hebrew collaborator's tragic death. The novel portrays these desires as fruitless and destructive; it forwards a critique of such relationships. But where do we locate Bikhovsky's secular Hebrew project—her attempt to sever Hebrew from its relationship to Jewish nationalism and traditional Jewish culture? We can contextualize her project in relationship to Hebrew modernism through Leah Goldberg, who a decade later would grapple with the relationship between Hebrew modernism and Orientalism in her unpublished novel *Avedot*. Goldberg attempts to move beyond the tension between Hebrew secularism and Christian Orientalism by envisioning the future of secular Hebrew in the hands of Jewish women readers. Bikhovsky, on the other hand, represents the future of the language in the hands of a non-Jewish woman, writing from the Jewish national center but divorced from its ethnic loyalties. Her tragic end might bespeak the failure of her project, but the novel represents her attempts to realize her modernist vision of a secular, cosmopolitan, minority aesthetic.

Both Ludmilla and Edward distance Hebrew from its Jewish roots, whether as an act of self-alienation (Ludmilla) or Russian cultural renaissance (Edward). Hebrew survives only after the Hebrew original is subsumed through translation into Russian and the Hebrew writer dies. Beneath these personal romantic gestures is skepticism toward Hebrew nationalism. Zionism and Palestine are mentioned only briefly in the novel. The decline of Hebrew in Russia contrasts with its flourishing in Palestine. Bikhovsky's novel embraces the idea of Hebrew and gestures toward its future in Palestine, while also imagining the language as a denationalized medium of modernist art. By envisioning a Hebrew culture not bound to the limits of ethnonationalism in the Soviet Union, Bikhovsky offers an alternative vision of Hebrew culture in Palestine. Her novel's distance from the Hebrew cultural world of Palestine, its disinterest in the heroic figure of the new Jew settling a Jewish homeland, and its attention to the aspirations of young women artists and writers offer a subtle critique of Hebrew nationalist literary culture. Bikhovsky immigrated to Palestine with her husband and pursued her career as a Hebrew writer in an embrace of Zionism. Her novel calls into question this choice, even before his death and her regret.

Simṭa'ot concludes with a departure and uncertain futures. Ludmilla leaves Moscow for Paris, a journey that recalls the mass exodus of Russian intellectuals and artists to that city in the 1920s, including such luminaries as Marina Tsvetaeva, Marc Chagall, and Viktor Shklovsky. Daniel and Ludmilla meet once before they say goodbye at the train station, and their strange encounter epitomizes Ludmilla's ambivalence toward Hebrew. Daniel knows that even in Russia there is nothing to be gained by knowing Hebrew. Yet, as the two stare out into the sun setting over the city, she confesses to Daniel: "Perhaps in a short while I will stand on some bridge in Paris and will gaze at the expanse of the Seine decorated with the colors of the sunset . . . Royter, my heart trembles" (330). In this confessional moment, Ludmilla expresses her fascination with the iconic romantic and artistic vistas of the city. Does Ludmilla long for a cosmopolitan Parisian world, or does Paris represent the continuation of Russian imperial culture, as it did for many émigré Russian writers who fled the Soviet Union and its revolutionary milieu?[44] If Ludmilla allies herself with the romance of Paris and its cosmopolitan artistic dreams, Daniel remains firmly connected to the alleyways of Moscow, to Russian life, and to minority Jewish culture. Daniel confesses that he will begin writing in Yiddish, turning to a Jewish language with a more robust audience in the Soviet Union. Daniel's turn to Yiddish is a compromise. Earlier in the novel he describes himself as alienated from Yiddish literary culture. Unable to continue his Hebrew aspirations or become a Russian writer, Yiddish presents a possible alternative. Yiddish allows him to remain in Moscow, to continue to publish, and to be a Jewish and a Soviet writer. If France represents the capital of what Pascale Casanova has termed the "world republic of letters,"[45] Yiddish is the Jewish equivalent of a cosmopolitan language that is not tied to national borders. Hebrew recedes in the novel, a language with no future, attached to the dead and the starving—and in a reversal that recalls Goldberg's novel, with no remaining connection to women.

Bikhovsky's novel gestures toward a cosmopolitan Hebrew culture not linked to Jewish tradition or practices. But Ludmilla also embodies the failure of this vision.[46] The novel concludes with a strange moment of antisemitic spite. After Ludmilla's train departs, Karavtsov turns to Daniel and calls him "Peter Schlemihl." Daniel is stunned by the term that—unbeknownst to him—Karavtsov has picked up from Ludmilla. Karavtsov then asks him one final time with biting irony when he will travel to Palestine. In this concluding encounter between the two men, Daniel angrily rejects Ludmilla's strange vision of him as a "Peter Schlemihl," calling into question Ludmilla's literary and cultural project of self-minoritization. He remains behind, rooted in Moscow's alleyways and tied to the future of the Soviet Union. Ludmilla's words, parroted by Karavtsov, take on a more ominous meaning, hinting at the darker fate of Soviet Jewry to come. It is in this ending that Palestine, a destination for no one in the novel, takes on a new meaning as a possible refuge. Yet Daniel rejects Mandatory Palestine as a destination, fervently making Soviet Russia his literary and cultural home. Ironically, in this modernist Hebrew novel penned by a non-Jewish Hebrew author residing in Palestine, neither character chooses Hebrew. Yet the novel proposes that this very lack of attachment might make possible another future for Hebrew.

Ten years after the publication of *Simṭa'ot* Leah Goldberg explored related questions about language, gender, and minority identity. In *Avedot*, Goldberg engages in an extended dialogue with Bikhovsky, whom she found to be a compelling figure of Hebrew modernity. Goldberg's novel reimagines Daniel Royter in the guise of Elhanan Kron, exchanging the Soviet Jew for the

Russian immigrant Hebrew poet and scholar in Berlin. In Goldberg's 1930s novel, National Socialism, not Soviet national minority politics, threatens Hebrew and Jewish culture in Europe. Despite these historical differences, both novels sought to rescue Hebrew from the forces of fascism and nationalism, and both envisioned the role that women might play in this project. Yet, at the same time, each novel features a male Hebrew writer. Both Bikhovsky and Goldberg grapple with the male legacy of Hebrew culture through their protagonists, and also ask whether that legacy can be overcome, and by whom. Unlike the protagonists of their novels, Goldberg and Bikhovsky succeed in writing Hebrew modernist texts that endeavor to think an alternative Hebrew modernist future that awaits its moment to be heard.

Chapter 7

Debora Vogel's Montage Democracy

Between 1935 and 1938 the Lwów-based avant-garde poet and art critic Debora Vogel corresponded regularly with Aaron Glanz-Leyeles, the editor of the modernist New York literary journal *In zikh* (In oneself). Vogel found artistic and literary kinship with *In zikh* and in New York modernist Yiddish literary circles. New York had a more developed avant-garde culture than the Galician Yiddish scene in Lwów, situated at the edges of 1930s Poland in a Ukrainian stronghold of the former Habsburg Empire.[1] Through Vogel's correspondence with Glanz-Leyeles, we gain a sense of her despair as she stood on the precipice of imminent catastrophe for European Jewry.

The letters highlight her abiding frustration with Galician Yiddish culture and the feeling of *fremdkayt* (alienation) she experienced in the largely conservative Galician Yiddish literary scene.[2] They also register her deep commitment to Yiddish as her language of modernist experimentation. With one foot in Polish leftist circles and the other in an international Yiddish modernist milieu, she had no fixed literary home but regularly participated in multilingual and multiethnic artist communities. By 1936, her access to left-wing Polish venues, particularly the Lwów arts journal *Sygnały*, had dwindled. As Yiddish critics turned their backs on her avant-garde prose writing, the leftist Polish press, with whom she identified politically, rejected her as a Jewish writer whose interest in Jews was by default nationalist. She explains in a letter to Melekh Ravitch that "they discontinued the column on Jewish affairs, since Marxism does not want 'any nationalism' that lets you know something about the times!"[3] All that remained for her was an increasingly vulnerable international Yiddish audience and a handful of publications in New York. She relied on New York at the very moment when Europe was about to enter a war that would cut off all contact with her diasporic interlocutors. These historical cirucmstances shaped the crisis faced by Jewish modernist writers during the 1930s in a hostile Europe. This crisis was compounded for women writers, who were subject to a literary scene dominated by men who devalued their contributions.

On May 23, 1939, months before the German and Soviet invasions of Poland, Debora Vogel wrote her penultimate letter to Glanz-Leyeles, congratulating him on his fiftieth birthday. Her world was rapidly closing in as borders in Europe realigned and her family faced serious economic hardship. On the face of it, however, the letter appeared to address a different set of concerns. It describes the greatest obstacle that Vogel faced as the fact of being born a woman:

> I also have this talent in me, but it has not been able to find its full expression, because . . . because—I'm going to make a risky statement—because of the miserable fortune [*shlemazeldikn mazel*] it is to be a woman. The "metaphysical" role of a woman flows in a stream of daily trifles. And my professional work, which barely pays me anything—the same amount of money that I could earn by writing just two articles per month—completely absorbs me. But male competition does not allow a woman to improve her position. A few newspapers have written about the fact that men, even those who have nothing to say and are talentless scribblers, receive money for their writing, while women are rewarded merely with respect.[4]

In 1939, trapped by war and poverty, Vogel expresses what she believes is the greatest barrier to her ability to make a living as a writer—the "shlemazeldikn mazel" of having been born a woman. If her venues are limited by language and aesthetic choices—she is too avant-garde for Polish Yiddish journals and too Jewish for the Polish art scene—she also struggled as a woman to earn a living as a writer and gain critical recognition. Women, she writes, are held back from their intellectual and artistic endeavors by "a stream of daily trifles"—the domestic demands unfairly made upon them—and the social norms that restrict their activities. Moreover, women's aesthetic labor goes unrecognized and uncompensated, accorded "respect," but no substantive economic support. Historically, writing Yiddish literature was rarely a profitable endeavor. In New York many Yiddish writers supported themselves through manual labor, in sweatshops or the trades; H. Leyvik, for instance, worked as a wallpaper hanger. The economic crisis in Europe affected Vogel as a woman struggling to support herself in a literary scene hostile to women, while writing in a minority language.[5]

The historical context for Jewish belonging amid the fervor of competing nationalisms in Poland exponentially compounded Vogel's marginalization as a woman writer. It is from this double bind that she created modernist montage works that capture her feminist and Marxist aesthetic. In her prose montage she develops a feminist and minority narrative form that rejects social hierarchies by refusing the traditional tools of plot and narrative. She repudiated the novel, with its expansive realist pretensions and reliance on the point of view of a central protagonist, turning to a nonhierarchical aggregation of images and events that penetrate collective forms of experience. Her work investigates the forms of women's aesthetic labor that so fascinated

Baron and Shtok, though with a greater emphasis on the commodification of women's bodies and the ways women can resist by transforming themselves into artists.

Vogel's Illegibility in the Modernist Yiddish Poetry Scene

A multilingual writer with a PhD in philosophy, Vogel forged a difficult path writing avant-garde poetry, criticism, and montage prose. Her criticism cemented her place in the Polish art scene in Lwów, and her two collections of avant-garde Yiddish poetry—*Tog figurn* (Day-figures, 1930) and *Manekinen* (Mannequins, 1934)—received positive reviews. Ber Shnaper, for example, writing in *Der morgn* in 1930, described *Tog figurn* as "daring" and "successful."[6] Despite these reviews, she had difficulty selling copies, commenting in a letter to Glanz-Leyeles, "I did not get a single *zloty* for all three books."[7]

Her prose experiments were roundly misunderstood and dismissed. Apparently, she had crossed the line of female literary decorum. Whereas male poets like Peretz Markish and Jacob Glatstein wrote wild and ambitious poetry in line with early twentieth-century fragmentation and dislocation, the "archetypal female modernist voice spoke erotically,"[8] as in the works of Anna Margolin or Celia Dropkin. The literary establishment recognized women poets who wrote from the subjective voice of a lyrical "I" to describe women's private experience. Vigorous debates took place about the value and substance of women's poetry in Yiddish. In his essay "Kultur un di froy," Glanz-Leyeles famously critiqued the staleness of the Yiddish poetry scene, which he blamed on the absence of women poets. He sought to encourage women's creativity: "Woman must be who she is! Then she will be able to be great, to create a new world for us, and become a blessing for us men."[9] In his poetic call to arms, he dreams that women can transform Yiddish by creating new worlds for their male compatriots. Ironically, as Hellerstein notes, too often when writing about women, he actually diminished their achievements and discouraged them, as in the case of Fradl Shtok.[10] In the eyes of male writers and critics, women were expected to play a specific poetic literary role as creative muses to male writers. Indeed, this is the role that Vogel apocryphally played for her friend and literary interlocutor, the celebrated Polish modernist writer Bruno Schulz. Despite the Polish narrative that Vogel was merely "addressee, lover, and muse" to Schulz, the two shared a "dialogical" literary and intellectual exchange that proved fertile to both artists.[11] Both writers emerged from and participated in a post-Habsburgian Galician cultural world that included many Jewish and non-Jewish writers and intellectuals, who were shaped by the distinct nonnational provincial identity of the region.[12]

Vogel's aesthetic and political project was illegible to Jewish critics, who could not fathom that her intellectualism and avant-garde practices were anything but difficult and derivative. For example, Y. Rappaport, in his 1936 review in the Romanian journal *Shoybns*, read her experiments in cubist terms, finding them narrow and limiting. Her montages are "laboratory experiments" that are not viable because they do not contribute to "normal word craft [*normelen vort shaft*]."[13] For Rappaport, Vogel had breached the social and aesthetic norms of the craft, using language in a deviant fashion. In effect, she was too avant-garde for a woman. B. Alkvit, a member of *In zikh*'s editorial board, meanwhile, bemoaned her lack of originality. He claimed, "It is quiet by us on the prose front. There is no news."[14] Yet he dismissed her attempts to revolutionize Yiddish prose, deeming her montages belatedly surrealist.

Vogel's prose also drew criticism for inadequately representing the Jewish community and not being sufficiently nationalist. Alkvit was troubled by what he perceived to be the nonnationalist content of her montage, accusing Vogel of trying to hide from the circumstances of Jews in the 1930s: "A Jewish writer cannot escape the influences of a specifically Jewish reality, which demands a certain dose of rationalism every time."[15] He cannot comprehend her political engagement with the social conditions of labor, her feminist critique of capitalist commodification, and her antinationalist minority aesthetic—these are not properly political or Jewish. Instead, he wants her prose to be avant-garde, realist, and decidedly Jewish. He defines the quality of being Jewish as an explicit nationalist politics that she rejects, and thus overlooks the complex minority attachment central to her embrace of Yiddish as a Jewish language of modernist experimentation.

Vogel participated in the cosmopolitan literary and intellectual circles of her time but has not been written into their intellectual histories. Prior to recent feminist scholarship, Vogel's posthumous reception, where it does exist, has focused on her relationship to her close friend and collaborator, Bruno Schulz. Schulz's biographer, Jerzy Ficowski, perhaps most crudely exemplifies the barriers facing women when he writes of Vogel, "Her literary output—inferior to that of Schulz—is not of primary importance. Above all, Debora Vogel was the best, the most intellectually stimulating and creative muse for Bruno Schulz."[16] Ficowski could not fathom that Vogel was Schulz's equal, an important writer on her own merit. Thanks to the work of Polish and German critics and historians, including Karolina Szymaniak, Anna Maja Misiak, Karen Underhill, Anna Torres, and Anastasiya Lyubas, Vogel's participation in the Jewish Polish avant-garde has finally received recognition, and her work has been made available to new reading publics through Misiak's German and Lyubas's English translations.[17] A 2017 exhibit at the Museum Sztuki in Lodz, *Montages: Deborah Fogel and the New Legend of the City*, showcased the importance of her work in the history of Polish modernism and in the larger narrative of the Polish avant-garde.[18] Yet Vogel remains on the margins of modern Jewish and European intellectual and cultural histories.

Lwów, Modernism, and Jewish Minority Aesthetics

Debora Vogel's Yiddish experimentation unfolded against the historical and cultural backdrop of interwar Lwów's competing Ukrainian, Polish, and Jewish nationalisms. The city was on the front lines of World War I and frequently changed hands. It was first occupied by the Russians; the Austro-Hungarian Empire retook the city in 1915 and held it until the empire's demise in 1918, when it passed through Ukrainian and Polish control.[19] Vulnerable Jewish residents were caught between warring Polish and Ukrainian factions. Once Habsburg protections were no longer in place, the province erupted in ethnic violence, and "a savage assault of the triumphant Poles upon the Jews of the city" ensued.[20]

In 1919, Poland signed the Polish Minority Treaty, which was meant to protect racial, religious, and linguistic minorities within Polish borders but ultimately sowed greater ethnic conflict and strife. The Polish state viewed the treaty as a threat to national sovereignty, and thus the treaty sowed greater resentment toward the minorities it was meant to protect. During these tumultuous times, Lwów nurtured an array of artists, writers, intellectuals, and legal thinkers. Notably, Raphael Lemkin and Hersch Lauterpacht, two Jewish law students at the university in Lemberg (Lwów's name under Austro-Hungarian rule) during these crises of "group identity and autonomy," would go on to develop the legal concepts of crimes against humanity and genocide—the charges brought against the Nazis at Nuremberg.[21] As James Loeffler has shown, it was in this city at the edge of empire that the very notion of a national minority was formed by Lauterpacht and others who believed in a Jewish nationalism that included both the creation of a territorial state and the existence of a diasporic minority.[22]

Under Polish rule, Lwów nurtured its own unique modernist culture, distinct from that of the Polish national center in Warsaw. Central to the scene was the multiethnic group Artes, founded by Jerzy Janisch, Aleksander Krzywobłocki, and Mieczysław Wysocki in 1929 after they returned from an extended period in Paris, where they studied with Fernand Léger. The group grew to include a number of other artists, including Vogel. In the 1930s, Vogel, along with Henryk Streng, Otto Hahn, Margit Reich-Sielska, and others, studied in Paris, many with Léger.[23] Expressionism and constructivism dominated art in interwar Poland, but Artes artists embraced a mix of styles and were influenced by both Western and Eastern European movements, including cubism, surrealism, and the new realist movements in France and Germany, particularly *neue Sachlichkeit* and Léger's "New Realism." The group's members embraced montage techniques, incorporating "a surrealist juxtaposition of everyday images: photomontage and collage."[24] They were particularly attentive to post-expressionist trends in Germany, and to the work of art critics like Franz Roh and Gustav Friedrich Hartlaub.

Vogel read Roh's influential 1925 work *Nach-Expressionismus, Magischer Realismus: Probleme der neuesten Europäischen Malerei*, in which he coined the term "magical realism" to describe the work of German post-expressionism. In *Nach-Expressionismus, Magischer Realismus*, Roh critiques the ways expressionism "resorts to the everyday and the commonplace for the purpose of distancing it, investing it with shocking exoticism."[25] Vogel shared Roh's distaste for such exoticism and was similarly drawn to the return to realism that characterized interwar modernist art, including heightened attention to the object and the adoption of a stance of impersonal objectivity, at odds with the subjective and abstract style of expressionism. This body of art offered, in the words of the critic Irene Guenther, "a definition of the object, clinically dissected, coldly accentuated, microscopically delineated."[26] In Roh's view, the "real world" reemerges in this new realism but does so in a way that differs from traditional realism, through images of a strange and spellbinding material world.

Lwów also served as an incubator for a new Yiddish culture that strove to be both Jewish and cosmopolitan. The city nurtured a multiethnic, modernist literary and artistic milieu that represented a nonchauvinistic embrace of minority language and culture. Jewish artists created institutions to reinvigorate Jewish culture in a region devastated by war and interethnic strife. These included the Jewish Literary-Artistic Circle, which was founded in 1925 and modeled on the successful efforts of the Kiev Kultur Lige (Culture League).[27] Uncertainty remained about what form this Yiddish culture should take—should it be a monolingual nationalist endeavor or multilingual and cosmopolitan? At the 1929 Galician Writers Conference in Lwów, "some participants believed that only writers who wrote in Yiddish should be part of the movement, while those publishing simultaneously in Hebrew or Polish should be rejected."[28] They argued for Yiddish as the language of a Jewish diasporic nationalism. Among the discussants were the editors of the newly founded Yiddish journal *Tsushtayer*, a project undertaken by Rachel Auerbach, Melekh Ravitch, and others to rehabilitate Galician Yiddish culture and envision its future.

Vogel was born within five years of Raphael Lemkin and Hersch Lauterpacht and was a product of the same Jewish cultural and creative milieu. Like her male contemporaries, she was a multilingual intellectual seizing the moment of nascent national minority thinking, a moment when one could be at once a Yiddish modernist poet, Zionist, and socialist, writing avant-garde feminist poetry for New York, Polish, and Romanian journals. Born to Polish-speaking parents in 1902 in the city of Burshtyn in Galicia (now Ukraine), Vogel was educated in Polish, German, and Hebrew. The family moved to Vienna during World War I and then settled in Lwów, where she studied in the Jewish gymnasium.[29] During Vogel's time in the gymnasium, she became a member of Ha-shomer ha-tsair, a Zionist youth organization, and later taught at the Hebrew teacher's college in Lwów. She received her

PhD in 1926, writing a dissertation that charted the influence of Hegel's aesthetics on Józef Kremer, a prominent Polish philosopher and art theorist. Vogel was simultaneously a Hebrew-speaking Zionist, a scholar of Polish aesthetics, and a modernist Yiddish poet—a dizzying combination of intellectual, political, linguistic, and aesthetic commitments. Her story highlights a brief and extraordinary opportunity that emerged out of the collapse of empire and the throes of competing nationalisms, which led to the creation of new nation-states, including Poland and Lithuania, and ignited aspirations for the creation of a Jewish state in Palestine. For a brief moment amid this realignment of national and cultural identity, new rich and productive forms of minority identities became possible.

Vogel actively participated in Lwów's interwar modernist and avant-garde artistic institutions and saw herself as part of an ethnically mixed arts community. Responding to the creative fervor of interwar Lwów, she embraced Yiddish as her literary language, while nurturing her burgeoning feminist and Marxist commitments. Her editorial work for the short-lived Yiddish journal *Tsushtayer* emblematized her belief in the possibilities of Yiddish in Galicia. *Tsushtayer* stood out in the world of Yiddish modernist publishing for the leadership roles that women played on its editorial board, the number of women it published, and the feminist themes that appeared in its pages. The lion's share of modernist periodicals of the period, including *Ringen*, *Albatros*, *Shtrom*, *Eygns*, *Yung Vilne*, and *In zikh*, did not include women on their editorial board, even if they did occasionally publish them in their pages. Kadia Molodowsky's later journal *Svive* stands out as another exception to the rule.[30]

In *Tsushtayer*, Rachel Auerbach's reviews of women writers extended a feminist narrative of world literary history as she surveyed a group of women writers, including Fradl Shtok and the Polish writer Ewa Szelburg-Zarembina. Auerbach's essays detail the frustrating patriarchal landscape of literary publishing in at least three languages. These essays also underscore the challenges Vogel faced as a bilingual Polish Yiddish writer in a literary-critical scene contemptuous of women's writing. We can see this in the Yiddish critical response to Vogel and in the failure of Polish critics to recognize Polish-language women writers such as Szelburg-Zarembina.

Vogel curated *Tsushtayer*'s section on the arts and contributed essays on Marc Chagall and Artes members, such as the Polish-Jewish artists Henryk Streng and Otto Hahn. Not only did she write about Polish arts in Yiddish, but she also published Polish translations of Yiddish modernist writers in the pages of the leftist journal *Sygnały*, the same journal that discontinued its section on Yiddish culture in 1936 for fear of appearing "nationalist." While Vogel chose Yiddish, she continued to publish in Polish for both practical and cultural reasons. It was easier for her to find Polish venues for her work and to be compensated for that work. At the same time, it also allowed her to bridge the divide between the two languages through translation.

In 1935 she published her only collection of prose montage, *Akatsyes blien* (Acacias blooming). One year later, she self-translated the collection into Polish, published under the title *Akacje kwitną*. Writing in both languages, she resisted "the emerging zero-sum proposal that posited belonging to either Polish or 'nationally-Jewish' cultural spheres: Vogel belonged and felt a desire to be recognized in both."[31] Vogel found that her work was more welcome in Polish circles than Yiddish ones. In a letter to Glanz-Leyeles, she wrote, "I am too often forced to approach Polish journals with my essays on art where I am a welcome, popular contributor, and where they also pay me."[32] Vogel found the Polish press more open to her avant-garde approach to art and her critical writing about Jewish culture, as well as her art criticism. Publishing in Polish might have been an economic necessity for Vogel, but it also attested to her desire to find a broad Jewish and non-Jewish audience for her work. Although the montages rarely touch on Jewish themes or a traditional Jewish vocabulary, the language of their creation—the raw material used in their production, Yiddish—was inextricably Jewish. As Karen Underhill argues, "The very Jewishness of the text, as well, was given expression only through formalist means—in the forms, lines and shapes of the Hebrew letters in which it was printed; and in the sounds of the Yiddish language in which it was read."[33] In their 1919 Manifesto, *In zikh* writers declared: "We are 'Jewish poets' simply because we are Jews and write in Yiddish. No matter what a Yiddish poet writes in Yiddish, it is ipso facto Jewish. One does not need any particular Jewish themes."[34] Their journal was the primary outlet for her work in the United States. Vogel, whose first languages were Polish, German, and Hebrew, chose Yiddish as her language of modernist experimentation. Szymaniak argues that Vogel turned to Yiddish as an act of "self-marginalization" and "self-modernization."[35] Yet, by embracing Yiddish, she aligned herself with a language that spoke to Jews internationally across oceans and that linked her to a tradition of Jewish women's modernist writing. The diasporic language enabled her to collaborate, for example, with her friend, editor and critic Rachel Auerbach. Moreover, writing in Yiddish, she sought to express her own sense of minority belonging as a Jewish writer in the former Habsburg Empire, producing art in Yiddish over Hebrew. I suspect that her affinity for Yiddish went hand in hand with her deep attachment to the multilingual, multiethnic legacy of Galicia, against an emerging monolingual Hebrew nationalism.

Yiddish led her down a road that may have been even more challenging than she expected. According to Auerbach, Vogel learned Hebrew from her father, who had what Auerbach characterized as an "aristocratic" (i.e., snobbish) relationship to Yiddish.[36] Auerbach takes credit for convincing Vogel to learn Yiddish. When Vogel returned from her European travels to Stockholm and Paris, she decided to continue with Yiddish, publishing her first poems in the Yiddish press. Auerbach recalls the difficulties that Vogel faced: "I thought that perhaps I had done her a well-intentioned but ill-fated favor: she was isolated and separated from a cultural milieu and community that was essentially much more suitable and intimate to her than our Jewish 'Yiddishist' environment."[37] In 1938 Debora Vogel wrote to Bruno Schulz, describing her abiding frustration as an avant-garde Yiddish poet in Lwów in the 1930s. "For whom am I writing in Yiddish?"[38] she asks, recounting her disappointment at a recent evening of poetry. Those who attended were interested in her poetics but could not understand Yiddish, and no one among the "so-called Yiddishists" attended the event. Her friend Henryk Streng was furious on her behalf. Having an audience mattered to Vogel. She chose Yiddish not as an act of self-marginalization but as part of a greater movement for a Galician Jewish cultural renaissance.

Despite the frustrating challenges she faced, Vogel was committed to Yiddish as a Galician minority language. She discusses the Jewish minority question in two essays that she wrote on Polish Jewry: "Human Exotics" and her encyclopedia entry on Lwów Jewry for *The Almanac and Lexicon of Polish Jewry*.[39] In "Human Exotics," Vogel positions Jews as colonial others within Europe's borders. The essay opens as a critique of the Polish writer and adventurer Jerzy Giżycki, and his racist travelogue of his journeys in colonial Africa, which indiscriminately juxtaposes tales of racial violence with happy quotidian scenes without a critical framework to critique the injustice and exploitation of colonialism.[40] Vogel then provocatively observes, "One does not need Africa in order to exoticize people, to reduce them to beings of incomprehensible mentality, whom one may only approach with mixed feelings of pity and contempt; it might even be unclear whether pity is only a milder form of disdain. One does not need to search for Blacks. There are Jews."[41] She then pivots from Giżycki's Africa to Wanda Melcer's dehumanizing depictions of Warsaw Jews in reportage pieces published in *Wiadomości literackie* (Literary news). She links Melcer's and Giżycki's writing to draw attention to the many Orientalist and racist representational practices in Poland that produced and sustained racial difference, linking the Jewish other with the colonial other. These ideas were reified by an international system of hierarchies between civilizations that arose at the hands of the European powers in the wake of World War I. In her reading of this reportage, she illuminates how racism is concealed behind "a smoke screen of pity, rationalized as the need for the 'white civilizing mission,' a gesture of pity for all the black continents in this world!" She expresses solidarity with Africans and other colonial subjects who are forced to submit to racist and Orientalizing practices.

In her careful analysis of both Giżycki's and Melcer's works, Vogel articulates a minority practice of reading and writing that penetrates the colonial antipathy for the Other that lies beneath these exoticized portraits. As a reader with a keen eye, honed by her own minority perspective, Vogel easily recognized the racialized character of these representations. She critiqued the way both writers transformed living communities into objects, molding them into exotic subjects. Moreover, she traced how these racist forms of representation are also imposed upon Jewish bodies.[42] Her montage techniques sought to highlight these forms of objectification and to find alternative aesthetic practices to represent minority experience.

In her entry on the city of Lwów for *The Almanac and Lexicon of Polish Jewry*, Vogel purposely resists the racist ethnographic reportage style of the Polish writers she criticizes. Instead she introduces an alternative narrative approach to describe the Jewish neighborhoods of her city. The essay travels street by street, promising to take the reader to Dragon Street, a mystical and exotic-sounding location. At the end of the essay, Vogel deflates all exotifying expectations: "Finally, I find the street, and it is disappointing, as was to be expected. Its name does not correspond to banal and crooked houses or toy-like signs."[43] Here she mobilizes the readers' affective disappointment because, as she writes, it "calls us to order, it helps overcome the counterfeit exotic we're inclined to wrap around foreign cities and streets."[44] The corrective to such exoticism is the acknowledgment that "this life is an ordinary life"—recalling Vogel's interest in a realist practice that penetrates all imposed interpretive frames. Her outrage at exotified portrayals of everyday urban Jewish life informs her montage practice, with its attention to ordinary life and its refusal of the exotic. Her understanding of Jewish difference was interlinked with her feminist and avant-garde aesthetic practices. She developed montage as the technique to resist these exoticizing and racist narrative practices.

Montage as Social Form

Vogel's prose montage broke with grand narrative structures and objectifying representational practices to imagine expansive and radically equalizing forms of collectivity. Her montages grapple with the linked concerns of women's aesthetic labor, Jewish minority culture, and the condition of art in late capitalist modernity. Vogel innovates a radical and nonhierarchical approach to narrative form, producing a minority aesthetic that reframed the multiple identarian and national ideologies whose hold she sought to escape. Underhill describes this aesthetic as "diasporist" to highlight Vogel's cosmopolitan affinity with an international Yiddish and European modernist literary community.[45] Vogel's position, I argue, is not only diasporic; it is also feminist in the way she resists the privileging of the bourgeois male subject, while seeking to equalize the representation of experience by foregrounding a minority perspective. The result is a montage aesthetic that resists traditional narrative forms and avoids privileging select experiences.

By 1935, the year she published these montages, she had ceased to compose poetry. She wrote to Glanz-Leyeles that she was now working on "poetic prose [*poetisher proze*] in the genre of *Acacias*." Naming her genre "poetic prose," she blurs the boundaries between the two genres. In her 1937 essay "The Literary Genre of Montage," Vogel describes her montage practice as a form of "constructivist realism," aligning herself with trends in Polish and Russian art. Members of Artes likewise embraced montage as a technique to overcome the traditional dichotomy between "life" and "art" and a means by which to undermine the organic unity of the work of art.[46] Peter Bürger traces the origins of montage in painting to cubism, particularly Picasso's and Bracque's collages, contending that montage introduced the "reality fragment" into painting to challenge a vision of the painter as the transposer of reality.[47] Rearranging these reality fragments, artists sought not only to transform the work of art but also to participate in the formation of revolutionary visions of new social possibilities.

Fearing the premature publication of her new prose montage work, Vogel was anxious to familiarize her readers with *Acacias* and help her audience to "adjust to the form of them."[48] We will never know what the full trajectory of Vogel's avant-garde montage project might have been had her life not been cut short in the Lwów ghetto in 1942, when Nazis murdered her, along with her husband and son. It is clear that Vogel had a vision for a new form of writing that she had only just begun with *Acacias Blooming* and that she hoped would create new readers.

Inspired by the work of visual artists, Vogel discovered in montage a tool to move beyond the social conventions of narrative, which shape our quotidian understanding of the real. Vogel's critical writing on the montage form theorizes new narrative structures that can break down the boundaries between art and life central to the novel. Vogel critiques the contemporary novel's desire for closure and its reliance on traditional mimetic practices that smooth over the fragmentation and alienation of modern life. Montage afforded the possibility of new narrative forms that could harness the disruptive power of photomontage in particular. As Patrizia McBride argues, the techniques of montage served as "a means for rethinking narrative beyond the conceptual and experiential constraints imposed by the novel and other literary genres bound to the print media."[49] Alfred Döblin, who also wrote a travel narrative of his journeys through Galicia, *Reise in Polin* (1924), embraced these techniques for their capacity to transform language, "likening narrative to a concrete activity akin to building and making, which made it possible to wring out of language artifacts endowed with utmost plasticity and vividness."[50] Echoing Döblin, Vogel argued that the medium of the novel must change; its focus on plot and a central protagonist did not suffice to represent the contemporary moment. Literary montage links events without relying on plot, and allows the "empty spaces" between events to speak. In contrast to the novel, she argues, montage is endowed with "epic expression." Her interest in the epic resonates with the work of Walter Benjamin, who was also invested in "the possibility of grounding narrative in revived epic forms."[51] Moreover, Vogel's montage disrupts the narrative biases that privilege male experience over women's. It afforded Vogel a political and social lens through which to critically view the everyday, displaced from a privileged male subjectivity and distanced from ethnic and national conflicts. Her prose cuts through the chauvinism of individual subjectivities, envisioning alternatives to the social conventions of narrative prose fiction. It also offers a feminist articulation of the avant-garde dream of breaking down the distinctions between art and life.

In *Acacias Blooming*, Vogel reclaims the domestic and the everyday as urgent subjects of both poetry and prose. *Acacias Blooming* contains three separate montages: "Dear boy fun a banstantsye" (1931; The building of a train station), "Akatsyes blien" (1932; Acacias blooming), and "Blumengesheftn mit azalyes" (1933; Flower shops with azaleas). Each prose montage is written in a distinct modernist style—for example, a geometric cubist approach in "The Building of a Train Station" and what Vogel terms "constructivist montage" in "Flower Shops with Azaleas." In "The Building of a Train Station," Vogel describes the construction of a train station, juxtaposing careful descriptions of raw materials and defamiliarized images of laboring bodies, all filtered through her geometric language of description. Offering a verbal parallel to the photomontages of the 1920s, she layers images, physical details, temporal perspectives, and human actions, producing a lyrically dizzying depiction of a living earth shaped into industrial form. The other two montages focus on women's bodies in an urban landscape. Vogel viewed the entire collection as an image of modern experience and a narrative of aesthetic history, offering a panoramic account of cubism and its decline. The history culminates in the final montage, "Flower Shops," which portrays "the new value that persists after the exhaustion of earlier possibilities."[52] She defines this new value as the rehabilitation of the banality of everyday life: "A consequence of a worldview that tries to level the hierarchy of events."[53] No detail, no event is endowed with more meaning than any other. Specks of dust and fragments of popular music are as important as world historical events and serve as windows into the reality of human experiences that have been disguised by narrative conventions.

"Flower Shops" focuses on the aesthetic labor of the female artist and experiments with a nonhierarchical narrative mode of representation. Although the narrative unfolds chronologically between April and November 1933, the montage eschews plot; instead, it records, from a collective perspective, impressions and details from an urban landscape, including the experience of economic crisis and impending war. Vogel depicts women's bodies in public space. She collates fragments of cheap novels, popular tango lyrics, advertisements, and dolled-up mannequins that construct a cityscape of commodified femininity, offering women a vision of themselves as mannequins and the goods that are sold back to them. Vogel also describes the hidden feminine labor behind this process of commodification: women whose labor drives this commodification are artists of a kind. She does this by paying attention to the small details of urban life that capture perspectives not normally seen in conventional narrative. Through these perspectives she creates an aesthetic practice that does not commodify and objectify women.

Each section of "Flower Shops" is composed using a restrained descriptive vocabulary in which images of people and places in the city are juxtaposed with images of the natural world. Soldiers marching on the street are characterized in the language of geometry—they are like "blue rectangles"—and are juxtaposed with blooming jasmine, acacias, and linden trees. The mechanical and the organic are rendered in a visual language of shapes and colors that links the urban and natural worlds. Interspersed throughout is the narrator's commentary on the collective experience of the urban world—for example, "And suddenly it becomes self-evident that happiness is needed for life. At the same time, it turns out that there are plenty of passersby on the streets who have 'broken hearts.' "[54] Vogel blends reflections on this meaning of life with images of women wandering through the streets changing hats and clothes. The metaphysical, the poetic, and the everyday are described in the same terms; they are equivalent.

The montage also juxtaposes broken female bodies against an urban landscape as it changes over the course of the year, shaped by natural, political, and economic forces. The juxtaposition highlights women's exploitation under the conditions of capitalism from the factory floor to the art studio, offering a feminist critique of capitalism at a moment of economic crisis in an effort to reimagine women's experience. In representing the work of the artist, she also reflects on her own labor as a Yiddish writer struggling to survive in a literary marketplace that devalued women as well as Yiddish. In doing so, she sheds light on the relationship of the woman artist to the conditions of her aesthetic labor. A feminist critique of women's labor animates her critical dialogue with the novel's narrow representation of human experience. She demands that we rethink our mode of representing human experience to capture everything that is left out of view in the plot-driven narrative construction of the modern novel.

Woman Artists and the Feminist Avant-Garde

Vogel embraced prose montage as a tool to record everyday life, gathering together the small, the insignificant, the impersonal, and the feminine. Anna Torres astutely observes that her approach to the monotony of women's everyday lives "anticipated the postwar emergence of experimental representations of domestic temporality and women's labor, as exemplified by the films of Chantal Akerman and Trinh Minh-ha."[55] Vogel herself described the montage in contrast to the bourgeois novel: "There [in literary montage] individual situations are linked directly, without the circular wallpaper of a sequel that we know from traditional novels."[56] Whereas plot detours are linked to events as experienced by specific individuals, montage frees Vogel to adopt an entirely impersonal perspective with which to move among crowds and nameless faces in the urban world. Whereas plot imposes artificial structures of meaning, Vogel's montage attempts to offer more capacious descriptions of reality as experienced by the masses.

Vogel envisions an aesthetic avenue through which women can be not only useful objects of exchange value but also subjects producing art through their aesthetic labor within the world of capitalist decay. In her "poetic prose" she conceptualizes a metapoetic path for the female artist. We can see this in sections 15, 16, and 17 of the montage "Flower Shops with Azaleas," which are separated by their titles: "Der traktat fun lebn ershter kapitl" (Treatise on life: first chapter), "Fun traktat der tsveyter kapitl" (From the second chapter of the treatise), and "Driter zats traktak" (Third sentence of the treatise). In these sections of the montage, Vogel uses the visual language of modern art to meditate on the complex relationship between women's bodies, their labor, and the commodification of both in the creation of a feminine aesthetic.

"Treatise on Life: First Chapter" describes a dusky evening in a beauty salon. The montage reflects on beauty and the commodification of women:

> One only needs to go out into the streets, into the amber-yellow October dusk. Then, between four and five o'clock, life is always "broken" regardless of what happens to us.
>
> In the Salon de Beauté, 25 Karmelitska Street, there is a manicurist who looks like she's made of wax, like a fashionable doll from 1924. The hairdresser has a wavy hairdo scented with Milles Fleurs perfume, and the owner of the salon looks for anything like a heavily retouched photo of a woman circa 1900, with a deeply cut waistline and a stiff whalebone collar, the latest fashion of the 1900s.
>
> And it was just such a yellow dusk, between four and five o'clock, when the owner of the beauty salon on 25 Karmelitska Street—without ceremony and in front of all her customers—raised the subject: "For what must I live?"
>
> At that moment, as if answering the question, the waxen manicurist under the purple lampshade stood and gave the lady in black an aluminum bowl with water for her nails. Then with a lot of noise and pomp the hairdresser started working on one hairstyle after another with unusual tenderness, paying attention to the shape of each and every wave.
>
> A female apprentice began to set up and arrange canisters of black and brown henna hair dye, making an absolutely unjustified amount of noise.
>
> That is how the fact that there is something to live for in this world comes to be expressed either on a cheap postcard with a picture of a

> woman on it or on tins of hair dye exhibited in prime locations. And how could it be otherwise in such a place and under such conditions?
>
> And so it has always started with the statement: "Why live." That's how the course of every single life began in the autumn treatise on life. (61–62)

The section begins, as many others do, with a nonfocalized description of people walking the city streets. The October dusk captures the feeling of brokenness that overcomes all at this hour. Emotion is not an individual interior experience but is externalized into the city streets. The montage moves to the inside of a salon, describing the female owner and her employees. The women are characterized as outdated reproductions from the past, like a "retouched photo of a woman circa 1900," as though they were on a turn-of-the-century postcard. Here Vogel distills the imitative work of the beauty salon, its desire to reproduce women's fashion and beauty. The montage shifts from the present continuous to a specific moment: "And it was just such a yellow dusk, between four and five o'clock, when the owner of the beauty salon on 25 Karmelitska Street—without ceremony and in front of all her customers—raised the subject: 'For what must I live?' " The proprietress's question is answered by the actual labor of the salon workers. The hairdresser moves from hairstyle to hairstyle, tending to individual waves, and an apprentice sets up the cannisters of henna. Vogel draws attention to these women's labor, which both mirrors and produces social standards of beauty. The manicurist sways and works on her customer's nails, the hairdresser uses her imagination to tend carefully to her client's hair, and even the apprentice who displays the henna contributes a loud noise to the scene. These women's work is a form of aesthetic labor; they paint and shape, and they make sound. Their labor answers the owner's question: the meaning of life is found in women's aesthetic labor, a possibility reborn from the monotony of women's work. Even as Vogel critiques the practice of commodifying women's beauty, she finds potential in her practice of chronicling that labor.

Vogel returns the animated scene to a two-dimensional image, explaining: "That is how the fact that there is something to live for in this world comes to be expressed on a cheap postcard with a picture of a women on it or on primly exhibited tins of hair dye. And how could it be otherwise in such a place and under these conditions?" The apprentice's work and the postcard merge. She is both real and reproduced, flattened onto a postcard that wants to sell her products without acknowledging the monotony of her labor. In the juxtaposition, Vogel extracts the tension between the labor of producing beauty and the project of selling beauty. The postcard is a reminder of the banal cliché of women's work, aestheticized to sell products, and the possibility that the work might signal its opposite, the possibility of art. It represents life as it is lived and commodified. She also captures women's artistic bind:

How to step outside the restraints of the market to produce art that works against these aesthetic norms?

In her essay "Women on the Market," Luce Irigaray describes how capitalism depends on the exchange of women. If, as Marx argues, a commodity is produced through the social relations of labor, then women as commodities are produced through their social relationship with other things. According to Irigaray, "*Women-as-commodities are thus subject to a schism* that divides them into the categories of usefulness and exchange value; into matter-body and an envelope that is precious but impenetrable, ungraspable, and not susceptible to appropriation by women themselves; into private use and social use."[57] This abstraction of women as objects of exchange precludes their taking on the position of the laboring subject who produces art. Only as subjects can they create art. Anna Torres has observed how Vogel's poetry documents the fraught relationship between women and commodities without disavowing the pleasures of consumption. In her reading of *Manekinen*, she argues that "Fogel examines what it means to be a feminine commodity gaining voice through the eloquent vulgarity of consumption."[58] Kathryn Hellerstein contends that "Fogel's poems describe the contorted physical appearances of women—in beauty parlors and brothels—who attempt to please the gaze of men by imitating the mannequins through which modern society represents them."[59] As Torres and Hellerstein argue, Vogel's poetry and montage prose critique the commodification and instrumentalization of women's bodies and their sexual desires as depicted in the romantic narratives of cheap novels, popular music, and the display windows of women's clothing shops. But in *Acacias Blooming*, Vogel provides a much colder account of this project. Whereas in *Manekinen* Vogel critiques "the objectification of the body wrought by capitalism without disavowing the pleasures of kitsch and consumption," as Torres puts it, in *Acacias Blooming*, these pleasures are absent from view.[60] Instead, Vogel imagines the role of the woman artist who produces art with the commodity as her reality fragment. The montage is less interested in preexisting use value than in the spaces made possible by shedding light on the aesthetic labor of commodification. These practices create new narrative forms to capture and undo this bind.

The section of "Flower Shops" titled "From the Second Chapter of the Treatise" focuses on women's disarticulated bodies and imagines these partial bodies as sensate. Vogel both documents the violence against women inherent in these portrayals and tries to undo that violence:

> "And yet life is worth living."
>
> And thus the second section of the treatise and of life has always begun.
>
> Of course it is an ordinary summer, and all the sticky, dense, and outspread matter of the world is fermenting with promise, aromas, and possibilities. It is divided up and dissected into different piles:

> dense clumps, flabby and shapeless; sheets as taut and elastic as anticipation; and other sheets, insignificant, anonymous pieces of sheet metal, and scraps of ample, self-confident life-matter that is nearly brazen from its pure self-certainty.
>
> All of this matter resolves into things: the smart contours of bodies and breasts; of weeds, leaves, walls, bottles, and events. And then there is a reason to live in the world.
>
> Along the alleys of the city park stroll heavy torsos with round breasts. The bodies' wide, dishonest layers and waves are squeezed into brocade corsets the color of flesh and apricots.
>
> There is too much body. The body smells of ample leaves. It sparkles with possibilities.
>
> They watch the old ladies in dresses that are too wide and loose, especially sagging in the bust. And they watch people who "don't know how to live."
>
> And then one needs to be sure that every passerby thinks about one and the same thing: that life passes, and one cannot change its course; that such a single honeysweet day, full of a thousand possibilities and promises, will also pass.
>
> There is always a bronze heat; the world is a hot ball of metal, and life becomes time. (63)

In this montage, Vogel reduces the summer urban landscape into piles of flabby clumps, taut sheets, metal, and life matter, and so the organic and inorganic matter blends into abstraction. Bodies, leaves, bottles, and events are all gathered together as objects that form the substance of the meaning of life. Meanwhile, women roam the parks and alleys as "heavy torsos and round breasts." These bodies overwhelm the public space: "The bodies' wide, dishonest layers and waves are squeezed into brocade corsets the color of flesh and apricots. There is too much body." The fragmented bodies are both the objects of description and the subjects of sensory experience: "They [the torsos] watch the old ladies in dresses that are too wide and loose, especially sagging in the bust. And they watch people who 'don't know how to live.' " The bodies, both alive and inanimate, overwhelm the public sphere. This monstrous femininity is a product of the commodification and disarticulation of the female body by male artists, as well as a site of possible resistance.

Torsos and mannequins permeate Vogel's oeuvre. In "Flower Shops with Azaleas," the mannequin serves as a double figure for the crisis of the female artist and the Yiddish writer.[61] In the montage Vogel imagines women as both objects of violence and subjects who participate in the visionary reordering of a modernist language of sexual degradation. In section 4 of "Flower Shops," titled "Spring and Small Boxes," Vogel links these disarticulated women's bodies to the fate of the woman artist. The montage describes the arrival of spring with the lush greenery of the natural world invading the urban landscape. The perspective pivots to city streets littered with paper and cardboard from women's hat boxes, signs of springtime consumption. Shop windows are filled with partially dressed mannequins—the "female torsos" that "spin in finger wave updos: ancient torsos without eyes." Vogel takes these women's bodies seriously, imaging their inanimacy in the language of animate life: "However, women's torsos were shoving their way over the sidewalks and across the squares: torsos without eyes to see the waves of the lush greenery and multitudes of diverse and delicate matters that were happening around them and that were to change shortly." In this portion of the montage, Vogel describes the mannequins' failure to see as a product of their incompletion; no one had bothered to give them eyes or mouths. Nor can they complete themselves if they are deprived of hands to hold writing utensils. She captures the violence inflicted upon women when they are excluded from literary and artistic labor. Although the mannequins cannot experience the sensorium of spring, neither do the city dwellers, who are mired in the artificial blossoms of cardboard boxes. Whereas the mannequins are blind, the city dwellers can see only the artificial world of commodities.

The imagery of a torso with empty eyes recalls Vogel's poem "Ferd un torsn" (Horses and torsos) from her collection *Manekinen*.[62] The poem is dedicated to Giorgio de Chirico, and the torso image in the montage, as Lyubas insightfully notes, evokes "de Chirico's 'The Seer,' a picture of mannequin-prophet, bereft of sight, yet charged with insight."[63] Invoking de Chirico's visual vocabulary, Vogel filters the images of kitsch and consumerism through a de Chirico–like juxtaposition of classical imagery with reality fragments of modern-day life. She distills this male imagery of female bodies into her own feminist modernist language. Through fragmented bodies, Vogel ironizes what it means to be alive. These "porcelain torsos with breasts cannot properly receive life unless they are wearing new, unworn dresses" (48). They cannot see because they have no eyes, but they are bestowed with life by the new fashionable dresses they wear. If fashion bestows life on the golem-like figures, it does the opposite to the living women on the streets.

Vogel not only cites these modernist male influences on her work but also offers a critique of their masculinist assumptions regarding female bodies. In section 3 of "Acacias Blooming," Vogel describes doll-like mannequins that walk out of a shop window: "And there among them a pear-like head with the round lazy eyes of Picasso's women, and the uncertain, flustered mask color of faded roses and greenery. (She was once painted by Toulouse-Lautrec and is now presented anew by Pascin)" (24). In this scene, the mannequins resemble the distorted female subjects of male artists. Through these mannequins she draws attention to how male artists instrumentalize female bodies in order to give voice to their own anxieties about the transformations of modernity.

Notably in "Flower Shops with Azaleas," Vogel describes the mannequins as grotesque mirror images of women: "melancholy is crammed in" their made-up faces, their lips are outlined with "Chameleon-brand" lip liner. In section 6 of "Acacias Blooming," "Necklace, a Lyrical Intermezzo," Vogel engages in dialogue with modernist visual imagery: "Women plunge into the caressing metallic bustle," which she compares to images of Leda and the swan, a motif in Polish modernist art, and to "Max Ernst's women—blind, fleshy, brutal" (27). Describing these women using the visual language of male painters, Vogel invokes an iconography of subjected women who are objects of the male gaze. The mannequin, the puppet, the doll—inanimate representations of bodies—permeate modernist writing and visual art of the period. These proliferating images offered an avant-garde critique of what Andreas Huyssen terms "bourgeois enlightenment,"[64] so often figured in the inanimate bodies of women. For surrealist artists, Ghislaine Wood argues, the mannequin "represented the human form as a commodity," and in the work of male artists "women became the vessel through which to explore a variety of psychological and emotive states."[65] Vogel presents us with a vision of this modernist landscape as a dystopian space of broken and dismembered bodies in which women are transformed into abstract commodities or used as raw material for the art of others. However, unlike the passive objects of modernist desire—the women in the paintings of de Chirico, Ernst, or Picasso—these torsos long for expression—to be viewed not as objects of exchange but as subjects.

In "Third Sentence of the Treatise," Vogel offers a vision of a woman whose movements through the city are endowed with narrative agency: the female flaneur or flaneuse. We might read in this figure a representation of the author herself. As Szymaniak argues, "Her thought is born of movement, walking, traveling, and experience of space."[66] Walking and thought are inseparable, and an aesthetic of walking the city is central to Vogel's montage: "Along Karmelitska street that gray afternoon hour, a woman walks by" (64). She is described as beautiful: "Her complexion is the color of brown tree bark, lowered on a pink apricot." The woman walks "as if floating, lightly rocking on her nicely arched feet, with her step pouring over every gray board of sidewalk" (65). The female flaneur's body wanders the city freely: "And it is clear that she left the house with a plan for a long stroll in accidental streets that arrive unexpectedly." Her accidental wandering produces its own new narrative: "And thanks to the lady in brown and the sentimental Karmelitska Street, cheap delights and needs of our souls, which we always prefer to 'forget,' take shape in words" (66). This woman, both painterly and painter, muse and poet, ambles through the city. Wandering animates a new language for her to describe the anonymous passersby on the street. She overhears music emanating from the Femina Bar, which becomes a commentary on life, on par with a philosophical treatise. Vogel registers the ambivalence of its reception as both wisdom and vernacular or low culture. Her montage finds meaning through juxtaposition, endowing what has been extraneous to representation: snippets of popular music overheard on the street, or the path of the flaneuse through the city, take on a new importance. In this section of the montage, Vogel collects and collates impressions to capture what is lost in traditional narrative—to give credence to forms of culture directed at women and derided as feminine.

Montage, the Novel, and Democratic Form

Focusing on women's experiences and their aesthetic labor enables Vogel to radically rethink the role of narrative. With the montage, Vogel not only theorizes the role of the woman artist but also rethinks the genre of the novel.[67] Schulz immediately grasped this about her work: "The true originality of Debora Vogel's book and that which disorients the reader—pushes him unlike the ground under his feet—is the complete breaking with the stated form and principle of the traditional novel."[68] Having dispensed with plot, Vogel can replace the individual protagonist with an anonymous person who, as she describes in her essay on montage, "has the same role as an impersonal situation: a fatalistic role to exemplify an impersonal process."[69] According to Vogel, "The actual protagonist in a montage is the process of life with its dialectic and two main tendencies: the biological (stable) and social (timely)."[70] Vogel jettisons the conventional protagonists of prose fiction, making life itself the hero of her montages. She collates fragments of lived reality as an answer to the modern novel, whose reliance on romantic individualism and heroic events were anathema to her understanding of life. Her montage is a direct rebuke of the novel as an enclosed hermeneutic form. However, Vogel is drawn to the mimetic impulses and social affordances of novelistic prose.

In the opening section of "Flower Shops with Azaleas," she contrasts the third-person male subjectivity of the bourgeois novel to her own method in the montage, an impersonal and collective narrative of sensation. The narrative voice describes how passersby wander the city, longing to lose themselves in "an old-fashioned novel [*altmodish roman*]," whose conventional protagonist is described: "A man in a gray coat and a black bowler hat was walking on L. Street, weighing his life to that point" (43). In contrast to the bourgeois novel with its focus on social norms and assimilation into an established social world, Vogel's montage depicts these passersby through "the new novel of everyday life." This new novelistic form registers anonymous and pedestrian sensations available for ambulatory city dwellers to discover and immerse themselves. She describes these depersonalized sensations collectively experienced in everyday life: "The streets of that novel smell of elasticity, of glass, and of walking [*dem geyn*]. Smell of something unusual: of the hardness and roundness of things" (44). Stickiness hardens into spheres and flat planes; white canvases are synonymous with walls "whiter than in reality, melancholy white or hard white." The walls are "dense with longing and heat"—this object world produces its own desires. She translates her geometric terms into the language of everyday life, both domestic and urban; the things in the novel are "spherical, square, rectangular (according to everyday nomenclature: furniture, clothing, sidewalks, figures)." Bruno Schulz characterizes the tension between her geometric language and surrealist style: "It is as if we are in a surrealistic landscape bordered by flat homes without windows, by figures from commercials and shop signs, under the textured and lacquered sky, in a late and extravagant light."[71] Vogel transcribes life into an idiosyncratic stylized language: "In gray skies walls rise, smooth like satin. Walls rise, similar to lacquer or paper. Figures walk the streets: figures taken from a novel called 'life' " (44). Moreover, she creates an interior collectivity that operates according to a different temporal logic from that of the bourgeois novel and pushes beyond the technique of Flaubert's mode of free indirect discourse. Rather than focus on the simultaneity of events in different locations—the feature of the national novel that Benedict Anderson so aptly describes—she looks at the simultaneity of interior experience.[72] She explains, "What is important is not the fact that space can simultaneously contain multiplicity, but that the inner space of experience can simultaneously incorporate strikingly different areas and contents, dimensions and directions of psychic events."[73] Here she sets the stage for imagining new forms of collectivity organized around shared sensations and impressions that emerge from montage, and are not registered by the national novel.

In "Flower Shops with Azaleas," Vogel develops techniques to capture the simultaneity of interiority in the city. We can see this beautifully in section 6, which describes a series of rainy days when one leans back against the "the dazzling wall of posters, pretending to wait for someone with whom one had arranged a meeting, although there was no one to wait for" (50). Against this backdrop of urban advertising, the afternoons are experienced as "an old-fashioned hit song about 'always waiting, waiting again, not knowing what one is waiting for.' " This song's lyrics signal not only the romantic longings that underwrite a commercialized culture but also their opposite: "The sticky and resigned odor of dresses, worn until finally threadbare. They also recalled the former withered and helpless situations one carries in one's soul—one does not know how to live" (50). The lyrics reference both romance and despair amid the Great Depression: threadbare dresses and feelings of helplessness. But Vogel imagines the potential aesthetic rehabilitation of this despair: "However, on those rainy days in 1933 the fatalism that was then rife among people was rehabilitated. And as usual with such banal matters, such an event did occur far from life and as if imagined." The rain, the posters, the afternoon—these are not sensations experienced by individuals. They are sensations of the city that collide and reverberate. They represent the collective interior life of the city, rather than the interiority of an individual protagonist.

In describing a banal event unfolding so distant from life, Vogel invokes plot only to subvert it. These events do not produce individual meaning but rather appear "so far from life as if imagined." It is at this moment that the clichéd lyrics from popular songs—" 'broken hearts,' 'streets that want nothing more' and 'waiting for life' "—become part of life (51). These phrases fill the commercialized landscape of life with haunting echoes of their meaninglessness, and this meaninglessness takes on a new significance. The lyrics are no longer about women's unfulfilled desires but the echoes of those desires circulating collectively in the atmosphere of life. A similar refrain reappears in the next section, when Vogel meditates on the azaleas in the flower shops on Boulevard Montparnasse; beautiful and fragrant, they are perfectly lovely in their idyllic and bohemian contexts, but "suddenly enormous sadness passes, a tin sea of melancholy. It bursts forth, no one knows how, from the azalea shop" (51). Here Vogel captures the affective experience of the city; the sadness that reverberates in disembodied fragments, the sadness which belongs to everyone and no one.

These affective experiences float on the surface of the city and are shared by passersby. As these once elegant azaleas become "unbearable," other desires emerge for "missed opportunities," "failed romances," and "unhappy loves" (51). Vogel characterizes these desires and disappointments as the "tandeyte moto far a bilikn roman"—that is, the "shoddy tagline of a cheap novel" (52). These meaningless events and trite words recall their opposite and speak to the reality of the moment, not through the desires of an individual hero, but through the collective longing and disappointment of the city streets filled with anonymous passersby: "Yet that's how life works: the most meaningless things remind us of the most important things in life" (53). But whose truths lie in the bouquets of beautiful flowers, the romantic tunes of popular music, and trashy novels? These are the collective spaces of women's desires, speaking to the romantic longings of women who have been sold the idea of beautiful things and romantic desire as an antidote to the bleak reality of their everyday lives. Vogel juxtaposes fragments of these popular narratives of women's desire in order to reveal the conditions that control women's subjectivity and their agency.

Vogel, writing in 1933, three years prior to Walter Benjamin's well-known essay "The Storyteller," characterizes the novel as a clichéd performance of empty meaning. In her montage she describes the masses, who in looking for the "old-fashioned novel" are searching for meaning in familiar narratives because they are searching for direction. The old-fashioned novel does not answer the desire for meaning but rather raises another set of questions: "And like the matter, not yet settled (although many years have passed), a long-forgotten question, 'How does one live?' was asked as if for the first time. The question was so banal like before, and so ignorant of its own banality" (43–44). This circulating question of "How does one live?" echoes Benjamin's reflections on the novel in "The Storyteller." Benjamin diagnoses the rise of the novel as a form of private reading that accompanies the death of communal storytelling. The rise of the novel for Benjamin is a symptom of the alienation inherent in modern life. The novel emerges from "the individual in his isolation, the individual who can no longer speak of his concerns in exemplary fashion, who lacks counsel and can give none."[74] If the novel is about a search to recoup lost meaning, this search "is no more that the initial expression of perplexity with which its reader sees himself living this written life."[75] Vogel's answer to meaninglessness that haunts is montage. She looks to reorient the novel to the everyday life. To achieve this, she rejects the perspective of the man in the bowler hat, embracing instead the woman floating over the city or the broken mannequins in the park—and all in Yiddish, the language of minority identity.

Rather than offer meaning in the life narrative of a single individual, Vogel seeks to locate new meaning in the state of meaninglessness through attention to microevents. For example, in section 2 of "Flower Shops," titled "Street and Dust," Vogel turns to a moment when "on the very outer edge of the pavement a handful of dust swirled and scattered into the still pale air" (45). The dust disappearing in the air is an unremarkable event that takes on a powerful resonance: "And thus certainly, this same event became important suddenly, since many things have already disappeared from people's lives forever." The dust captures the experience of the fleeting and temporary, of the irretrievable nature of one's life, constructed of fleeting events of little significance. We can see an echo here between Vogel's and Flaubert's aesthetics. In his essay on *Madame Bovary*, Jacques Rancière meditates on swirling dust to describe the gap between Flaubert's aesthetic vision and Emma's perspective: "The Flaubertian characters," he writes, "don't even understand what kind of happiness can be enclosed in swirls of dust and bubbles on wavelets. They want those microevents to be linked together in a real plot. They want the swirls and bubbles to be turned into properties of real things that can be desired and possessed, into features of individuals that they can love and who love them."[76] Flaubert's characters still long for the old novel with its language of fate and personal destiny, a desire that Flaubert ironizes. Instead, according to Rancière, Flaubert "makes us feel the music of the impersonal, the music of true life, through the noise of her [Emma's] misfortunes."[77] If Flaubert, as Rancière argues, pushes beyond his readers' expectations of plot to transcend the narrow view of art as embodied by Emma, Vogel achieves something very different, envisioning a world that can incorporate Emma's aesthetic desires in the first place.

Moreover, Vogel's montage, with its attention to the microevent, ironizes the emplotted and clichéd language of individual experience. Happiness and joy, for example, are as substantive as scattered dust: "Every year has a given plan of happiness and something squandered. And from the muddy handful of dust a fragrance was emitted of yellow heat and concealed possibilities. And there was no more time left to lose" (45). The theme of squandered time recurs throughout the montage. What is being laid bare by the image of the dust and the repeating notions of happiness and time wasted? The scattered dust upends the conventional idea of meanings that can be materially grasped and preserved. Plot produces the fiction of a temporal unfolding of profound meanings, whereas the image of swirling dust more accurately captures the arbitrariness of everyday life.

At the conclusion of her montage, Vogel returns to the subject of the novel and its failures. She makes the case for a return to the chronicle as the structuring principle for montage. In the last section, titled "Second Commentary," the narrator returns to the topic of the novel:

> This is still not the novel for which we were seized with a sudden, sweet passion right at the beginning of the year, on a day with gray skies and streets like seas and skies.
>
> Yet every future novel has to handle life in this and similar ways: like a chronicle that always has material to jot down, and where, as a result, one never runs out of sequels.
>
> This chronicle knows no events more important than any others. Everything is equally important and necessary.
>
> This chronicle does not consider sharp contours of tragic experiences nor heaps of resignation. Everything plays itself out like a continuation, without hierarchy. That's where the monotony begins, and that often unbearable repetition.
>
> Life is like a chronicle: an anonymous and undemanding heap. Only upon a closer examination can the glutinous and undemanding mass of life be arranged into individual fates and particular subjects. Just as one divides the mass of green in June or July into individual leaves and branches.
>
> At every point life can be interrupted and then picked back up again: like the chronicle of a year, interrupted in November, made from copper brass, sad and fantastical, "like life itself." (74)

The reader is reminded that this montage is not the equivalent of the novel, the novel that everyone longs for in the opening section, "Streets and Sky." Instead Vogel informs us that this montage will be like the novel of the future, "like a chronicle that always has material to jot down, and where, as a result, one never runs out of sequels." In contrast to the novel, the chronicle accumulates details and events and has no endings, no meaningful conclusions. Vogel describes a chronicle as a narrative that refuses to make distinctions between experiences, whether profound or mundane. The coordinates of the montages are not determined by the novel's diegetic and spatiotemporal axes, but rather are unstructured and adjacent to the material world. The result is "monotony" and "unbearable repetition." But Vogel reminds us that life is also monotonous and unbearable, such that "at every point life can be interrupted and then picked back up again: like the chronicle of a year, interrupted in the month of November, made from copper brass, sad and fantastical, 'like life itself.'" In this way, there is no development of meaning and no editing out of the repetitive events that structure daily life, as there is in the novel. Vogel here articulates a modernist, democratic aesthetics of monotony. This is her project: to reimagine the novel appropriate to a revolutionary moment that seeks to break down social hierarchies.

In her 1935 essay, "The Romance of the Dialectic," published after *Acacias Blooming*, Vogel describes the novel as a genre intent on capturing certain forms of historical experience. The typical novel is about the themes of "love, failures, and frustrations," and focuses on heightened individual experience, which is reduced to these affective events.[78] In the essay, Vogel praises "the documentary novel," using the example of Rudolf Brunngraber's novel *Karl und das zwanzigste Jahrhundert* (*Karl and the Twentieth Century*). She reads Brunngraber's novel as a Marxist critique of novelistic romantic individualism. According to Vogel, the novel's male protagonist, Karl Lakner, grows up in an atmosphere in which "individualism is marked by a faith in the world and in life and in the conviction that each individual decides about his own life and is responsible for its success or failure. This individualism is furthermore full of optimism, conditioned by a faith in one's own strength" (245). But Vogel is drawn, in particular, to how the narrator frames this optimism: "And this very optimism isolated him from the real connections of events in the world—indeed, Karl did not have a clue about their totality" (246). In effect, the novel is about a man whose individualism and agency are subject to question. She continues, "Karl Lakner, the hero of romance, experiences in himself the thesis of the author that 'the economic conditions of his desires are at least equal in value to those that are biologically conditioned'" (245). The true protagonist of that novel, according to Vogel, is not Lakner but "impersonal time"; it is not an agent of history but rather a "passive product" (243).

The second aspect of the novel that attracts Vogel is its documentary aspirations, its reliance on "dry numbers and dates" as the organizing principle (246). She explains, "This intricate knot of causes and results called life, this gray rhythm and fatalism are represented here as impersonal lists of numbers and an enumeration of facts." What appeals to her are what she terms the "banal gestures," because for her, these bring her closer to "that thing that is undefined at the micro-level and misunderstood in its meaning but yet is well understood, known as 'life.'" These dry details move attention away from the frameworks of meaning that structure our perceptions and our prejudices; she wants details before interpretation. This monotonous and egalitarian approach to narrative is not an easy read, but easy reading was never Vogel's interest.

Vogel wants to get closer to life, which means departing from the mediating frameworks that shape our understanding. She writes, "I adopt a very proximate perspective to these things. It consists of discarding the familiar distance to things, the distance becomes filled with interpretation, which becomes so deeply intertwined with the thing itself and taken for it."[79] This impulse to a radical realism stripped of interpretive prejudices mirrors a politics that refuses judgment and prejudice. If montage is the technique suited to the temporality of the twentieth century, then so too is it suited to an art practice that refuses to hierarchize and discriminate against its subjects, that refuses to privilege the bowler-hat-wearing man over the woman manicurist. Montage is an equalizing force if it breaks through grand narrative structures. Montage is also the culmination of the work of the women writers, like Fradl Shtok and Dvora Baron, who too were fascinated by women's object worlds, and who sought new forms of narration that might give voice to the experience of these women.

Conclusion

Grace Paley's Modernist Legacy

Debora Vogel's prose-montage experiments represent the apotheosis of the feminist aesthetic projects laid out in this book. Vogel's work investigated women's aesthetic desires, the exploitation of women's labor, and narrative form. She linked these formal and aesthetic concerns to the political questions of minority identity and citizenship. Her work emerges from the crucible of the aesthetic, social, and political crises from which all of these women wrote. Vogel shows us the links between the narrative techniques employed by Baron and Shtok, as well as the thematization of minority literature, the future of Jewish languages, and the crises of Jewish national belonging that appear in Goldberg and Bikhovsky's work. These writers shared a keen awareness of narrative's social power to reconfigure social norms, to imagine new national and minority communities, and to seize cultural authority.

Vogel and the other women writers in this book turned to prose fiction to establish their literary authority at the very moment when Jewish men sought to reconstitute their cultural authority in the secular world of Jewish letters. The everyday and the prosaic served as an ideal stage on which to bring women's experiences into the world of aesthetic representation from which they had been excluded. They gravitated to the thin wall between literary and social convention, hoping that by breaking one they would break the other. They addressed political questions about women's role as artists in the context of rapidly shifting definitions of minority and national culture, and in doing so they were writing about the radical political and social transformations of the interwar period. These writers' response to their historical moment captured the conflict between Jewish nationalism and various modes of internationalism, asking not how Jewish literature should serve Jewish national strivings, but rather how literature might break the boundaries between Jewish and non-Jewish culture.

The women in this book experienced the possibilities of freedom and liberation, including sexual liberation, gender equality, and democratic representation, that modernity promised as a tantalizing potentiality, but which was never fully achievable. They gained new access to education, citizenship, and legal rights, but even when that access was real, they were not able to fully capitalize on it. The societies they lived in devalued women's labor and refused them opportunities to make a living or gain sufficient recognition and support for their work. In response, their writing challenged the social hierarchies that excluded them as women and as Jews. This is the other story of modernity, a story of the violence committed against women and other marginalized peoples who sought to grab hold of the possibilities that citizenship promised.

These writers chose prose fiction not only as the means to contest social and aesthetic norms but also as a medium of historical authority and knowledge. Historical knowledge was a central thematic of the creation of modern Hebrew and Yiddish literature, which aimed to insert Jews into history. "Classic" male writers understood the power of prose narrative, casting themselves as the keepers of Jewish memory and the arbiters of the linked projects of literary and national revival. They invented new masculine discourses, reconstituting modernity as Jewish men's struggle to become men, and they claimed this authority for themselves. S. Y. Abramovitsh once famously told the Russian Jewish historian Simon Dubnow, "I am also an historian, but after another fashion. When you come to the history of the nineteenth century, you will have to consult my works to depict the lifestyle of those generations."[1] The Hebrew writer and critic David Frishman wrote that should a deluge overtake the small towns of the Pale of Settlement, then "the future scholar would be able to reconstruct the entire map of Jewish shtetl life in Russia of the first half of the nineteenth century in such a manner that not even one iota would be left out" by turning to Abramovitsh's work.[2] These claims placed Abramovitsh and his male contemporaries as the heirs to a traditional Jewish world that authorized their work and whose memory they crafted.

In response, women writers offered counter-narratives of Jewish experience that highlighted the gendered dimensions of Jewish modernity. Baron and Shtok focused on women's desires and aesthetic experiences. Goldberg and Bikhovsky probed the place of women in modern Jewish letters. Each of these writers challenged the social norms embedded in the conventions of literary narrative. Among them, Vogel's work pushed literary and historical narrative to a radical extreme. She dispensed with plotted narrative, arguing that plot produces an artificial representation of everyday life and imposes arbitrary meaning. Instead she turned to the chronicle—a historical genre that includes lists of chronological events without interpretation. Vogel held that the structure of the chronicle is more suited to document everyday life than narrative fiction: "Every future novel has to handle life in this and similar ways: like a chronicle that always has material to jot down, and as a result one never runs out of sequels."[3] In arguing for a turn to the chronicle against plot-based forms of the novel, Vogel envisioned a genre with the capacity to describe marginalized forms of collective experience; to document the tensions between bodies and social forces; and also to record the encounter between bodies, the natural world, and the built environment. Her intention was to disrupt normative narrative authority, to dispel the myth that a single body of work told from the perspective of one individual could speak to the varieties of human experience.

In dispelling with plot, Vogel saw an avenue through which to rethink not only literary but also historical narrative. Hayden White gives voice to a similar set of concerns about modern historiography's reliance on the techniques of narrative storytelling. The emplotment of history, according to White, imposes artificial coherency on historical events:

> The notion that sequences of real events possess the formal attributes of the stories we tell about imaginary events could only have its origin in wishes, daydreams, reveries. Does the real world present itself to perception in the form of well-made stories, with central subjects, proper beginnings, middles, and ends, and a coherence that permits us to the see "the end" in every beginning? Or does it present itself more in the forms that the annals and chronicles suggest, either as mere sequence without beginning or end or as sequences of beginnings that only terminate and never conclude? And does the world, even the social world, ever really come to us as already narrativized, already "speaking itself" from beyond the horizon of our capacity to make scientific sense of it? Or is the fiction of such a world, capable of speaking itself and of displaying itself as a form of story, necessary for the establishment of that moral authority without which the notion of a specifically social reality would be unthinkable?[4]

White grapples with how the narrative techniques of historiography rely on fictional narrative forms: Does the imposition of plot, with its coherent focus on events around shared meaning, distort our understanding of history? Or rather, is historiography more akin to the novel, a fictional representation of historical events structured by a plot and imbued with moral authority? White proposes that the chronicle and the annals offer us a more accurate or realistic depiction of history that is not mired in moral authority or social convention. In White's view, history and the novel impose artificial structures of meaning onto the everyday lives of individuals. Just as White recognized the dangers of emplotted historiographies, Vogel and the other women writers in this book took issue with the emplotment of literary narrative that privileged men's experiences and often doomed women to tragic ends.

These women writers were ahead of their time in drawing attention to the crisis of narrative history and linking it to a critique of narrative prose fiction. The insights that Hayden White raises were abundantly clear to them five decades earlier. They understood that the social norms governing the narration of Jewish modernity excluded their experiences and silenced their voices. Introducing new narrative techniques and new plot structures, and drawing attention to women's artistic possibilities, they created radical new Jewish literary forms and a feminist and democratic aesthetic that demands our attention.

✦

The legacy of their modernist, feminist aesthetic lives on in Grace Paley's innovative English-language prose fiction. We can see in her metaliterary reflections on narrative, voice, and the writing of both literature and history a radical continuation of the writers in this book. Paley produced her work in the post–World War II era, after the decline of the transnational Jewish language literary world that this book documents. She was born in the Bronx to socialist Russian Jewish immigrants who spoke Russian at home. She studied poetry at the New School with W. H. Auden. She published three collections of highly acclaimed stories: *The Little Disturbances of Man* (1959), *Enormous Changes at the Last Minute* (1974), and *Later the Same Day* (1985). She wrote and published poetry and was a prominent peace activist, from the 1960s onward, speaking vociferously against war and nuclear weapons.[5] Paley received grants and honors during her lifetime, including a Guggenheim award, a PEN/Faulkner prize, and an NEH Art award. In her short stories, written over several decades, she explores the multiple voices of women in her neighborhood in New York, examining their lives, friendships, and disappointments, and in doing so, reflects on the social role of storytelling.

Paley started her career as a poet, like many of the writers I discuss. In a 1987 interview with Jacqueline Taylor, she explained why she turned to prose: "In a way what made me write fiction is that I was really thinking an awful lot about women's lives, and I wasn't able to get it into poems somehow."[6] Paley's simple explanation conceals a more complex relationship to narrative prose. Paley turned to prose as a tool for documenting everyday experience and women's voices. In the 1950s, men dominated the American literary scene and the Jewish American literary scene was no different. Paley wanted to create a literary stage for the everyday life of the women whom she observed on her block. In doing so, she challenged the gendered aesthetic norms of the period.

This literary moment dovetailed with the canonization of American Yiddish literary history and the erasure of women from that literary history. In the 1950s, Yiddish was memorialized in English by a generation of male critics and scholars who did not read women. Saul Bellow's 1953 translation of Isaac Bashevis Singer's "Gimpel the Fool" for the *Partisan Review*, which established Yiddish and Singer in the literary milieu of *Partisan Review* and the intellectual left, captures the problem. Irving Howe, the author of *The World of My Fathers*, invited Saul Bellow to translate the work for a major anthology of Yiddish literature he edited with Eliezer Greenberg, *A Treasury of Yiddish Stories*, which contained not a single work by a woman author. The anthology and the story were a success, and they established Singer as a singular voice in American literature. Both Bellow and Singer later won Nobel Prizes for their work, canonizing them as the central protagonists in American letters.

The 1950s and 1960s also saw the rise of a new male canon of Jewish American writers. Philip Roth became the heir to Bellow's and Singer's legacy, and for years, until his death, his name circulated as a potential Nobel awardee. This was the Jewish literary world as described by Alfred Kazin in 1966: "What saved Jewish writing in America from its innate provincialism, what enabled it to survive the moral wreckage of the 30s, was the coming of the 'intellectuals'—writers like Delmore Schwartz, Saul Bellow, Lionel Trilling, Karl Shapiro, Harold Rosenberg, Isaac Rosenfeld, Lionel Abel, Clement Greenberg, Bernard Malamud, Irving Howe, Philip Rahv, Leslie Fiedler, Robert Warshow, Paul Goodman, Norman Mailer, Philip Roth, William Phillips."[7] These seventeen Jewish men represented the best of "modern literature," upholding "the primacy of intelligence and the freedom of the imagination."[8] Kazin argued that a diet of Jewish tradition and Jewish revolutionary thinking placed American Jews, or at least American Jewish men, in a position to ascend to the pantheon of postwar American literature. Kazin's starting point for the ascendancy of English-language, American Jewish writing was the men who transcended the immigrant world of Jewish writing, a generation that included significant women writers such as Mary Antin and Anzia Yezierska. Notably, the list of the new intellectuals that he celebrates as the future of American writing does not include a single woman. Missing for example are Paley or Tillie Olsen. Kazin could not conceive of the idea of intellectual women writers, especially those that take women as their subject.

In 1959 Philip Roth and Grace Paley both published acclaimed collections of short fiction: *Goodbye, Columbus* and *The Little Disturbances of Man*, respectively. Paley was eleven years older than Roth. His first book appeared when he was twenty-six years old, while Paley waited until the age of thirty-seven to publish hers. The two collections share a fascination with language and orality, capturing forms of Jewish speech as it registered in English among second-generation immigrants. Both writers described East Coast Jewish life from the perspective of young Jews grappling with their place in Christian America, though Paley, unlike Roth, also wrote about women from other immigrant communities. Both writers explored the taboo of sexuality, though through very different lenses. In his review of the collections, Harvey Swados describes their shared "nervous muscular prose perfectly suited to the exigencies of an age which seems at once appalling and ridiculous."[9] If 1959 was the meeting point of those two writers, whose collections were reviewed together, it was also a defining moment of splitting that would propel Roth to the novel and Paley to short fiction and political activism. Roth continued to work through the conundrums of his contemporary moment through the guise of Jewish men: these include the recurring protagonist of many of his novels, Nathan Zuckerman; Mickey Sabbath in *Sabbath's Theater*; and Roth himself, who appears in *Operation Shylock*. Roth came to be seen as Bellow's heir, the voice of Jewish America and a great American writer. Paley would take a dramatically different path. In a talk at Barnard College in the mid-1960s, she explained that in *The Little Disturbances of Man* she was drawn to explore subjects because she felt like an outsider in her Jewish neighborhood, where her family spoke Russian, "but the street spoke Yiddish. There were families of experience I was cut off from. You know it seemed to me that an entire world was whispering in the other room. In order to get to the core of it, I used all those sibilant cues. I made fiction."[10] Here she explains her fascination with voices, voices that she overheard and later translated onto the page in Jewish-accented English. Unlike Roth, Paley did not exclude non-Jewish voices from her work, paying attention to the multitude of communities she lived among. In her talk, she asserts that she's done with Jewish voices: "But the truth of the matter is, I have probably shot my Jewish bolt. I had better recognize that fact and remember it."[11] Nancy K. Miller interprets Paley's enigmatic statement as a call to arms, as if Paley were to proclaim, "I hereby take my distance from those who pay no attention to what I write, I take myself out of the story."[12] On the face of it, the statement is ludicrous because Paley continued to write about Jewish women—not exclusively, but their lives continued to matter and be of interest in her stories. Yet Paley no longer wanted to be viewed in these terms, in part because these had become the terms of Jewish men.

Paley's emergence as a writer coincided with her coming into being as a woman. In her 1981 essay "Of Poetry and Women in the World," Paley describes how growing up, she felt she was a boy, "like a lot of little girls who like get into things and want to be where the action is, which is up the corner someplace, where the boys are."[13] But Paley was transformed into a woman when she became a mother, "and it wasn't really until I began to live among women, which wasn't until I had children, that I began to look at that life and began to be curious about it."[14] Once she found women's lives, wrote and documented them, she recognized their absence in the literary world. Reading the intellectual boys' club as outlined by Kazin, she observes, "But what I thought to myself was: am I tired of some of these books that I'm reading! Some of them are nice, and some of them are exciting, but really, I've read about this stuff already. And who's this guy Henry Miller? You know, big deal. He's not talking to me. My life's not going to get a lot sexier on account of him. His is, no question about it. Maybe."[15] Henry Miller's sexy writing is for men. It is about their fantasies. Miller might get off on it, but Paley's sexual life had no place in Miller's universe. She went on to say similar things about the Beats, referring to them as the boys. Paley located herself outside of this male Jewish literary tradition. In a 2006 interview with Ilya Kaminsky and Katherine Towler, Paley explained:

> I read a lot. In poetry, I liked W. H. Auden more than anyone. I loved British writers and the novels I grew up with, Twain, Dickens, and so on. I was not influenced say by Walt Whitman or anyone like that. His freedom was not my freedom, and so it didn't affect me. But Saul Bellow had begun to write already. He freed the Jewish voice in some ways that I didn't even recognize, but his work was all about men. Still, for Jews who are crazy about the English language, he was the one.[16]

Paley identifies the men who loosened up the tight strictures of English-language writing, but she is not their heir. Their freedoms were not hers; she could not enjoy them, just as the women writers of the interwar period did not enjoy the same freedoms as their male contemporaries.

Although Paley's work attracted acclaim, similar to the women writers I have discussed in this book, she remains a somewhat marginal figure in American letters. Despite the many advances of the feminist movement in the post–World War II era, the canon of Jewish writing has remained male-dominated. Jacqueline Taylor offers a useful frame to understand Paley's ambiguous place in American and American Jewish literary history:

> Despite widespread acknowledgment of Paley's originality, critics have seemed at a loss to account for the power of her work. Her published volumes are widely reviewed and often acclaimed, and she regularly appears in literary anthologies, but she has attracted little scholarly attention. This is due in part, no doubt, to her relatively slight output and the simple fact that short stories rarely receive the critical attention accorded to novels and poetry. But a more important reason for the critical silence towards Paley's work is that her writing does not fit readily into the established literary frameworks. Somewhat too innovating to conform to the conventions of reality mimetic fiction, she nevertheless shares little with the modernists and metafictionists.[17]

Taylor ascribes the critical silence toward Paley as a sign of her illegibility to the literary establishment. Critics celebrate Paley's collection and yet find it difficult to locate her in "the established literary frameworks" because, as Taylor argues, she was both "too innovating" to be a realist storyteller and too idiosyncratic to be considered part of the modernist literary world.

I locate Paley's illegibility in the vexed meeting place between Jewish American writing and feminist literature. Paley, despite her claims that she "shot her bolt," continued to explore both Jewish lives and women's lives. Her work does not fit into the narrow conception of Jewish American writing centered on a genealogy that moves from Bellow to Roth to contemporary writers like Jonathan Safran Foer or Nathan Englander. Even though, as

Hammerman and Seidman argue, Paley's literary experiments were more radical than her male peers and "Paley's innovative literary style and her attention to the voices of women on the social margins are, in fact, intricately related," she remains on the margins of the American and Jewish American canons.[18] Yet she embodies a century of female Jewish writers whose style and prose challenged establishment literary institutions and norms. Her experiments recall the work of the writers in this book, and when we read Paley in the context of their feminist experiments, her work becomes much more legible. Like them, she develops innovative narrative techniques to capture the porous boundaries between the private world and the public sphere, between Jew and gentile.

Grace Paley's oeuvre engaged in a dialogue with this legacy of Yiddish culture. Her story "A Conversation with My Father" from her 1974 collection, *Enormous Changes at the Last Minute*, reflects on the subversive role of the woman writer who takes women's lives as her subject. In the story, the daughter, an American short-story writer, writes literary works that disappoint and frustrate her father. Jewish writing from the early of the part of the century was filled with conflicts brought about through the tensions between novel-reading daughters and their traditional Jewish fathers. In Paley's story, the dialogue and tension are between a novel-reading father and his short-story-writing daughter. The father's cultural compass is Russian realist literature; he reads novels (and short stories) to confirm what he knows about morality and fate. The daughter, by contrast, embraces a feminist and avant-garde narrative style.

What's fascinating about this tension is that postwar American Jewish literature has been dominated by narratives that highlight the generational and gendered tensions between overbearing mothers and their neurotic Jewish sons. This trope pervades Philip Roth's *Portnoy's Complaint* and is visually realized in Woody Allen's short film *Oedipus Wrecks*. This phenomenon of the postwar period diverged from the sympathetic portraits of Jewish mothers produced in the 1920s, for example in "My Yiddishe Momme," the jazz song made famous by Sophie Tucker.[19]

Paley's choice to return to a different generational tension, between father and daughter, harkens back to the early twentieth century. Jewish-language writing from that time was filled with conflicts brought about through the tensions between novel-reading daughters and their traditional Jewish fathers. For example, Sholem Aleichem's story cycle, *Tevye the Dairyman*, dramatizes the transformation of Jewish literature through Tevye's daughters' rejection of their father's matches. The cycle, though it focuses on the daughter, is largely about Jewish male anxiety in response to the gendered transformations of Jewish modernity.[20] In her story, Paley both mirrors and flips the script. Rather than giving us a view of the novel-reading daughters who came to figure the tensions of a modernizing Jewish literary culture, she offers a daughter who is already an author in conversation with her novel- (and short-story)-reading father. What ensues is a metaliterary dialogue that sheds light on the gendered norms of European and American realism. In this dialogue her father represents the very literary authority she is challenging with her writing.

"A Conversation with My Father" is a frame tale. In the frame story, the narrator sits at her dying father's bedside, as he offers last-minute literary advice. The advice comes in the form of a request for a story: "'I would like you to write a simple story, just once more,' he says, 'the kind de Maupassant wrote, or Chekhov, the kind you used to write. Just recognizable people and then write down what happened to them next."[21] Her father wants sequentially ordered, plot-based stories with characters from nineteenth-century fiction. The narrator wants to please her dying father, but she also rejects the literary principles he's describing with a powerful statement about narrative fate: "I *would* like to try to tell such a story, if he means the kind that begins: 'There was a woman . . .' followed by plot, the absolute line between two points which I've always despised. Not for literary reasons, but because it takes all hope away. Everyone real or invented deserves the open destiny of life" (162). On the one hand, the narrator wants to indulge her father's passion for Russian and French nineteenth-century literature. But she takes an ethical stand against such narratives. The problem with plot, she tells us, is the way it interferes with the "open destiny of life." The narrator warns against such a definitive arc and ending. A character's destiny should not be foreclosed because of their background. Paley resists the sociological narratives internalized as fate by realist fiction, narratives that impose unfair endings, not only in fiction but also in real life.

The daughter decides to tell her father a story, one that might please him, although she must know from the start that this is impossible. In this enclosed story, the central narrative tension is between a mother and her son, an aspiring writer. The first version of the story is a short paragraph and describes the mother who turns to drugs to stay close with her drug-addicted son. Then her son gives up drugs and leaves his addicted mother hopeless and alone. The narrator adds at the end of the story, "We all visit her" (162). That last sentence signals that the story is about someone Paley knows, not an imagined life. It is one of many moments when Paley references extraliterary events to resist forms of narrative closure. This woman is real and known to the narrator. In an interview with Leonard Michaels, Paley explained, "What I don't like is the word 'fiction.' I think it's a false word, and it's led to 'non-fiction.' I mean you're either a storyteller, an inventor in language or event or whatever, or a poet of storytelling—or you're not."[22] Paley conceives of storytelling as an art form that rejects the arbitrary boundary between fiction and history or fiction and nonfiction. She sees her job as documenting historical experience; the job of the writer, she says, is "to tell the story of the people of the life of your time."[23] In this way, she echoes Abramovitsh's reflections on his oeuvre as a form of historical documentation. Paley, however, wants to give voice to everyday women's experiences outside of the sociological norms according to which such women are understood.

Paley's enclosed story references a real life, a portrait captured by an artist of a woman who exists. She is a woman Paley visited, and Paley's job is to artfully tell her story. For her father, though, the story is a failure. He wants the accumulation of realist detail, but not reality. He condescendingly tells her, "There are Russian writers you never heard of, you don't have an inkling of, as good as anyone, who can write a plain ordinary story, who would not leave out what you have left out. I object not to facts but to people sitting in trees talking senselessly, voices from who knows where" (162). According to the father even the most minor Russian writer can write an "ordinary" story better than his daughter. In particular, he takes issue with stories about "people sitting in trees talking senselessly, voices from who knows where." His synopsis matches the plot of Paley's story, "Faith in a Tree," from the very same collection. In that story, Paley experiments with narrative perspective in inventive ways that recall Shtok's, Baron's, and Vogel's work. Just as male writers in the early twentieth century found it difficult to read experimental fiction by women, so too does Paley's fictionalized father. He is both her actual father, and a figure for male literary authority. Paley artfully captures the blurred boundaries of art and life in a conversation between herself and her father about narrative fiction and social reality.

In the ensuing conversation, the father poses more questions about the protagonist that seek to locate her in relationship to class and race: Who were her parents? What was her background? How will her ancestry determine her future? Is she from a good family? He imagines that character is fate, and the more we know about this mother, the more we will understand her life as fated. Fate here is both destiny and morality. It is what must happen, and it is a moral judgment imposed on the woman. It represents the literary and social norms that Hebrew and Yiddish writers recognized and resisted. They sought to find avenues for women's expression that were not linked to the social fates of women and did not depend on marriage, family ties, and the bonds that kept women tied to the domestic realm. They rejected the morality imposed on them by fates they hoped to overturn. In the same spirit, Paley exposes how her father's understanding of the literary is driven by his morality. She gently mocks his conservatism. The boy is born out of wedlock; her parents are divorced. Again her father objects: "For God's sakes, doesn't anyone in your stories get married? Doesn't anyone have the time to run down to City Hall before they jump into bed?" (163). Her father wants the characters to observe bourgeois social norms. He wants to believe that addicts are addicts because of their moral failings, and children are born out of wedlock because of their mothers' depravity. That is, he judges the literary world by the heteronormativity of the social world he inhabits.

In the second version of the story that the narrator tells her father, she works to humanize the mother, highlighting her love for her son. The son is not only an addict, but also a writer. He writes for the school newspaper and starts his own periodical, *Oh Golden Horse!*. Although the mother also suffers from addiction, she takes care to nurture her son and his friends with healthy foods and vitamins. The boy falls in love and gets clean. He invites his mother to join him, but unlike her son, she cannot overcome addiction. So the son and his girlfriend cut her off; she remains at home alone, crying for her son: "My baby, my baby" (166). The father rejects this version as well, insisting that his daughter cannot tell "a plain story." But the father is contented, at the very least, by the ending of the story: he muses, "Poor woman. Poor girl to be born in a time of fools. To live among fools. The end. The end. You were right to put that down. The end." (166). The poor woman has met her tragic end, and the narrator's father approves of this tragic ending, a poetic justice that fits the narrative of classical tragedy.

Paley's narrative genius is that she refuses her father the neat structure of tragedy. The narrator turns to her implied audience and says, "That woman lives across the street. She's my knowledge and my invention. I'm sorry for her. I'm not going to leave her there in that house crying. (Actually neither would Life, which unlike me has no pity)" (167). The narrator employs the phrase "my knowledge and my invention" to capture a vision of narrative art that is tied to knowledge of the world, even as it invents details. The woman is both neighbor and fiction, and the story is both imagined and real. The narrator/author feels a deep responsibility to the story and her character, to not abandon her and women like her to the fate that others feel they deserve. Her father wants to see the addict mother punished, but his daughter refuses. This is the fantasy about narrative that Hayden White describes, in which the conventions of realist fiction and historical narrative are more akin to fantasy and "daydreams" than to the ways that life unfolds in reality. Paley resists such fantasies, telling her father that the woman overcomes addiction. Whereas White is concerned with the moralism that clouds our understanding of history, Paley recognizes the violence of narratives that condemn their subjects to real-life tragedies. The woman will recover and go to work as a receptionist at a community clinic. She will thrive.

The narrator's refusal to end the story of the mother comes up against her refusal to recognize her father's death. "'How long will it be?' he asked. 'Tragedy! You too. When will you look it in the face?'" (167). Paley contrasts the story of a mother who loves her son and supports his writing without judgment to the frame story of a father who derides his daughter's writing. She explains in an introduction to the story for an edited volume, "My father liked me a lot, but was for many years disappointed in me."[24] Despite his failure to recognize and support her art, in the story he does force her to confront his imminent death. Just as she declines to give the mother a tragic ending, she hopes to do the same for her own father. However, narrative play cannot protect her from his mortality. Paley, I argue, is confronting the death of the father, and the freedoms and constraints that such a death might pose.

Paley's oeuvre embodies the feminist ethos that emerged in the interwar period, when women writers experimented with realist prose fiction to capture women's lives beyond the canned plots and narrow fates open to women in literature. Paley, like the writers in this book, conceived of the aesthetic as intricately connected to the social. Though this perception was shared by male writers, Jewish women writers embraced the literary as a frontier and a site of social and political transformation for women and for Jews. In this way they revolutionized Hebrew and Yiddish literature, and it is high time that we recognize these women's struggles as central to Jewish historical experience. We must rewrite the narratives of Jewish modernity from their perspectives and rethink modern Jewish experience through their eyes.

NOTES

Introduction

1. Vogel, letter to Aaron Glanz-Leyeles, May 23, 1939, RG 556, box 4, folder 5, Glanz-Leyeles Collection, YIVO Institute for Jewish Research, New York.

2. Ewa Płonowska Ziarek, *Feminist Aesthetics and the Politics of Modernism* (New York: Columbia University Press, 2012), 2.

3. Ruth Hemus, *Dada's Women* (New Haven, CT: Yale University Press, 2009). For another take on surrealism and women, see Paula Kamenish, *Mamas of Dada: Women of the European Avant-Garde* (Columbia: University of South Carolina Press, 2015). For scholarship on women and Surrealism, see Whitney Chadwick, *Women Artists and the Surrealist Movement* (London: Thames Hudson, 1985); Mary Ann Caws, Rudolf E. Kuenzli, and Gwen Raaberg, eds., *Surrealism and Women* (Cambridge, MA: MIT Press, 1991).

4. Bonnie Kime Scott, "Introduction," in *The Gender of Modernism: A Critical Anthology*, ed. Bonnie Kime Scott (Bloomigton: Indiana University Press, 1990), 2.

5. Anne Fernald, "Women's Fiction, New Modernist Studies, and Feminism," *Modern Fiction Studies* 59, no. 2 (2013): 229. This critique is echoed by numerous others: Urmila Seshagiri, "Mind the Gap! Modernism and Feminist Praxis," *Modernism/Modernity Print Plus Forum* 2, no. 2 (2017), doi:10.26597/mod.0022. Also see Tory Young and Jeff Wallace, eds., "The Future of Women in Modernism," special issue, *Literature Compass* 10, no. 1 (2013). Rebecca Walkowitz and Douglas Mao introduced the term "new modernist studies" to describe the transnational and postcolonial turns in modernist studies that sought to expand the field beyond its provincial investment in a select group of men. See Douglas Mao and Rebecca Walkowitz, "The New Modernist Studies," *PMLA* 123, no. 3 (2008): 737–48.

6. Seshagiri, "Mind the Gap!" In the editor's introduction to the first issue of *Feminist Modernist Studies,* Cassandra Laity underlines the role that feminist scholarship played in transforming modernist studies, making possible its global expansion and yet failing to transform the central literary historical narratives that continue to elide women's contributions. "Editor's Introduction: Toward Feminist Modernisms," *Feminist Modernist Studies* 1, nos. 1–2 (2018), DOI:10.1080/24692921.2017.1390870. Jessica Berman also argues for the centrality of feminist thought to transnational turn in modernist studies. "Practicing Transnational Feminist Recovery Today," *Feminist Modernist Studies*1, nos. 1–2, (2018): 9–21, DOI: 10.1080/24692921.2017.1382968.

7. See, for example, Janet Lyons, *Manifestoes: Provocations of the Minor* (Ithaca, NY: Cornell University Press, 1999); Ziarek, *Feminist Aesthetics*; and Jill Richards, *The Fury Archives: Female Citizenship, Human Rights, and the International Avant-Gardes* (New York: Columbia University Press, 2020).

8. Paula Hyman, "Two Models of Modernization: Jewish Women in the German and the Russian Empires," in *Jews and Gender: The Challenge to Hierarchy*, ed. Jonathan Frankel (New York: Oxford University Press, 2000), 50.

9. Rita Felski, *The Gender of Modernity* (Cambridge, MA: Harvard University Press, 1995), 30.

10. For a discussion of these portrayals, see Sander Gilman, *The Jew's Body* (New York: Routledge, 1991); Ann Pellegrini, *Performance Anxieties: Staging Psychoanalysis, Staging Race* (London: Routledge, 1996), 17–66; Daniel Boyarin, *Unheroic Conduct: The Rise of Heterosexuality and the Invention of the Jewish Man* (Berkeley: University of California Press, 1997), 7–37. Boyarin (*Unheroic Conduct*, 4, 23) contends that Jewish culture also produced its own internal counterpart to the non-Jewish idea of manliness by embracing an ethos of *eydelkeyt* (gentleness).

11. See Todd Presner, *Muscular Judaism: The Jewish Body and the Politics of Regeneration* (London: Routledge, 2007); Boyarin, *Unheroic Conduct*; Oz Almog, *The Sabra: The Creation of the New Jew* (Berkeley: University of California Press, 2000); Yaron Peleg, "Heroic Conduct: Homoeroticism and the Creation of Modern Jewish Masculinities," *Jewish Social Studies* 13, no. 1 (2006): 31–58.

12. Among these works: Norma Fain Pratt, "Culture and Radical Politics: Yiddish Women Writers," *American Jewish History* 70, no. 1 (1980): 68–90; Naomi Sokoloff, Anne Lapidus, and Anita Norich, eds. *Gender and Text in Modern Hebrew and Yiddish Literature* (New York: Jewish Theological Seminary of America, 1992); Freeda Forman, Ethel Raicus, and Sarah Silberstein Swartz, eds. *Found Treasures: Stories by Yiddish Women Writers* (Toronto: Second Story Press, 1994); Yaffa Berlovitz, *She-ani adamah ve-adam: Sipure nashim ʻad ḳum ha-medinah* (Tel Aviv: Ha-kibbutz ha-me'uchad, 2003); Wendy Zierler, *And Rachel Stole the Idols: The Emergence of Modern Hebrew Women's Writing* (Detroit: Wayne State University Press, 2004); Tova Cohen and Shmuel Feiner, eds., *Kol ʻalmah ʻivriyah: Kitve nashim maskilot ba-me'ah ha-tesha'-'eśreh* (Tel Aviv: Ha-kibbutz ha-me'uchad, 2006); Orly Lubin, *Ishah koret ishah* (Haifa: University of Haifa Press, 2006); Orian Zakai, "Zion of Their Own: Hebrew Women's Nationalist Writing" (PhD diss., University of Michigan, 2012); Kathryn Hellerstein, *A Question of Tradition: Women Poets in Yiddish 1586–1987* (Stanford, CA: Stanford University Press, 2014); Carole B. Bailin and Wendy Zierler, eds., *"To Tread on New Ground": Selected Hebrew Writings of Hava Shapira* (Detroit, MI: Wayne State University Press, 2014).

13. Several recent translations have made women's prose more widely available for syllabi and should help change this trend. These include Kadia Molodowsky, *A Jewish Refugee in New York*, trans. Anita Norich (Bloomington: Indiana University Press, 2019); Miriam Karpilove, *Diary of a Lonely Girl, or The Battle against Free Love*, trans. Jessica Kirzane (Syracuse: Syracuse University Press, 2020); Yenta Mash, *On the Landing*, trans. Ellen Cassedy (DeKalb: Northern Illinois University Press, 2018); Blume Lempel, *Oedipus in Brooklyn and Other Stories*, trans. Ellen Cassedy and Yermiyahu Ahron Taub (Simsbury, CT: Mandel Vilar Press, 2016). Anita Norich discusses the translation of Yiddish women's prose and the syllabi question in "Translating and Teaching Yiddish Prose

by Women," *In geveb*, April 2, 2020, https://ingeveb.org/blog/translating-and-teaching-yiddish-prose-by-women.

14. Irena Klepfisz, "Di Mames, Dos Loshn/The Mothers, The Language: Feminism, Yidishkayt, and the Politics of Memory," *Bridges* 4, no.1 (1994): 17–18.

15. For a discussion of how male writers turned to prose fiction to assert themselves as new secular authorities on everyday life in competition with women, see Allison Schachter, "Men Reading Women: Secularism and Literary Modernity in the Writings of Abraham Cahan and Sholem Aleichem," *Jewish Quarterly Review* 111, no. 4 (2021), forthcoming.

16. Eva Broido, *Memoirs of a Revolutionary* (Oxford: Oxford University Press, 1967), 9.

17. Mary Asia Hilf and Barbara Bourns, *No Time for Tears* (New York: Thomas Yoseloff, 1964), 17.

18. Puah Rakovsky, *My Life as a Radical Jewish Woman: Memoirs of a Zionist Feminist in Poland*, ed. Paula Hyman, trans. Barbara Harshav and Paula Hyman (Bloomington: University of Indiana Press, 2001).

19. The collection housed at the YIVO Institute in New York contains over three hundred first-person accounts from Jewish youths about their experience in Europe from the 1930s and 1940s.

20. "Esther," in Jeffrey Shandler, ed., *Awakening Lives: Autobiographies of Jewish Youth in Poland before the Holocaust* (New Haven, CT: Yale University Press, 2002), 343.

21. "Esther," 343.

22. Allison Schachter, "Modernist Indexicality: The Language of Gender, Race, and Domesticity in Hebrew and Yiddish Modernism," *MLQ* 72, no. 4 (2011): 493–520.

23. Leah Goldberg, "Pirḳei zikhronot meḳuṭa'im," in *Hekhal she-shaka': Ha-ḥinukh ha-'Ivri be-Ḳovna mosadot ve-ishim*, ed. Y. Yablokovsky (Tel Aviv: Irgun bogre ha-gimnasyon ha-'Ivri be-Ḳovna, 1962), 126–34.

24. Yaffah Berlovitz, "Elisheva Bichovsky," *Encyclopedia of Jewish Women*, Jewish Women's Archive, https://jwa.org/encyclopedia/article/elisheva-bichovsky.

25. Rachel Auerbach, "Nisht-oysgeshpunene fedem," *Goldene keyt* 50 (1964): 135.

26. Laura E. Thomason, *The Matrimonial Trap: Eighteenth-Century Women Writers Redefine Marriage* (Lewisburg, PA: Bucknell University Press, 2014), 1.

27. Christine Delphy, *Close to Home: A Materialist Analysis of Women's Oppression* (London: Verso, 2016), 20.

28. Dan Miron offers an important account of Bikhovsky's contributions to Hebrew modernist poetry and her later rejection by the Hebrew elite following her husband's death. See *Imahot meyesdot, aḥayot ḥorgot* (Tel Aviv: Ha-kibbutz ha-me'uchad, 1991).

29. Bikhovsky, letter to British High Commission of Refugees, June 12, 1947, Elisheva Bikhvosky Papers, Archive of the Hebrew Writers Association, Binder 7, Folder 5555170.

30. For a discussion of Goldberg's relationship to women writers, see Allison Schachter, *Diasporic Modernisms: Hebrew and Yiddish Literature in the Twentieth Century* (New York: Oxford University Press, 2012), 133–37.

Chapter 1

1. Dorrit Cohen, *Transparent Minds: Narrative Modes for Presenting Consciousness in Fiction* (Princeton, NJ: Princeton University Press, 1978), 100.

2. Frances Ferguson, "Jane Austen, *Emma*, and the Impact of Form," *Modern Language Quarterly* 61, no. 1 (2000): 158. Ferguson writers about Jane Austen's development of this technique decades before Flaubert.

3. Patricia Howell Michaelson, *Speaking Volumes: Women, Reading, and Speech in the Age of Austen* (Stanford, CA: Stanford University Press, 2002); Suellen Diaconoff, *Through the Reading Glass: Women, Books, and Sex in the French Enlightenment* (Albany: State University of New York Press, 2005).

4. Jacques Rancière, "Why Emma Bovary Had to Be Killed," *Critical Inquiry* 34, no. 2 (2008): 236.

5. Jacques Rancière, *Dissensus: On Politics and Aesthetics* (London: Bloomsbury, 2015), 3.

6. Na'ama Rokem, *Prosaic Conditions: Heinrich Heine and the Spaces of Zionist Literature* (Evanston, IL: Northwestern University Press, 2013).

7. For a discussion of male anxiety about women's new role in Jewish literary culture, see Schachter, "Men Reading Women."

8. Jordan Finkin, *A Rhetorical Conversation: Jewish Discourse in Modern Yiddish Literature* (University Park: Penn State University Press, 2010), 2.

9. Finkin, *A Rhetorical Conversation*, 2.

10. Chava Weissler, "'For Women and for Men Who Are Like Women'": The Construction of Gender in Yiddish Devotional Literature," *Journal of Feminist Studies in Religion* 5, no. 2 (1989): 9.

11. Naomi Seidman, *A Marriage Made in Heaven: The Sexual Politics of Hebrew and Yiddish* (Berkeley, University of California Press, 1997), 1–8.

12. Robert Alter, *The Invention of Hebrew Prose: Modern Fiction and the Language of Realism* (Seattle: University of Washington Press, 1988), 3.

13. For an account of the role that educated women played in the rise of modern Hebrew and Yiddish literature, see Iris Parush, *Reading Jewish Women: Marginality and Modernization in Nineteenth-Century Eastern Europe* (Waltham, MA: Brandeis University Press, 2004).

14. Irena Klepfisz, "Queens of Contradiction: A Feminist Introduction to Yiddish Women Writers," in *Found Treasures: Stories by Yiddish Women Writers*, ed. Frieds Forman, Ethel Raicus, Sarah Silberstein Swartz, and Margie Wolfe (Toronto: Second Story Press, 1994), 37.

15. Tova Cohen, "Portrait of the Maskilah as a Young Woman," *Nashim: A Journal of Jewish Women's Studies and Gender Issues* 15 (2008): 11.

16. Zierler, *And Rachel Stole the Idols*, 31.

17. Wendy Zierler, "Hava Shapiro's letters to Reuven Brainin," *Nashim: A Journal of Jewish Women's Studies and Gender Issues*, no. 16 (2008): 67–68.

18. Pratt, "Cultre and Radical Politics"; Klepfisz, "Di Mames, Dos Loshn"; Norich, "Translating and Teaching Yiddish Prose by Women."

19. Dorothy Bilik, "Yente Serdatzky," in *Encyclopedia of Jewish Women*, Jewish Women's Archive, https://jwa.org/encyclopedia/article/serdatzky-yente.

20. I thank Anita Norich for sharing her new bibliographic work on Yiddish women's publications.

21. Pratt, "Culture and Radical Politics," 77.

22. Yente Serdatzky (1877–1962) left her husband and children to become a writer, first in Warsaw in 1905 and then in New York in 1907. She worked on the editorial staff of the *Forverts*, and in 1913 she published a collection of short stories entitled *Geklibene shriftn.* Rokhl Brokhes (1880–1942) was born in Minsk and studied Hebrew; in 1896 she began writing short fiction in Yiddish, and in 1922 published a collection of her stories, *A zamlung dertseylungen.* Miriam Karpilove, born in Minsk in 1888, emigrated to the United States in 1905. She published her first book, *Tog-bukh fun an elende meydel*, in the 1910s (its publication date is not given), and numerous serialized novels in the *Forverts.*

23. Pratt, "Culture and Radical Politics," 77.

24. Klepfisz, "Queens of Contradiction," 54.

25. See Zelda Kahn Newman, "The Correspondence between Kadya Molodowsky and Rokhl Korn," *Women in Judaism* 8, no. 1 (2011): 1–26. Other women's groupings can be found surrounding the modernist journal *Tsushtayer* in 1930s Lwów. See Anastasiya Lyubas, "Gender, Language, and Territory: *Tsushtayer* Literary Journal in Galicia and Contributions of Yiddish Women Writers," *Nashim: A Journal of Jewish Women's Studies and Gender Issues*, no. 37 (2020).

26. Ezra Korman, *Yidishe dikhterins antologye* (Chicago: L. M. Shteyn, 1928).

27. See, for example, Aaron Glanz-Leyeles [A. Glanz], "Kultur un di froy," *Di fraye arbiter shtime*, October 10, 1915, 4–5; Melekh Ravitch's review of Ezra Korman's *Yidishe dikhterins*, "'Den mir hobn zunshtn keyn andri (mekhaye) in der velt': E. Korman *Yidishe dikhterins*," *Literarishe bleter*, 5, no 42 (October 19, 1928): 830–31.

28. Hellerstein, *Question of Tradition.*

29. Irving Howe and Eliezer Greenberg, *A Treasury of Yiddish Poetry* (New York: Holt, Rinehart, and Winston, 1969); Joseph Leftwich, *The Golden Peacock: A Worldwide Treasury of Yiddish Poetry* (New York: T. Yoseloff, 1961).

30. Naomi Seidman, *A Marriage Made in Heaven*, 17. See also Weissler, "For Women and for Men Who Are Like Women," 9.

31. Naomi Seidman, *A Marriage Made in Heaven*, 18.

32. I. L. Peretz, "Speech at the 1908 Czernowitz Language Conference," in *Selected Work of I. L. Peretz*, ed. Marvin Zuckerman and Marion Herbst (Malibu: Simon/Pangloss, 1996), 384–87.

33. Norma Fain Pratt's groundbreaking essay, "Culture and Radical Politics," represents an important step at filling these silences, gathering historical details of the lives of Yiddish women writers.

34. Alan Mintz, *"Banished from Their Father's Table": Loss of Faith and Hebrew Autobiography* (Bloomington: University of Indiana Press, 1989), 4–5.

35. Shachar Pinsker, *Literary Passports: The Making of Modernist Hebrew Fiction in Europe* (Stanford, CA: Stanford University Press, 2010), 9.

36. Michael Gluzman, *The Politics of Canonicity: Lines of Resistance in Modern Hebrew Poetry* (Stanford, CA: Stanford University Press, 2002), 104.

37. On women's participation in the Haskalah, see Tova Cohen, "Portrait of the Maskilah"; Cohen and Feiner, *Kol 'almah 'Ivriyah.* On women's participation in the Hebrew renaissance in Europe, see, for example, Bailin and Zieler, *"To Tread on New Ground."* On women's participation in Hebrew culture in Ottoman and Mandatory Palestine, see Berlovits, *She-ani adamah ve-adam*; Berlovitz, "Literature by Women of the First Aliyah: The Aspiration for Women's Renaissance in Eretz-Israel," in *Pioneers and Homemakers: Jewish Women in Pre-State Israel*, ed. Deborah

Bernstein (Albany: State University of New York Press, 1992), 49–73; Tamar Hess, *Ḥeḳ-ha-em shel zikhronot: Nashim, oṭobiyografyah veha-'aliyah ha-sheniyah* (Or Yehuda: Dvir, 2014); Lubin, *Ishah ḳoret ishah*; Zakai, "Zion of Their Own."

38. One recent contribution to this field is Zohar Weiman-Kelman's queer reading of Hebrew and Yiddish women's poetry, *Queer Expectations: A Genealogy of Jewish Women's Poetry* (Albany: State University of New York Press, 2018).

Chapter 2

1. Although most date Shtok's birth to 1890 and her arrival in the United States to 1907 at the age of seventeen, her naturalization papers list her birth year as 1889. National Archives and Records Administration, Washington, DC, Petitions for Naturalization from the U.S. District Court for the Southern District of New York, 1897–1944; Frances Zinn, Application for Social Security Number, August 18, 1943, copy in my possession. The year of her birth is difficult to pin down with certainty. There are several birth dates listed for Shtok: 1888, 1889 and 1890. The 1888 date is listed on the Jewish Records Index (JRI Poland) website https://jri-poland.org/databases/jridetail_2.php. Numerous sources also list 1890, including the as yet unrevised entry for the Jewish Women's Archive: Ellen Kellman, "Fradel Shtok," *Jewish Women: A Comprehensive Historical Encyclopedia*, December 31, 1999, https://jwa.org/encyclopedia/article/shtok-fradel. In her naturalization papers and documents requesting a social security number, Shtok lists her date of birth as January 11, 1889. Jordan Finkin and I listed 1890 in our translation of Shtok's stories, *From the Jewish Provinces: The Selected Stories of Fradl Shtok* (Evanston, IL: Northwestern University Press, 2021). A grave marker at Blaisdell Cemetery at Rockland Psychiatric Center, where she was institutionalized in the 1960s, lists the dates 1900–1990 for a Freidel Stock. If this is indeed Fradl, then the date of her death would suggest she was likely born after 1890.

2. As Kathryn Hellerstein notes, Fradl Shtok was the only woman poet well represented in both M. Bassin's 1917 *Antologye* and Ezra Korman's influential volume of Yiddish women poets, *Yidishe dikhterins antologye*.

3. A. Tabatshnik, *Dikhter un dikhtung* (New York: David Ignatov literatur fund, 1949), 205–7.

4. Glants, "*Kultur un di froy*," 4–5. Kathryn Hellerstein discusses this quote in *A Question of Tradition*, 30.

5. Norma Fain Pratt calls the story "apocryphal" in "Culture and Radical Politics," 79. However, Jacob Glatstein cites it in his 1965 essay, "Tsu der biografye fun a dikhterin," *Tog-morgn-zhurnal*, Sunday supplement, September 19, 1965, 7. Avraham Novershtern writes about the episode without questioning its veracity. "Ha-ḳolot ṿeha-makhela: Shirat nashim be-yidish ben shtei milḥamot ha-'olam," *Biḳoret u-farshanut*, no. 40 (2008): 67–68.

6. A. Tabatshnik, "Fradl Shtok," *Leksikon fun der nayer yidisher literatur*, ed. Shmuel Niger and Jacob Shatsky (New York: Congress for Jewish Culture), 8:607. The online translation of the *Leksikon* by Josh Fogel adds: "This appears to have transpired in Hollywood." Fogel does not offer any source for this information. See Josh Fogel, "Fradl Shtok," *Yiddish Leksikon* (blog), August 12, 2019, https://yleksikon.blogspot.com/2019/08/fradl-shtok.html.

7. Melekh Ravitch, "Meydlekh, froyen, vayber—yidishe dikhterins," *Literarishe bleter* 4, no. 21 (May 27, 1927): 395–96.

8. Mikhail Krutikov, *Yiddish Fiction and the Crisis of Modernity, 1905–1914* (Stanford, CA: Stanford University Press, 2002), 168.

9. Krutikov, *Yiddish Fiction*, 168.

10. Kathryn Hellerstein is one of the few scholars to have interviewed Yiddish women writers, including Malka Hefetz Tussman.

11. See Joachim Neugroschel, ed. and trans., *No Star Too Beautiful: An Anthology of Yiddish Stories from 1382 to the Present* (New York: W. W. Norton, 2002), 463. Sonia Gollance notes that Joachim Neugroschel was the first to publish a reference to the 1942 letter to Cahan, although she acknowledges that Pratt may have first discovered the letter. See Sonia Gollance, "A Dance: Fradel Shtok Reconsidered," *In geveb*, December 3, 2017, https://ingeveb.org/articles/a-dance-fradel-shtok-reconsidered.

12. Helene Kenvin, "Fradel Shtok: Author and Poet," Jewish Gen Shtetl-Links, accessed May 15, 2019, https://kehilalinks.jewishgen.org/SkalaPodol/FradelShtok.html. Gollance follows Helene Kenvin's posting on the genealogy website JewishGen to suggest that Frances Zinn died in California in 1952. See Gollance, "'A Dance' Reconsidered."

13. New York State Census, 1915, E.D. 16, Assembly District 3, New York City, p. 27, Ancestry.com.

14. Pratt, "Culture and Radical Politics," 79.

15. Shachar Pinsker, *A Rich Brew: How Cafés Created Modern Jewish Culture* (New York: New York University Press, 2018), 212.

16. Pinsker, *A Rich Brew*, 214.

17. Ruth Wisse, *A Little Love in Big Manhattan* (Cambridge, MA: Harvard University Press, 1988), 17.

18. Pratt, "Culture and Radical Politics," 82.

19. New York Extracted Marriage Index, 1866–1937, Ancestry.com, https://www.ancestry.com/search/collections/9105/.

20. Glatstein, "Tsu der biografye fun a dikhterin," 7. Also see Shtok's naturalization document.

21. "A pekl nayes fun yidish teater," *Forverts*, August 24, 1923, 3. The copyrighted manuscript resides in the Lawrence Marwick collection in the Library of Congress. Sonia Gollance also mentions this play in "A Dance."

22. "A Distracted Woman: Review of *Musicians Only*," *New York Times*, February 6, 1927, BR22.

23. U.S. Federal Census for 1930, Kings County, New York, E.D. 1312, FHL microfilm 2341233, Ancestry.com; U.S. Federal Census for 1940, Kings County, New York, E.D. 24–760, Roll m-t0627–02565, Page 2B, Ancestry.com.

24. U.S. Federal Census for 1930.

25. Frances Zinn, Application for Social Security Number, August 18, 1943, copy in my possession. The document lists her maiden name as Fradi Stock and her parents' names as Simon Stock and Dina Gauberg.

26. Form OAC-790, a request for Social Security benefits, was filed under the name Fradel Stock on March 30, 1966. The remarks section of the form additionally lists the name Francis Zinn and the words "mental institution case." The Social Security Administration sent me a copy of the form in response to my Freedom of Information request.

27. Susan Glenn describes the trajectory of many young immigrant woman who began their careers in the garment industry, became active in the labor

movement, and then married and left the industry. *Daughters of the Shtetl: Life and Labor in the Immigrant Generation* (Ithaca, NY: Cornell University, 1990).

28. Kathryn Hellerstein offers a careful reading of Shtok's poetry in *A Question of Tradition*, 37–39. Sonia Gollance writes about Shtok's depiction of dance and her male protagonists in "A Dance Reconsidered."

29. Rachel Auerbach, "Fradl Shtok," *Tsushtayer*, no. 2 (1930): 40. Auerbach wrote feminist reviews of women writers in the three issues of the journal. See my discussion of *Tsushtayer* in chapter 5.

30. Glatstein, "Tsu der biografye fun a dikhterin," 7.

31. Glatstein, "Tsu der biografye fun a dikhterin," 7.

32. Shmuel Niger came closest to understanding the ways she sought to bridge the divide between art and life, describing her protagonists as "monomaniacal people who continually look in one corner, people who are seized and mesmerized by one thought, by one wish. And the meaning, the purpose of this one thought, this one desire is to whiten the greyness and make festive the everydayness of real life." Shmuel Niger, "Di Ertseylungen fun Fradl Shtok," *Tsukunft* (1920), 609.

33. Aaron Glanz-Leyeles [A. Glanz], "Temperment," *Der Tog*, December 7, 1919, 9.

34. M. Olgin, "Pesimizm," *Di Naye velt*, January 9, 1920, 16.

35. Olgin, "Pesimizm," 16.

36. Rancière, "Why Emma Bovary Had to Be Killed," 233.

37. Friedrich Schiller, *On the Aesthetic Education of Man*, trans. Reginald Snell (New York: Frederick Ungar, 1964), 27.

38. Asher Biemann, *Inventing New Beginnings: On the Idea of Jewish Renaissance in Modern Judaism* (Stanford, CA: Stanford University Press, 2009), 296–7.

39. Biemann, *Inventing New Beginnings*, 297; Paul Mendes-Flohr, "Zarathustra's Apostle: Martin Buber and the Jewish Renaissance," in *Nietzsche and Jewish Culture*, ed. Jacob Golomb (London: Routledge, 1997), 235–36.

40. "Friedrich Schiller," in *Gezamalte ertseylungen* (New York: Farlag Nay Tsayt, 1919). All translations by Allison Schachter and Jordan D. Finkin, in Fradl Shtok, *From the Jewish Provinces: The Selected Stories of Fradl Shtok* (Evanston, IL: Northwestern University Press, 2021), 38. Parenthetical citations refer to the English translation *From the Jewish Provinces*.

41. Notably, although Yiddish authors wrote about educated Jewish women, they are typically marginal characters whose self-realization is never explored. For example, see David Bergelson's *Nokh Alemen* and *In a fargrebter shtot*. Shotk plays with this absence in her stories.

42. Daniela Mantovan convincingly traces Bergelson's stylistic debt in *Nokh alemen* to Flaubert's novel, noting in particular Bergelson's innovative use of Flaubert's narrative techniques. "Language and Style in *Nokh alemen* (1913): Bergelson's Debt to Flaubert," in *David Bergelson: From Modernism to Socialist Realism*, ed. Joseph Sherman and Gennady Estraikh (Leeds: Legenda, 2007), 89–112.

43. Dovid Bergelson, *The End of Everything*, trans. Joseph Sherman (New Haven, CT: Yale University Press, 2010), 99.

44. Bergelson, *The End of Everything*, 204.

45. Bergelson, *The End of Everything*, 205.

46. Seidman, *The Marriage Plot*, 127.

47. Sartre, *What Is Literature and Other Essays* (Cambridge, MA: Harvard University Press, 1988), 34.

48. Sartre, *What Is Literature*, 37.
49. Jacques Rancière, *The Politics of Aesthetics*, trans. Gabriel Rockhill (London: Continuum, 2000), 7.
50. Rancière, *The Politics of Aesthetics*, 11.
51. Ziarek, *Feminist Aesthetics and the Politics of Modernism*, 13.
52. Ziarek, *Feminist Aesthetics and the Politics of Modernism*,15.
53. Klepfisz, "Queens of Contradiction," 40.
54. "Der ertsbishop," *Gezamlte ertseylungen*, "The Archbishop," *From the Jewish Provinces*, 31. Parenthetical page numbers refer to the English translation, *From the Jewish Provinces*.
55. Catherine Gallagher, "The Rise of Fictionality" in *The Novel,* ed. Franco Moretti (Princeton, NJ: Princeton University Press, 2006), 1:356.
56. Gallagher, "The Rise of Fictionality," 356.
57. Cohen, *Transparent Minds*.
58. D. A. Miller, *The Novel and the Police* (Berkeley: University of California Press, 1989).
59. Anne-Lise François, *Open Secrets: The Literature of Uncounted Experience* (Stanford, CA: Stanford University Press), 2008.
60. Ferguson, "Jane Austen, *Emma,* and the Impact of Form," 157–78.
61. Ferguson, "Jane Austen, *Emma,* and the Impact of Form," 165.
62. Robert Alter, *The Wisdom Books: Job, Proverbs, and Ecclesiastes: A Translation with Commentary* (New York: Norton, 2010), 16.
63. Violet Lutz, "Fradel Shtok," *Yiddish-Modern Jewish Studies* 17, nos. 3–4 (2012): 95.
64. Ziarek, *Feminist Aesthetics*, 12.
65. Ziarek, *Feminist Aesthetics*, 13.
66. Ziarek, *Feminist Aesthetics*, 3.

Chapter 3

1. Historically, Hebrew-language critics have referenced Baron's dialogue with Flaubert. However, they have limited their observations to the artistry with which she portrays provincial Jewish life and have not addressed her substantial engagement with larger aesthetic questions. See Ada Pagis, ed., *Dvora Baron: Mivḥar ma'amare biḳoret 'al yetsiratah* (Tel Aviv: Am oved, 1974), especially Tuvia Reuvner, "Midanim u-fiyus"; Asher Barash, "Ha-meshoreret be-prozah"; and Yeshrun Keshet, "'Al Dvora Baron." Wendy Zierler's recent work dynamically engages the connections between Flaubert and Baron: "Breaking the Idyll: Rereading Flaubert's *Madame Bovary* and Agnon's *Sippur Pashut* through Devorah Baron's 'Fradl'" *Prooftexts: A Journal of Jewish Literary History* 37, no. 3 (2019): 607–41. Also see Zierler's chapter on barrenness in *And Rachel Stole the Idols,* 192–201.
2. For example, she was referred to as a "poet in prose" by Asher Barash. "Ha-meshoreret be-prozah," in Pagis, *Dvora Baron*, 46–47.
3. Anita Shapira, *Yosef Haim Brenner: A Life* (Stanford, CA: Stanford University Press, 2015), 173.
4. Nurith Govrin, *Ha-maḥatsit ha-rishonah: Dvora Baron* (Jerusalem: Mosad Bialik, 1988), 35.
5. Govrin, *Ha-maḥatsit ha-rishonah*, 38.
6. Govrin, *Ha-maḥatsit ha-rishonah*, 77.

7. Ben-Zion Katz was in touch with Ben Avigdor about publishing Baron's collected stories. Avigdor agreed, but nothing came of the volume. Govrin, *Ha-maḥatsit ha-rishonah*, 123.

8. Govrin, *Ha-maḥatsit ha-rishonah*, 93.

9. Speculation about Baron's retreat into her home has played an outsized role in biographical criticism of Baron. For a discussion of her seclusion, see Amia Lieblich, *Conversations with Dvora: An Experimental Biography of the First Modern Hebrew Woman Writer* (Berkeley: University of California Press, 1997).

10. See Dvora Baron, *Agav orḥa: Asufah me-'izbonah 'al D. Baron umi-sevivah* (Merhavya: Sifiyat poalim, 1961), 9.

11. See "Language Insomnia," trans. Benjamin Harshav, in Benjamin Harshav, *Language in Time of Revolution* (Berkeley: University of California Press, 1993), 183–94.

12. Roni Henig, "Life of the Non-Living: Nationalization, Language, and the Narrative of 'Revival' in Modern Hebrew Literary Discourse" (PhD diss., Columbia University, 2018), 128–80.

13. Katznelson-Shazar previously published key sections of the Yiddish version under the title *Divre po'alot* [Woman Workers Speak] in 1928. Mark Raider traces the history of the volume in "Between Text and Context," in Mark A. Raider and Miriam B. Raider-Roth, eds., *The Plough Woman: Records of the Pioneer Women of Palestine; A Critical Edition* (Waltham, MA: Brandeis University Press, 2002), xli–xlii.

14. Rachel Katznelson-Shazar, "'Im ha-sefer 'Keṭanot,'" *Davar,* May 17, 1934, 71–72.

15. For a discussion of Baron's use of these traditional sources for her modernist project, see Shachar Pinsker, "Unraveling the Yarn: Intertexuality, Gender, and Cultural Critique in the Stories of Dvora Baron," *Nashim: A Journal of Jewish Women's Studies and Gender Issues*, no. 11 (2006): 244–79.

16. See, for example, the volume of essays on her work edited by Ada Pagis: *Dvora Baron: Mivḥar ma'amare biḳoret 'al yetsiratah*.

17. See Miron, "The Endless Cycle," 18.

18. Zierler, "Breaking the Idyll," 609–10.

19. See Sheila Jelen and Shachar Pinsker, eds. *Hebrew, Gender, and Modernity: Critical Responses to Dvora Baron's Fiction* (Bethesda: University Press of Maryland, 2000).

20. Sheila Jelen, *Intimations of Difference: Dvora Baron in the Modern Hebrew Renaissance* (Syracuse, NY: Syracuse University Press, 2007).

21. Pinsker, *Literary Passports*, 263. In contrast, Orly Lubin conceives of her as a diasporic writer. See "Tidbits from Nehama's Kitchen: Alternative Nationalism in Dvora Baron's The Exiles," in *Hebrew, Gender, and Modernity,* ed. Jelen and Pinsker, 7.

22. Zierler, *And Rachel Stole the Idols*; Orian Zakai, "A Zion of Their Own."

23. Shapira, *Yosef Haim Brenner*, 169.

24. See Wendy Zierler's discussion of their relationship in "Breaking the Idyll." Marc Bernstein analyzes how Baron's short story "'Agunah" was also written in a feminist dialogue with Agnon's well-known short story "'Agunot." "Midrash and Marginality: The Agunot of S. Y. Agnon and Devorah Baron," *Hebrew Studies* 42 (2001): 7–58.

25. Govrin, *Ha-maḥatsit ha-rishonah*, 233.

26. Quoted in Karen Grumberg, "Between the World and the Yishuv: The Translation of Knut Hamsun's *Markens grøde* as a Zionist Sacred Text," *Prooftexts: A Journal of Jewish Literary History* 36, nos. 1–2 (2017): 111.

27. Zohar Shavit, "The Status of Translated Literature in the Creation of Hebrew Literature in Pre-State Israel (the Yishuv Period)," *Meta: Journal Des Traducteurs / Meta: Translators' Journal* 43, no. 1 (1998): 2.

28. Lawrence Venuti, "Local Contingencies: Translation and National Identities," in *Nation, Language, and the Ethics of Translation*, ed. Sandra Berman and Michael Wood (Princeton, NJ: Princeton University Press, 2005), 178.

29. Shavit, "The Status of Translated Literature" 4–5.

30. Shlomo Tsemach, "*Madam Bovari* be-ivrit," *Moznayim* 30 (1931): 13.

31. Lori Chamberlain, "Gender and the Metaphorics of Translation," in *The Translation Studies Reader*, ed. Lawrence Venuti (New York: Routledge, 2000), 314–29.

32. Tsemach, "*Madam Bovari*," 13.

33. Dvora Baron, "Letter to the Editor," *Moznayim* 31 (1932): 15.

34. Baron's translation also mediated between French and Zionist socialist discourses. In her reading of the translation, Tir-Apelroit addresses the translation's dialogue with Zionist socialist discourse, contending that Baron translates the anti-Republican conservatism that is skewered in the agricultural scene into a Zionist-socialist idiom. "Ha-targum be-tselem uvi-demut" (PhD diss., Tel Aviv University, 2004), 136–37. Replacing one discourse (conservative monarchist) with its near opposite (Zionist socialist), Baron ironizes both, critiquing the dominant political ideology of her day at a moment when she divorced herself from the public political world. Baron's translation also forwards a feminist critique of Zionist socialism and its erasure of women. Drawing attention to women's domestic labor, she exposes the gap between socialist Zionism's egalitarian ideals and the lived experience of women who were relegated to uncompensated domestic tasks once arrived in Palestine.

35. Gustave Flaubert, *Madame Bovary* (Paris: Flammarion, 1979), 72.

36. Gustave Flaubert, *Madame Bovary*, trans. Eleanor Marx Aveling and Paul DeMan, ed. Margaret Cohen, Norton Critical Edition (New York: W. W. Norton, 2005), 50.

37. Gustave Flaubert, *Madam Bovari*, trans. Dvora Baron (Tel Aviv, Sifriyat Po'alim, 1966), 53. The novel was first published by Stybel in 1932.

38. I have translated Baron's Hebrew version into English.

39. Rancière, "Why Emma Bovary Had to Be Killed," 237.

40. Rancière, "Why Emma Bovary Had to Be Killed," 239.

41. Emily Apter, "Biography of a Translation: *Madame Bovary* between Eleanor Marx and Paul de Man," *Translation Studies* 1, no. 1 (2008): 75.

42. Rachel Holmes, *Eleanor Marx: A Life* (London: Bloomsbury, 2015, 249.

43. Apter, "Biography of a Translation," 76.

44. Apter, "Biography of a Translation," 79.

45. Apter, "Biography of a Translation," 79.

46. Emily Apter, "Taskography: Translation as Genre of Literary Labor," *PMLA* 122, no. 5 (2007): 1410.

47. Naomi Schor, *Breaking the Chain: Women, Theory, and French Realist Fiction* (New York: Columbia University Press, 1985), 19.

48. Ashley Hope Pérez, "Against 'Écriture Féminine': Flaubert's Narrative Aggression in 'Madame Bovary,'" *French Forum* 38, no. 3 (2013): 31.

49. Pérez, "Against 'Écriture Féminine,'" 32.

50. Jonathan Culler, *Flaubert: The Uses of Uncertainty* (Aurora, CO: Davies Group, 2006), 241.

51. Tir-Appelroit, "Ha-targum be-tselem uvi-demut," 182.

52. Tir-Appelroit, "Ha-targum be-tselem uvi-demut," 191.

53. Flaubert, *Madame Bovary*, 128.

54. Flaubert, *Madame Bovary*, trans. Aveling and DeMan, 79.

55. Flaubert, *Madam Bovari*, trans. Baron, 84.

56. I thank Chana Kronfeld for sharing her insightful reading of this term with me.

57. Rainer Warning, "Reading Irony in Flaubert," *Style* 19, no. 3 (1985): 312.

58. *Madame Bovary*, 155.

59. *Madame Bovary*, trans. Aveling and DeMan, 101.

60. *Madam Bovari*, trans. Baron, 109.

61. *Madame Bovary*, 155.

62. Flaubert, *Madame Bovary*, trans. Aveling and DeMan, 101.

63. Flaubert, *Madam Bovari*, trans. Baron, 109.

64. Dvora Baron, "Keṭanot," in *Parashiyot* (Jerusalem: Mosad Bialik, 2000), 41; "Trifles," in *The Thorny Path and Other Stories*, trans. Joseph Schachter (Jerusalem: Institute for the Translation of Hebrew Literature, 1969), 46. When citing in English, I put the Hebrew page number followed by the English parenthetically in the text. Wherever possible I have relied on the English translation. When necessary, I modified the translation to match the Hebrew more accurately.

65. Pérez, "Against 'Écriture Féminine,'" 44.

66. Pérez, "Against 'Écriture Féminine,'" 32.

67. Flaubert, *Madame Bovary*, trans. Aveling and DeMan, 131.

68. Flaubert, *Madam Bovari*, trans. Baron, 140.

69. Zierler, *And Rachel Stole the Idols*, 248.

70. Hannah Naveh and Tsila Abramovitz Ratner, *Tsenah, tsenah: Merḥav ha-nedunyah ba-sipurim me-et Dvora Baron, Y.D. Berḳovits ve-Ya'aḳov Shṭainberg* (Tel Aviv: Ha-kibbutz ha-me'uchad, 2015), 171.

71. *Madame Bovary*, trans. Aveling and De Man, 49.

72. Douglas Mao, *Solid Objects: Modernism and the Test of Production* (Princeton, NJ: Princeton University Press, 1998), 4.

73. Mao, *Solid Objects*, 40.

74. Mao, *Solid Objects*, 42.

75. Deborah Lupton, *The Emotional Self: A Sociocultural Exploration* (London: SAGE Publications, 1998), 144.

76. Elizabeth Wilson, *Adorned in Dreams: Fashion and Modernity* (New Brunswick, NJ: Rutgers University Press, 2003), 2.

77. Baron opined against marriage in her private correspondence. *Agav orḥa*, 109.

78. Rose L. Glickman, *Russian Factory Women: Workplace and Society, 1880–1914* (Berkeley: University of California Press, 1986), 60.

79. Glickman, *Russian Factory Women*, 60.

80. Glickman, *Russian Factory Women*, 61.

81. Susan Glenn (*Daughters of the Shtetl*, 16) argues that Jewish women found service a worse option than their non-Jewish counterparts, for "not only did it imply a loss of independence and an acknowledgment of inferiority, but it meant cleaning, sweeping, laundering, and other tasks labeled 'dirty work.' "

82. At the end of the nineteenth century and beginning of the twentieth, Jewish women's privileged access to foreign literature came to be viewed by male intellectuals as a threat to both literary cultures. See Schachter, *Diasporic Modernisms*, 135–36. Even later, in the 1950s, Leah Goldberg was attacked by the Hebrew critic Abraham Kariv for translating European literature into Hebrew and undermining the cultural authority of Hebrew. See Adrianna Jacobs, *Strange Cocktail: Translation and the Making of Modern Hebrew Poetry* (Ann Arbor: University of Michigan Press, 2018), 4–5.

83. Hess notes, "When a male character meets someone on a bench, as Michael meets Lotte, the consequences may be disastrous. Men sit alone, from the hero of Knut Hamsun's 1890 *Hunger*, to Oved Etsot reading *Faust* for the third time alone on a bench in the Galician town, in Brenner's *Mikan umi-kan*. Their sitting alone on a bench in public may be a moment of revelation, but it is self-reflexive." See Hess, "Empathy as the Origin of Narrative in Deborah Baron's Prose," presented at the Association for Jewish Studies annual conference, Boston, MA, December 2018, 6.

84. Flaubert, *Madame Bovary*, 109.

85. Zierler, *And Rachel Stole the Idols,* 248. In a forthcoming manuscript, Zierler offers a more detailed reading of the intertextuality in this story.

86. Jelen, *Intimations of Difference*, 27.

87. Baron, "Mah she-hayah," in *Parashiyot*, 128; Baron, "What Has Been," in *The Thorny Path*, 80. Subsequent parenthetical citations give the Hebrew followed by the English page number. Where necessary I have made changes to the English translation.

88. Jelen, *Intimations of Difference,* 61.

89. Seidman introduces this term in *A Marriage Made in Heaven*, 1–8. See my discussion of the changing social relations of Jewish languages as they were refracted through competing national, ethnic, and gender identities in "Modernist Indexicality."

Chapter 4

1. Salo W. Baron, "New Horizons in Jewish History," in *Freedom and Reason: Studies in Philosophy and Jewish Culture,* ed. Salo W. Baron, Ernest Nagel, and Koppel S. Pinson (Glencoe, IL: Free Press, 1951), 337.

2. Baron, "New Horizons in Jewish History," 338.

3. Cristanne Miller, *Cultures of Modernism: Marianne Moore, Mina Loy, and Else Lasker-Schüler* (Ann Arbor, MI: University of Michigan Press, 2007), 2.

4. Harshav elaborates on this revolution throughout his writing on Eastern European Jewish life. See, for example, *Language in Time of Revolution*, 3–26.

5. Alter, *The Invention of Hebrew Prose*, 3.

6. See, for example, Todd Hasak-Lowy, *Here and Now: History, Nationalism, and Realism in Modern Hebrew Fiction* (Syracuse: Syracuse University Press, 2008); Hannan Hever, *Producing the Modern Hebrew Canon: Nation Building and Minority Discourse* (New York: NYU Press, 2002); Dan Miron, *Bodedim*

be-mo'adam (Tel Aviv: Am oved, 1987); Kenneth B. Moss, *Jewish Renaissance in the Russian Revolution* (Cambridge, MA: Harvard University Press, 2009); Kalman Weiser, *Jewish People, Yiddish Nation: Noah Prylucki and the Folkists in Poland* (Toronto: University of Toronto Press, 2011).

7. Barry Trachtenberg, *The Revolutionary Roots of Modern Yiddish, 1903–1917* (Syracuse, NY: Syracuse University Press, 2008), 6.

8. Moss, *Jewish Renaissance in the Russian Revolution*, 4.

9. James Loeffler, *Rooted Cosmopolitans: Jews and Human Rights in the Twentieth Century* (New Haven, CT: Yale University Press, 2018), 5.

10. See Joshua Shanes, *Diaspora Nationalism and Jewish Identity in Habsburg Galicia* (Cambridge: Cambridge University Press, 2012), 1.

11. Deborah S. Bernstein, *Pioneers and Homemakers: Jewish Women in Pre-State Israel* (Albany: State University of New York Press, 1992), 15.

12. Anita Shapira, *Land and Power: The Zionist Resort to Force 1881–1948* (Stanford, CA: Stanford University Press, 1992), 123–24.

13. Terry Martin, *Affirmative Action Empire: Nations and Nationalism in the Soviet Union, 1923–1939* (Ithaca, NY: Cornell University Press, 2001), 32.

14. Deborah Bernstein, "The Women Workers' Movement in Pre-State Israel, 1919–1939," *Signs: Journal of Women in Culture and Society* 12, no. 3 (1987): 455.

15. Anna Żarnowska, "Women's Political Participation in Inter-war Poland: Opportunities and Limitations," *Women's History Review* 13, no. 1 (2004): 64.

16. Magdalena Kozłowska, "Did You Teach Us to Do Otherwise?" Young Women in the Tsukunft Youth Movement in Interwar Poland and Their Role Models," *Aspasia* 14, no. 1 (2020): 60.

17. Wendy Goldman, *Women, the State, and Revolution: Soviet Family Policy and Social Life, 1917–1936* (Cambridge: Cambridge University Press, 1993), 51.

18. Dagmar Herzog, *Sexuality in Europe: A Twentieth-Century History* (Cambridge: Cambridge University Press, 2011), 47.

19. Herzog, *Sexuality in Europe*, 53

20. Larry Wolff discusses the history of Galicia from its creation as a Habsburg province in 1772 to its dissolution in 1918, and finally traces its afterlife in the twentieth century. He focuses on the construction of a provincial identity in relationship to "the forces of the national and the imperial," arguing that "the provincial idea of Galicia remained fundamentally non-national." *The Idea of Galicia: History and Fantasy in Habsburg Political Culture* (Stanford, CA: Stanford University Press, 2010), 6. See also Shanes, *Diaspora Nationalism.*

21. Haiyan Lee, *Revolution of the Heart: A Genealogy of Love in China, 1900–1950* (Stanford, CA: Stanford University Press, 2006), 8.

22. Lee, *Revolution of the Heart,* 7.

Chapter 5

1. Goldberg, "Pirḳei zikhronot meḳuṭa'im," 129.

2. Goldberg, "Pirḳei zikhronot meḳuṭa'im," 129–31.

3. In "Pirḳei zikhronot" (134), Goldberg describes how she at first felt that the work of Hebrew prose writers was unequal to the prose of European writers such as Ibsen or Chekhov. Not until later in her studies in Kovno, when she discovered U. N. Gnessin's novellas and Yosef Chaim Brenner's novel *Shekhol ve-khishalon* did she change her opinion of Hebrew literature.

4. Barbara Mann, "Material Visions: The Poetry and Collage of Leah Goldberg's Native Landscapes," *Journal of Jewish Identities* 7, no. 1 (2014): 166.

5. Goldberg began writing the novel in 1936 shortly after she immigrated to Palestine. She published sections of it in various literary journals in Palestine in 1937–38. She ultimately abandoned the novel in 1939. A version was published in 2010, edited with an afterword by Giddon Ticotsky that includes a detailed history of the manuscript.

6. I discuss the novel's diasporic aesthetic and its dialogue with European literary culture in *Diasporic Modernisms*, 121–51.

7. Gil Anidjar, "Secularism," *Critical Inquiry* 33, no. 1 (2006): 60.

8. Vincent Pecora, *Secularization and Cultural Criticism: Religion, Nation, and Modernity* (Chicago: University of Chicago Press, 2006), 6.

9. Said has been amply criticized for ignoring German Orientalism in his work, *Orientalism.* Suzanne L. Marchand offers a recent critique of Said's historical argument without rejecting the politics of his project. *German Orientalism in the Age of Empire: Religion, Race, and Scholarship* (Cambridge: Cambridge University Press, 2009).

10. Jonathan Hess, *Germans, Jews, and the Claims of Modernity* (New Haven, CT: Yale University Press, 2002), 15.

11. Amnon Raz-Krakotzkin, "Orientalizm, mada'e ha-yahadut, ṿeha-ḥevrah ha-Yiśra'elit: Mispar he'arot," *Gama'ah* 3 (1998): 43.

12. Amnon Raz-Krakotzkin,"The Zionist Return to the West and the Mizrachi Jewish Perspective," in *Orientalism and the Jews*, ed. Ivan Davidson Kalmar and Derek J. Penslar (Waltham, MA: Brandeis University Press, 2005), 163.

13. Raz-Krakotzkin, "The Zionist Return to the West," 167.

14. Yfaat Weiss, "A Small Town in Germany: Leah Goldberg and German Orientalism in 1932," *Jewish Quarterly Review* 99, no. 2 (2009): 203.

15. Weiss, "A Small Town," 220. In a similar vein, John Efron asserts that Central European Jewish Orientalists had a vastly different relationship to their object of study than their Christian counterparts. According to Efron, Jewish Orientalists such as Abraham Geiger, Heinrich Graetz, and Ignaz Goldziher looked to Islam with a more sympathetic view. In part, this was because of their dual status as both European insiders and Orientalized others. John Efron, "From Mitteleuropa to the Middle East: Orientalism through a Jewish Lens," *Jewish Quarterly Review* 94, no. 3 (2004): 490–520. However, Goldberg's novel portrays Jewish participation in German Orientalism from a different perspective, calling into question the Orientalist endeavor.

16. Na'ama Rokem, "Questioning *Weltliteratur*: Heinrich Heine, Leah Goldberg, and the Department of Comparative Literature at the Hebrew University of Jerusalem," *Prooftexts: A Journal of Jewish Literary History* 36, nos. 1–2 (2017): 224.

17. Natasha Gordinsky, *Bi-sheloshah nofim: Yetsiratah ha-mukdemet shel Le'ah Goldberg* (Jerusalem: Magnes Press, 2016), 102–22.

18. Goldberg, "Le-or ha-raḥamim," in *Ha-omets le-ḥulin* (Tel Aviv: Sifriyat po'alim, 1975), 171.

19. Gordinsky, *Bi-sheloshah nofim*, 136–37.

20. Goldberg, "Eropah shelakhem," in *Ne'arot 'Ivriyot: Mikhteve Le'ah Goldberg min ha-provintsyah*, ed. Yfaat Weiss and Giddon Ticotsky (Tel Aviv: Sifriyat po'alim, 2009), 291.

21. Abraham Socher, *The Radical Enlightenment of Solomon Maimon: Judaism, Heresy, and Philosophy* (Stanford, CA: Stanford University Press, 2006), 4.

22. Hannah Arendt, "The Jew as Pariah: A Hidden Tradition," in *The Jewish Writings*, ed. Jerome Kohn and Ron Feldman (New York: Schoken, 2007), 275. In contrast, David Sorkin contends that Jews did not passively submit to the demands of Christian Europe to assimilate, but paradoxically in their efforts to assimilate formed a distinct Jewish-German "subculture." *The Transformation of German Jewry, 1780–1840* (Detroit, MI: Wayne State University Press, 1999), 6.

23. Goldberg, "Eropah shelakhem," 293.

24. Goldberg, "Eropah shelakhem," 293.

25. Carolyn Dinshaw, "Temporalities," in *Middle English: Oxford Twenty-First Century Approaches to Literature*, ed. Paul Strohm (Oxford: Oxford University Press, 2007), 112.

26. Weiman-Kelman (*Queer Expectations*, 45) elaborates further: "I will identify this queer history according to the widest meaning of the term *queer*—that is, disrupting of normative identity, desire, and temporality—while considering the poetic and political resonance of doing so in Hebrew."

27. Leah Goldberg, *Avedot: Roman ganuz*, ed. Giddon Ticotsky (Tel Aviv: Sifriyat po'alim, 2010), 39, henceforth cited parenthetically; all translations are my own.

28. Gershom Scholem, *Major Trends in Jewish Mysticism* (New York: Schoken, 1995), 204.

29. David Biale, *Gerschom Scholem: Kabbalah and Counter-History* (Cambridge, MA: Harvard University Press, 1979), 118.

30. David Biale, *Eros and the Jews: From Biblical Israel to Contemporary America* (Berkeley: University of California Press, 1997), 111.

31. Biale, *Eros and the Jews*, 112.

32. Paul Mendes-Flohr, *Divided Passions: Jewish Intellectuals and the Experience of Modernity* (Detroit, MI: Wayne State University Press, 1991), 78.

33. Marchand, *German Orientalism,* 120.

34. This fascination with Eastern European culture was integral to Weimar Jewish culture. See Michael Brenner's discussion of the importance of Hebrew and Yiddish language culture to this project: *The Renaissance of Jewish Culture in Weimar Germany* (New Haven, CT: Yale University Press, 1996), 185–211.

35. Biale, *Eros and the Jews*, 120.

36. Marchand, "Nazism, Orientalism, and Humanism," 272.

37. Ofra Yeglin, *Ulai mabaṭ aḥer: Ḳlasiyut modernit u-modernizm ḳlasi be-shirat Le'ah Goldberg* (Tel Aviv: Ha-kibbutz ha-me'uchad, 2002), 37–40.

38. In *Mimesis* Auerbach employs close readings of both the Hebrew Bible and the Gospels as part of his account of the rise of realism. Erich Auerbach, *Mimesis: The Represenation of Reality in Western Thought* (Princeton: Princeton University Press, 2003). Jacques Rancière offers an insightful reading of the book's Christian theological underpinnings in "The Body of the Letter: Bible, Epic, Novel," in *The Flesh of Words: The Politics of Writing* (Stanford, CA: Stanford University Press, 2004), 71–93.

39. Goldberg, "'Al ha-ḳomediyah ha-elohit," in *Mi-dor ume-'ever: Beḥinot u-te'amim be sifrut kelalit* (Tel Aviv: Sifriyat po`alim, 1977), 84.

40. Dina Berdichevsky discusses this at length in "Measuring Distances: Hebrew Essayists Reading World Literature," *Prooftexts: A Journal of Jewish Literary History* 36, nos. 1–2 (2017): 27, 38.

41. Berdichevsky, "Measuring Distances," 31.

42. Berdichevsky, "Measuring Distances," 39.

43. Maya Barzilai, "Ha-'ir ha-Germanit ha-avudah: Berlin shel Le'ah Goldberg" *Meḥkere Yerushalayim be-sifrut 'ivrit* 30 (2019): 143–68; Natasha Gordinsky, *Bi-sheloshah nofim.*

44. Leah Goldberg, *Mikhtavim me-nesi'ah medumah* (Tel Aviv: Sifriyat po'alim, 2007), 7. Subsequent citations in parentheses in the text.

45. Tamar Hess, "Peri bedidutah: 'Al siaḥ ha-ohavim ha-epistolari u-mikhtavim me-nesi'ah medumah le-Le'ah Goldberg," in *Pegishot 'im meshoreret*, ed. Ruth Kartun-Blum and Anat Weisman (Tel Aviv: Sifriyat po'alim, 2000), 160.

46. Giddon Ticotsky, "Afterword," 321.

47. Matthew Hoffman, *From Rebel to Rabbi: Reclaiming Jesus and the Making of Modern Jewish Culture* (Stanford, CA: Stanford University Press, 2007), 9.

48. Neta Stahl, *Other and Brother: Jesus in the Twentieth Century Jewish Literary Landscape* (New York: Oxford University Press, 2013), 10.

49. Barbara Mann, "Of Madonnas and Magdalenas: Reading Mary in Modernist Hebrew and Yiddish Women's Poetry," in *Leḳeṭ: Yiddish Studies Today*, ed. Marion Aptroot, Efrat Gal-Ed, Roland Gruschka, and Simon Neuberg (Düsseldorf: Düsseldorf University Press, 2012), 50.

50. Weiman-Kelman, *Queer Expectations*, 55.

51. Weiman-Kelman, *Queer Expectations*, 55.

52. Gordinsky, *Bi-sheloshah nofim*, 94–97.

53. See my discussion of Abramovitsh's complex play of authorial identities in his autobiographical novels *Ba-yamim ha-hem* and *Shloyme reb khayims. Diasporic Modernisms*, 29–54.

54. Barzilai, "Ha-'ir ha-Germanit ha-avudah," 23.

55. This turn to the Orient was a convention of Jewish modernism in the twentieth century. For example, Else Lasker-Schüler created an Oriental alter ego for herself named Prince Yussuf, who was situated "within an orient that functions as other to the West, and especially Germany during World War I." Antje Lindenmeyer, "'I am Prince Yussuf': Else Lasker-Schüler's Autobiographical Performance," *Biography: An Interdisciplinary Quarterly* 24, no. 1 (2001): 25–34. In the 1930s and 1940s, a group of Hebrew writers and artists asserted an Orientalized Canaanite identity as part of their attempts to construct a Hebrew culture that was native to the region rather than European.

56. Gordinsky, *Bi-sheloshah nofim*, 176.

Chapter 6

1. Not only did Hebrew critics use this term, but so did the Jewish press. During her book tour through Europe, the *Neues Viener Journal* and the *Viener Tag* referred to her as "Ruth van der Volga." See Archive of the Hebrew Writers' Association, Elisheva, folder 5608170. Also see M. Nivizky, "Rut me-gadot ha-Volga," in *Elisheva': Ḳovets ma'amarim odot ha-meshoreret Elisehva'* (Tel Aviv: Tomer, 1927), 15–18.

2. Dana Olmert, "Aḥarit devar," in *Simṭa'ot: Roman* (Tel Aviv: Ha-kibbutz ha-me'uchad, 2008), 348.

3. Rivka Alper, *Pirpure mahapekhah* (Tel Aviv: Mitspeh, 1930); Sarah Gluzman, *El ha-gevul* (Tel Aviv: Hotsa'at Yisraelit, 1938); Miriam Bernstein-Cohen, *Mefisto* (Tel Aviv: Mitzpeh, 1938); Elisheva Bikhovsky, *Simṭa'ot*. Published later: Mirele Blank, *Al gedot nahar Moskve* (Tel Aviv: Hotsa'at Neuman, 1964).

4. Goldman, *Women, the State, and Revolution*, 51.

5. Anita Shapira, *Ha-halikhah 'al ḳav ha-ofeḳ* (Tel Aviv: Am oved, 1987), 258–92.

6. David Biale, *Eros and the Jews: From Biblical Israel to Contemporary America* (Berkeley: University of California Press, 1997), 177.

7. Describing Zionism as an "erotic revolution," David Biale argues that "as long as Zionism was seen as the creation of a virile New Man against the allegedly feminine impotence of exile, women would have difficulty finding a truly equal place." *Eros and the Jews*, 187.

8. With the Hebrew poet Haim Nachman Bialik's assistance, her Russian translations found a publication home in a Russian monthly in Moscow. See Elisheva Bikhovsky, "Toldoti," in *Elisheva': Ḳovets ma'amarim odot ha-meshoreret Elisehva'* (Tel Aviv: Tomer, 1927), 5.

9. Quoted in Hillel Barzel, "Elisehva' ṿeha-roman shelah," in *Simṭa'ot* (Tel Aviv: Hadar, 1977), 297n16.

10. Quoted in Hillel Barzel, "Elisehva' ṿeha-roman shelah," 297–98.

11. Miryam Segal, *A New Sound in Hebrew Poetry: Poetics, Politics, Accent* (Bloomington: Indiana University Press, 2010), 77.

12. Dan Miron, *Imahot meyasdot, aḥayot ḥorgot* (Tel Aviv: Ha-kibbutz ha-me'uchad, 1991), 192.

13. Miron, *Imahot*, 180–81.

14. Elisheva Papers, Archives of the Hebrew Writers Association, Tel Aviv, file 5555170.

15. See Jeffrey Veidlinger, *The Moscow State Yiddish Theater: Jewish Culture on the Soviet Stage* (Bloomington: Indiana University Press, 2000), 3–4. David Shneer examines how Soviet Jews embraced Yiddish as a substitute for religion in defining their minority national identity. *Yiddish and the Creation of Soviet Jewish Culture: 1918–1930* (Cambridge: Cambridge University Press, 2004).

16. Ziva Galili, "Zionism in the Early Soviet State: Between Legality and Persecution," in *Revolution, Repression, and Revival: The Soviet Jewish Experience*, ed. Zvi Gitelman and Yaacov Ro'i (New York: Rowman and Littlefield, 2007), 38.

17. For example, He-Ḥaluts, the Zionist youth organization, operated freely until it was banned in 1922. It was reinstated in 1923, but only in Moscow. By 1925 those boundaries narrowed considerably. Galili, "Zionism in the Early Soviet State," 40, 44–46.

18. Elisheva Bikhovsky, *Simṭa'ot* (Tel Aviv: Ha-kibbutz ha-me'uchad, 2008), 11. Henceforth cited parenthetically; all translations are my own.

19. Elisheva Bikhovsky, "Letter to Gershon Shofman," *Gnazim* 1 (1961): 162.

20. See my discussion of the phenomenon in *Diaspora modernisms*, 99–100.

21. Galit Hasan-Rokem, "The Wandering Jew: A Jewish Perspective," in *Proceedings of the Ninth World Congress of Jewish Studies* (Jerusalem: World Congress of Jewish Studies, 1986), 195.

22. Sheila Jelen argues that despite the critical silence on the possibility of a *telushah*, female counterparts to the *talush* are to be found in works by Brenner and Berdichevsky. In *Intimations of Difference* she offers the first sustained consideration of the place of women in *talush* writing.

23. Olmert, "Aḥarit devar," 353.

24. See James Clifford, *The Predicament of Culture: Twentieth-Century Ethnography, Literature, and Art* (Cambridge, MA: Harvard University Press, 1988); Houston Baker, *Modernism and the Harlem Renaissance* (Chicago: University of Chicago Press, 1989); and Michael North, *The Dialect of Modernism: Race, Language, and Twentieth-Century Literature* (Oxford: Oxford University Press, 1998.

25. Paul Rabinow, "Representations Are Social Facts: Modernity and Postmodernity in Anthropology" in *Writing Culture: The Poetics and Politics of Ethnography*, ed. James Clifford and George E. Marcus (Berkeley: University of California Press, 1986), 234–61; Arjun Appadurai, "Cosmopolitanism from Below: Some Ethical Lessons from the Slums of Mumbai," *Johannesburg Salon* 4 (2014): 32–44; Bruce Robbins, *Perpetual War: Cosmopolitanism from the Viewpoint of Violence* (Durham, NC: Duke University Press, 2012).

26. Susan Koshy discusses the tensions between ethnic studies and cosmopolitanism, noting what she sees as the "marginalization of race, ethnicity, and non-Western cultures in discussions of cosmopolitanism." "Minority Cosmopolitanism," *PMLA* 126, no. 3 (2011): 594.

27. Robbins, *Perpetual War,* 16–17.

28. Koshy, "Minority Cosmopolitanism," 594.

29. Françoise Lionnet and Shu-mei Shih, *Minor Transnationalisms* (Durham, NC: Duke University Press, 2005): 6–7.

30. Caroline Humphrey, "Cosmopolitanism and Kosmopolitizm in the Political Life of Soviet Citizens," *FOCAAL—Journal of Global and Historical Anthropology* 44 (2004): 144.

31. Katerina Clark, *Moscow, the Fourth Rome: Stalinism, Cosmopolitanism, and the Evolution of Soviet Culture, 1931–1941* (Cambridge, MA: Harvard University Press, 2011), 5.

32. See Lee, *Revolution of the Heart*; Nancy Armstrong, *Desire and Domestic Fiction: A Political History of the Novel* (New York: Oxford University Press, 1987).

33. See my discussion of these critics in chapter 5.

34. Shneer, *Yiddish and the Creation of Soviet Jewish Culture*, 5.

35. For a history of the role Jews played in the translation of the Hebrew Bible, see Naomi Seidman, *Faithful Renderings: Jewish-Christian Difference and the Politics of Translation* (Chicago: University of Chicago Press, 2006).

36. Walter Benjamin, "The Task of the Translator," in *Walter Benjamin: Selected Writings*, ed. Marcus Bullock and Michael W. Jennings (Cambridge, MA: Harvard University Press, 1996), 1:255, 258.

37. Larry Rosenwald, "On the Reception of Buber and Rosenzweig's Bible," *Prooftexts: A Journal of Jewish Literary History* 14, no. 2 (1994): 150.

38. Seidman, *Faithful Renderings*, 163.

39. Seidman, *Faithful Renderings*, 178.

40. Ben Tran, "Negative Paradise: Rethinking Anglophone and World Literature as Literary Dubbing," *Modern Fiction Studies* 64, no. 1 (2018): 154–55.

41. Tran, "Negative Paradise," 154–55.

42. See my discussion of Brenner's novel *Shekhol ve-khishalon* in *Diasporic Modernisms*, 55–83.

43. Schachter, *Diasporic Modernisms*, 57–58.

44. For a discussion of émigré writers in Paris, see Robert Johnston, *New Mecca, New Babylon: Paris and the Russian Exiles, 1920–1945* (Montreal: McGill-Queen's University Press, 1988).

45. Pascale Casanova, *The World Republic of Letters* (Cambridge, MA: Harvard University Press, 1999).

46. We can see these concerns continuing in Hebrew literature into the late twentieth and early twenty-first centuries as non-Jewish Arab writers, such as Anton Shammas and Sayed Kashua, embrace and then repudiate their Hebrew literary careers.

Chapter 7

1. Galicia, the region where the lion's share of Jews lived in the Austro-Hungarian Empire, comprises what is now southeastern Poland and northwestern Ukraine. The city known as Lwów under Polish rule was named Lemberg in the Austro-Hungarian Empire, and is called Lviv in present-day Ukraine.

2. Debora Vogel, letter to Glanz-Leyeles, October 18, 1935, RG 556, box 4, folder 5, Glanz-Leyeles Collection, YIVO Institute for Jewish Research, New York. Anastasiya Lyubas translates Vogel's correspondence and her entire poetic and critical oeuvre in *Blooming Spaces: The Collected Poetry, Prose, Critical Writings, and Letters of Debora Vogel*, (Boston: Academic Studies Press, 2020). Unless otherwise noted, I have chosen to use my own translations for the clarity of my argument.

3. Debora Vogel, letter to Ravitch, September 10, 1936, ARC 4 1540, Melekh Ravitch Collection, National Library of Israel, Jerusalem.

4. Debora Vogel, letter to Glanz-Leyeles, May 23, 1939, RG 556, box 4, folder 5, Glanz-Leyeles Collection, YIVO Institute for Jewish Research, New York.

5. Kadia Molodowsky represents an interesting counterexample. Her husband played an important role in supporting her work on the journal *Svive*, helping to create the condition of possibility for her editorial labors.

6. Lyubas, "Plasticity of Language in Debora Vogel's Modernist Poetics," 658.

7. Debora Vogel, letter to Glanz-Leyeles, October 18, 1935, RG 556, box 4, folder 5, Glanz-Leyeles Collection, YIVO Institute for Jewish Research, New York.

8. Anna Torres, "Circular Landscapes: Montage and Myth in Dvoyre Fogel's Yiddish Poetry," *Nashim: A Journal of Jewish Women's Studies and Gender Issues*, no. 35 (2019): 45.

9. Glants, A. "Kultur un di froy," 4–5, translated and quoted in Hellerstein, *A Question of Tradition*, 30. For additional articles on women poets, see Ravitch, "Meydlekh, froyen, vayber," 396. Also see Kadya Molodowsky's response, "Meydlekh, froyen, vayber, un . . . nevue," *Literarishe Bleter*, 4, no. 22 (1927): 416.

10. Hellerstein, *Question of Tradition*, 31.

11. Karen Underhill, *Bruno Schulz and Galician Jewish Modernity* (Bloomington: University of Indiana Press, 2021), 229.

12. Larry Wolff (*The Idea of Galicia*, 395–419) describes this cultural milieu, invoking Schulz, S. Y. Agnon, and Josef Roth. He shows how their projects paid homage to the mythology of Galicia. Wolff does not consider women writers in

this circle of Galician writers, but Vogel's work can also be read as part of this post-Habsburgian milieu.

13. Y. Rappaport, "Vi a veverke in rod" [Like a squirrel in a circle], *Shoybns*, no. 4 (1936): 39.

14. B. Alkvit, "Moderne proze," *In zikh* 16, no. 7 (1935): 132.

15. Alkvit, "Moderne proze."

16. Jerzy Ficowski, *Regions of the Great Heresy: Bruno Schulz, a Biographical Portrait* (New York: W. W. Norton, 2003), 68.

17. Karolina Szymaniak, *Być agentem wiecznej idei: Przemiany poglądów estetycznych Debory Vogel* [*To be an agent of an eternal idea: The transformation of Debora Vogel's aesthetic views*] (Krakow: Universitas, 2006); Dvoyre Fogel, *Die Geometrie des Verzichts: Gedichte, Montagen, Essays, Briefe*, ed. Anna Maja Misiak (Wuppertal: Arco, 2015); Underhill, *Bruno Schulz*; Torres, "Circular Landscapes"; Dvoyre Fogel, *Blooming Spaces*.

18. Andrìj Boârov, Paweł Polit, and Karolina Szymaniak, eds., *Montages: Debora Vogel and the New Legend of the City* (Lodz: Museum Sztuki, 2017).

19. Phillipe Sands, *East West Street: On the Origins of "Genocide" and "Crimes against Humanity"* (New York: Vintage Books, 2016), 72–73.

20. Wolff, *The Idea of Galicia*, 373.

21. Sands, *East West Street*, 75.

22. Loeffler, *Rooted Cosmopolitans*.

23. Piotr Łukaszewicz and Zrzeszenie Artystów Plastyków Artes, *Zrzeszenie Artystów Plastyków Artes 1929–1935* (Wroclaw: Zaklad Narodowy im. Ossolinskich, 1975).

24. S. A. Mansbach, *Modern Art in Eastern Europe: From the Baltic to the Balkans, ca. 1890–1939* (Cambridge: Cambridge University Press, 1998), 133.

25. Franz Roh, "Magic Realism, Post-Expressionism," in *Magical Realism: Theory, History, Community*, ed. Lois Parkinson Zamora and Wendy B. Faris (Durham, NC: Duke University Press, 1995), 16.

26. Irene Guenther, "Magic Realism, New Objectivity, and the Arts during the Weimar Republic," in *Magical Realism*, 36.

27. Lyubas, "Plasticity of Language," 163.

28. Karolina Szymaniak, "On the Ice Floe: Rachel Auerbach—the Life of a Yiddishist Intellectual in Early Twentieth Century Poland," in *Catastrophe and Utopia: Jewish Intellectuals in Central and Eastern Europe in the 1930s and 1940s*, ed. Ferenc Laczó and Joachim von Puttkamer (Berlin: Walter de Gruyter, 2017), 329.

29. Yael Chaver, "Dvoyre Fogel," in *Encyclopedia of Jewish Women*, December 31, 1999, Jewish Women's Archive, https://jwa.org/encyclopedia/article/fogel-dvoyre.

30. See Schachter, *Diasporic Modernisms*, 152–82.

31. Underhill, *Bruno Schulz*, 223.

32. Vogel, letter to Glanz-Leyeles, October 18, 1935.

33. Underhill, *Bruno Schulz*, 231.

34. "Introspectivism," in Benjamin Harshav and Barbara Harshav, *American Yiddish Poetry: A Bilingual Anthology* (Stanford, CA: Stanford University Press, 2007), 780.

35. Szymaniak, *Być agentem wiecznej idei*, 211. All translations from the Polish, unless otherwise noted, are by Zach Mazur.

36. Auerbach, "Nisht-oysgeshpunene fedem," 132.

37. Auerbach, "Nisht-oysgeshpunene fedem," 135.

38. Bruno Schulz, *Księga listów*, ed. Jerzy Ficowski (Krakow: Wydawnictwo literackie, 1975), 173.

39. Debora Vogel, "Ludzkie egzotyki," *Przegląd Społeczny* 8, nos. 7–8 (1934): 150–59; Debora Vogel, "Lwowska Juderia," *Almanach i leksykon Zydowstwa Polskiego* (Lwòw, 1937), 1:88–96. An English translation, "Lwów's Jewish Quarter," trans. B. Paloff, can be found in Boârov, Polit, and Szymaniak, *Montages*, 277–88.

40. See Giżycki, *Biali i czarni: Fragmenty kolonjalne* (Warsaw: Gebethner and Wolff, 1934).

41. Debora Vogel, "Human Exotics," trans. Anastasiya Lyubas, *Blooming Spaces*, 92–93. I have modified the translation to hew more closely to the original, based on a version translated by Zachary Mazur.

42. Underhill, *Bruno Schulz,* 243.

43. "Lwów's Jewish Quarter," trans. Paloff, 288.

44. "Lwów's Jewish Quarter," trans. Paloff, 288.

45. Underhill, *Bruno Schulz*, 233.

46. Russell Berman, "Montage as a Literary Technique: Thomas Mann's 'Tristan' and T. S. Eliot's *The Waste Land*," *Selecta: Journal of the PNCFL* 2, no. 2 (1981): 20–23.

47. Peter Bürger, *Theory of the Avant-Garde* (Minneapolis: University of Minnesota Press, 1984), 78.

48. Vogel, letter to Glanz-Leyeles, October 18, 1935.

49. Patrizia McBride, *The Chatter of the Visible: Montage and Narrative in Modern Germany* (Ann Arbor: University of Michigan Press, 2016), 8.

50. McBride, *The Chatter of the Visible*, 7.

51. McBride, *The Chatter of the Visible*, 45.

52. Vogel, "A por bamerkungen vegn mayn bikhl, *Akatsyes blien*," *Shoybn*, no. 5 (March–April 1937): 39.

53. Vogel, "A por bamerkungen," 40.

54. Debora Vogel, *Akatsyes blien: Montazhn* (Lwów: POL, 1935), 58. Subsequent references in parentheses in the text.

55. Torres, "Circular Landscapes," 42.

56. Debora Vogel, "Di literarishe gatung montazh," *Bodn* 3, nos. 3–4 (1934): 99.

57. Luce Irigaray, *The Sex Which Is Not One*, trans. Catherine Porter (Ithaca, NY: Cornell University Press, 1985), 176. Emphasis in the original.

58. Torres, "Circular Landscape," 57.

59. Hellerstein, *Question of Tradition*, 147.

60. Torres, "Circular Landscape," 42.

61. Lyubas ("Plasticity of Language," 83) argues that "in *Acacias Bloom,* the mannequin is a highly formalized figure who acts as an ersatz for the protagonists in the unconventional novel." In this section the mannequin is more than a protagonist, but also a larger symbol of the woman as artist.

62. Debora Vogel, "Ferd un torsn," in *Manekinen* (Warsaw-Lemberg: Farlag Tsushtayer, 1934), 15–16.

63. Lyubas, "Plasticity of Language," 87.

64. Andreas Huyssen, *After the Great Divide: Modernism, Mass Culture, Postmodernism* (Bloomington: Indiana University Press, 1987), 11.

65. Ghislaine Wood, *The Surreal Body: Fetish and Fashion* (London: Victoria and Albert Museum, 2007), 42.

66. Karolina Szymaniak, "A Third District? Ethnicity, De-territorialization, Montage," in Boârov, Polit, and Szymaniak, *Montages*, 266.

67. In her response to B. Alkvit's review of her book in *In zikh* in 1935, Vogel distinguishes her montage from the cubists and the surrealists, describing her work as "realist montage." *In zikh*, no. 17 (1935): 63.

68. Bruno Schulz, "Akacje kwitną," *Nasza Opinja* no. 72 (1936), 199.

69. Debora Vogel, "Di literarishe gatung montazh," 100.

70. Vogel, "Di literarishe gatung montazh," 100.

71. Schulz, *Księga listów*, 199.

72. See Benedict Anderson, *Imagined Communities: Reflections on the Origin and Spread of Nationalism* (London: Verso, 1991).

73. Vogel, "Di literarishe gatung montazh," 104.

74. Walter Benjamin, "The Storyteller: Observations on the Work of Nikolai Leskov," in *Selected Writings*, vol. 3, ed. Howard Eiland and Michael W. Jennings (Cambridge, MA: Harvard University Press, 2002), 146.

75. Benjamin, "The Storyteller," 155.

76. Rancière, "Why Emma Bovary Had to Be Killed," 242.

77. Rancière, "Why Emma Bovary Had to Be Killed," 243. Drawing on Deleuze and Guattari, Anastasiya Lyubas ("Plasticity of Language," 73) remarks on the minute attention to dust in Vogel's montage, "precisely this impersonal flow of haecceities, or sensations of tangible micro-events in their relationships of movement and rest."

78. Debora Vogel, "Romans djalektyki," *Przegląd Społeczny* 9, no. 10 (1935): 243. Subsequent references given parenthetically in the text. Translation from Polish by Zach Mazur.

79. Debora Vogel, "Literarishe montazh: An araynfir," *Inzl* 3 (1938): 6. I use the translation from "Literary Montage: An Introduction," in Boârov, Polit, and Szymaniak, *Montages*, 393.

Conclusion

1. Quoted in Kenneth Frieden, *Classic Yiddish Fiction: Abramovitsh, Sholem Aleichem, and I. L. Peretz* (Albany: State University of New York Press, 1995), 93.

2. David Frishman, "Mendele, zayn lebn un zayn verk," in *Kritik iber mendele mokher sforim* (Warsaw: Farlag Mendele, 1911), 13.

3. Vogel, *Akatsyes blien,* 74.

4. Hayden White, *The Content of the Form: Narrative Discourse and Historical Representation* (Baltimore, MD: Johns Hopkins University Press, 1987), 24.

5. Anita Norich, "Grace Paley," in *Encyclopedia of Jewish Women*, Jewish Women's Archive, https://jwa.org/encyclopedia/article/paley-grace.

6. Jacqueline Taylor, "Interview: Grace Paley on Storytelling and Story Hearing," *Literature in Performance* 7 (1987): 52.

7. Alfred Kazin, "The Jew as Modern Writer," *Commentary* 41, no. 4 (1966): 40.

8. Kazin, "The Jew as Modern Writer," 40.

9. Harvey Swados, "Good and Short," *Hudson Review* 12, no. 3 (1959): 458.

10. Grace Paley, "The Value of Not Understanding Everything," in *Just As I Thought* (New York: Farrar, Straus, and Giroux, 1998), 188

11. Paley, "The Value of Not Understanding Everything," 188.

12. Nancy K. Miller, "Starting Out in the Fifties: Grace Paley, Philip Roth, and the Making of a Literary Career," *Contemporary Women's Writing* 3, no. 2 (2009): 140.

13. Grace Paley, "Of Poetry and Women in the World," in *Just As I Thought*, 167.

14. Paley, "Of Poetry and Women in the World," 168.

15. Paley, "Of Poetry and Women in the World," 170

16. Ilya Kaminsky and Katherine Towler, "An Interview with Poet and Fiction Writer Grace Paley," *Poets and Writers*, March, 17, 2008, https://www.pw.org/content/interview_poet_and_fiction_writer_grace_paley?.

17. Jacqueline Taylor, *Grace Paley: Illuminating the Dark Lives* (Austin: University of Texas Press, 1990), 3.]

18. Shaina Hammerman and Naomi Seidman, "Between Aunt and Niece," *Prooftexts: A Journal of Jewish Literary History* 32, no. 2 (2012): 178.

19. Jewish men figured their economic insecurities and sexual anxieties as the maternal grotesque and the passive body of the Jewish wife. By the postwar era, "the Jewish mother's fierce loyalty to her family, mixed with her pungent desire for its success, fueled the indictment that Jews themselves increasingly made of this indomitable matriarch: that by her overbearing control, she pushed and prodded her offspring to succeed but relegated them to a clinging dependency." Joyce Antler, *You Never Call! You Never Write! A History of the Jewish Mother* (Oxford: Oxford University Press, 2007), 11. Riv-Ellen Prell illuminates how the demonized Jewish mother and her "Jewish American princess" daughter represent Jewish male anxieties in "a consumption-driven economic system in which men are rendered as unproductive as surely women are. Work is abstract, its products difficult to identify. Consumption is almost infinitely variegated and as such, inevitably disappointing." "Why Jewish Princesses Don't Sweat: Desire and Consumption in Postwar American Jewish Culture," in *People of the Body: Jews and Judaism from an Embodied Perspective*, ed. Howard Eilberg-Schwartz (Albany: State University of New York Press, 1992), 345.

20. Schachter, "Men Reading Women."

21. Grace Paley, "A Conversation with My Father," in *Enormous Changes at the Last Minute* (New York: Farrar, Straus and Giroux, 1974), 161. Hereafter cited parenthetically.

22. Leonard Michaels, "Conversation with Grace Paley," in *Conversations with Grace Paley*, ed. Gerhard Bach and Blaine Hall (Jackson: University of Mississippi Press, 1997), 34.

23. Michaels, "Conversation with Grace Paley," 35.

24. Grace Paley, "Introduction to 'A Conversation with My Father,' " in *Fathers, Reflections by Daughters*, ed. Ursula Owens (New York: Pantheon, 1983), 233.

BIBLIOGRAPHY

Alkvit, B. "Moderne prose." *In zikh* 16, no. 7 (1935): 132.

Almog, Oz. *The Sabra: The Creation of the New Jew*. Berkeley: University of California Press, 2000.

Alper, Rivka. *Pirpure mahapekhah*. Tel Aviv: Mitspeh, 1930.

Alter, Robert. *The Invention of Hebrew Prose: Modern Fiction and the Language of Realism*. Seattle: University of Washington Press, 1988.

———. *The Wisdom Books: Job, Proverbs, and Ecclesiastes: A Translation with Commentary*. New York: Norton, 2010.

Anderson, Benedict. *Imagined Communities: Reflections on the Origin and Spread of Nationalism*. London: Verso, 1991.

Anidjar, Gil. "Secularism." *Critical Inquiry* 33, no. 1 (2006): 52–77.

Antler, Joyce. *You Never Call! You Never Write! A History of the Jewish Mother*. Oxford: Oxford University Press, 2007.

Appadurai, Arjun. "Cosmopolitanism from Below: Some Ethical Lessons from the Slums of Mumbai." *Johannesberg Salon* 4 (2014): 32–44.

Apter, Emily. "Biography of a Translation: *Madame Bovary* between Eleanor Marx and Paul de Man." *Translation Studies* 1, no. 1 (2008): 73–89.

———. "Taskography: Translation as Genre of Literary Labor." *PMLA* 122, no. 5 (2007): 1403–15.

Arendt, Hannah. "The Jew as Pariah: A Hidden Tradition." In *The Jewish Writings*, edited by Jerome Kohn and Ron H. Feldman, 275–97. New York: Schocken, 2007.

Armstrong, Nancy. *Desire and Domestic Fiction: A Political History of the Novel*. New York: Oxford University Press, 1987.

Asad, Talal. *Formations of the Secular: Christianity, Islam, Modernity*. Stanford, CA: Stanford University Press, 2003.

Auerbach, Erich. *Dante: Poet of the Secular World*. New York: New York Review of Books Classics, 2007.

———. *Mimesis: The Representation of Reality in Western Thought*. Princeton: Princeton University Press, 2003.

Auerbach, Rachel. "Fradl Shtok." *Tsushtayer*, no. 2 (1930): 39–45.

———. "Nisht-oysgeshpunene fedem." *Goldene keyt*, no. 50 (1964): 131–43.

Bacon, Gershon. "Woman? Youth? Jew?—The Search for Identity of Jewish Young Women in Interwar Poland." In *Gender, Place and Memory in the Modern Jewish Experience: Re-Placing Ourselves*, edited by Judith Taylor Baumel and Tova Cohen, 3–28. London: Vallentine Mitchell, 2003.

Bailin, Carole B., and Wendy Zierler. *"To Tread on New Ground": Selected Hebrew Writings of Hava Shapiro*. Detroit, MI: Wayne State University Press, 2014.

Baker, Houston A. *Modernism and the Harlem Renaissance*. Cambridge, MA: Harvard University Press, 1989.

Bar-Adon, Aaron. "S.Y. Agnon and the Revival of Modern Hebrew." *Texas Studies in Literature and Language* 14, no. 1 (1972): 147–75.

Barash, Asher. "Ha-meshoreret be-prozah." In *Dvora Baron: Mivḥar ma'amare biḳoret 'al yetsiratah*, edited by Ada Pagis, 46–47. Tel Aviv: Am oved, 1974.

Baron, Dvora. *Agav orḥa: Asufah me-'izbonah 'al D. Baron umi-sevivah*. Merhavya: Sifriyat po'alim, 1960.

———. *Ḳeṭanot* [Trifles]. Tel Aviv: Hotsa'at omanut, 1932.

———. "Letter to the Editor." *Moznayim* 31 (1932).

———. *Mah she hayah*. Jerusalem: Mosad Bialik, 1968.

———. *Mivḥar ma'amare biḳoret 'al yetsiratah*. Edited by Ada Pagis. Tel Aviv: Am oved, 1974.

———. *Parashiyot*. Jerusalem: Mosad Bialik, 2000.

———. *The Thorny Path*. Translated by Joseph Schachter. Jerusalem: Institute for the Translation of Hebrew Literature, 1969.

Baron, Salo W. "New Horizons in Jewish History." In *Freedom and Reason: Studies in Philosophy and Jewish Culture*, edited by Salo W. Baron, Ernest Nagel, and Koppel S. Pinson, 337–53. Glencoe, IL: Free Press, 1951.

Barzel, Hillel. "Elisheva' ṿeha-roman shelah." In *Simṭa'ot*, 280–95. Tel Aviv: Hadar, 1977.

Barzilai, Maya. "Ha-'Ir ha-Germanit ha-avudah: Berlin shel Le'ah Goldberg." *Meḥḳere Yerushalayim be-sifrut 'ivrit* 30 (2019): 143–68.

Bassin, M. *Antologye: Finf hundert yor yidishe poezye*. New York: Farlag Dos yidishe bukh, 1917.

Benjamin, Walter. *Selected Writings*. Edited by Howard Eiland and Michael W. Jennings, 143–66. Cambridge, MA: Harvard University Press, 2002.

———. *Walter Benjamin: Selected Writings*. Edited by Marcus Bullock and Michael W. Jennings. Vol. 1. Cambridge, MA: Harvard University Press, 1996.

Berdichevsky, Dina. "Measuring Distances: Hebrew Essayists Reading World Literature." *Prooftexts: A Journal of Jewish Literary History* 36, nos. 1–2 (2017): 27–52.

Bergelson, David. *The End of Everything*. Translated by Joseph Sherman. New Haven, CT: Yale University Press, 2010.

Berlovitz, Yaffa. "Elisheva Bichovsky." In *Encyclopedia of Jewish Women*. December 31, 1999. Jewish Women's Archive, https://jwa.org/encyclopedia/article/elisheva-bichovsky.

———. "Le-tivo shel ha-naraṭiv ha-tsiyoni ha-nashi—hatḥalat me'ah/sof me'ah: Ha-ḳol ha-biḳorti ha-ḥatrani." Edited by Yehudith Barel, Yigal Schwartz, and Tamar Hess. In *Sifrut le-ḥevrah ba-tarbut ha-'ivrit ha-ḥadashah: 'Ma'amarim mugashim Le-Gershon Shaḳed*, edited by Yehudith Barel, Yigal Schwartz, and Tamar Hess, 421–39. Tel Aviv: Ha-kibbutz ha-me'uchad: 2000.

———. "Literature by Women of the First Aliyah: The Aspiration for Women's Renaissance in Eretz-Israel." In *Pioneers and Homemakers: Jewish Women in Pre-State Israel*, edited by Deborah Bernstein, 49–73. Albany: State University of New York Press, 1992.

———. *She-ani adamah ṿe-adam: Sipure nashim 'ad ḳum ha-medinah*. Tel Aviv: Ha-kibbutz ha-me'uchad, 2003.

Berman, Jessica. "Practicing Transnational Feminist Recovery Today." *Feminist Modernist Studies* 1, nos. 1–2 (2018): 9–21. DOI: 10.1080/24692921.2017.1382968.

Berman, Russell. "Montage as a Literary Technique: Thomas Mann's 'Tristan' and T. S. Elliot's *The Waste Land*." *Selecta: Journal of the PNCFL* 2, no. 2 (1981): 20–23.

Bernstein, Deborah. *Pioneers and Homemakers: Jewish Women in Pre-State Israel*. Albany: State University of New York Press, 1992.

———. "The Women Workers' Movement in Pre-State Israel, 1919–1939." *Signs: Journal of Women in Culture and Society* 12, no. 3 (1987): 454–70.

Bernstein, Marc S. "Midrash and Marginality: The 'Agunot' of S. Y. Agnon and Devorah Baron." *Hebrew Studies* 42 (2001): 7–58.

Bernstein-Cohen, Miriam. *Mefisto*. Tel Aviv: Mitspeh, 1938.

Biale, David. *Eros and the Jews: From Biblical Israel to Contemporary America*. Berkeley: University of California Press, 1997.

———. *Kabbalah and Counter-History*. Cambridge, MA: Harvard University Press, 1979.

Biemann, Asher D. *Inventing New Beginnings on the Idea of Renaissance in Modern Judaism*. Stanford, CA: Stanford University Press, 2009.

Bikhovsky, Elisheva. "Letters to Gershon Shofman." *Gnazim* 1 (1961).

———. Papers. Archives of the Hebrew Writers Association, Tel Aviv.

———. *Simta'ot*. Tel Aviv: Ha-kibbutz ha-me'uchad, 2008.

———. "Toldoti." In *Elisheva': Ḳovets ma'amarim odot ha-meshoreret Elisehva'*. Tel Aviv: Tomer, 1927.

Bilik, Dorothy. "Yente Serdatzky." In *Encyclopedia of Jewish Women*. December 31, 1999. Jewish Women's Archive. https://jwa.org/encyclopedia/article/serdatzky-yente.

Blair, Sara. "Whose Modernism Is It? Abraham Cahan, Fictions of Yiddish, and the Contest of Modernity." *MFS Modern Fiction Studies* 51, no. 2 (2005): 258–84.

Blank, Mirele. *Al gedot nahar Moskve'*. Tel Aviv: Hotsa'at Neuman, 1964.

Boârov, Andrìj, Paweł Polit, and Karolina Szymaniak, eds. *Montages: Debora Vogel and the New Legend of the City*. Lodz: Museum Sztuki, 2017.

Boyarin, Daniel. *Unheroic Conduct: The Rise of Heterosexuality and the Invention of the Jewish Man*. Berkeley: University of California Press, 1997.

Brenner, Michael. *The Renaissance of Jewish Culture in Weimar Germany*. New Haven, CT: Yale University Press, 1996.

Broido, Eva. *Memoirs of a Revolutionary*. Oxford: Oxford University Press, 1967.

Brokhes, Rokhl. *A zamlung dertseylungen*. Vilnius: Kletzkin, 1922.

Bürger, Peter. *Theory of the Avant-Garde*. Minneapolis: University of Minnesota Press, 1984.

Cahan, Abraham. "The Imported Bridegroom." In *Yekl and the Imported Bridegroom and Other Stories of Yiddish New York*. Mineola, NY: Dover, 1970.

Casanova, Pascale. *The World Republic of Letters*. Cambridge, MA: Harvard University Press, 1999.

Caws, Mary Ann, Rudolf E. Kuenzli, and Gwen Raaberg, eds. *Surrealism and Women*. Cambridge, MA: MIT Press, 1991.

Chadwick, Whitney. *Women Artists and the Surrealist Movement*. London: Thames Hudson, 1985.

Chamberlain, Lori. "Gender and the Metaphorics of Translation." In *The Translation Studies Reader*, edited by Lawrence Venuti, 314–29. New York: Routledge, 2000.

Chametzky, Jules. *From the Ghetto: The Fiction of Abraham Cahan*. Amherst: University of Massachusetts Press, 1977.

Chaver, Yael. "Dvoyre Fogel." *Jewish Women: A Comprehensive Historical Encyclopedia*. December 31, 1999. Jewish Women's Archive. https://jwa.org/encyclopedia/article/fogel-dvoyre.

Chow, Rey. *Entanglements, or Transmedial Thinking about Capture*. Durham, NC: Duke University Press, 2012.

Clark, Katerina. *Moscow, the Fourth Rome: Stalinism, Cosmopolitanism, and the Revolution of Soviet Culture, 1931–1941*. Cambridge: Harvard University Press, 2011.

Clifford, James. *The Predicament of Culture: Twentieth-Century Ethnography, Literature, and Art*. Cambridge, MA: Harvard University Press, 1988.

Cohen, Dorrit. *Transparent Minds: Narrative Modes for Presenting Consciousness in Fiction*. Princeton, NJ: Princeton University Press, 1978.

Cohen, Tova. "Portrait of the Maskilah as a Young Woman." *Nashim: A Journal of Jewish Women's Studies and Gender Issues* no. 15 (2008): 9–29.

Cohen, Tova, and Shmuel Feiner, eds. *Ḳol 'almah 'Ivriyah: Kitve nashim maskilot ba-me'ah ha-tesha'-'eśreh*. Tel Aviv: Ha-kibbutz ha-me'uchad, 2006.

Culler, Jonathan D. *Flaubert : The Uses of Uncertainty*. Aurora, CO: Davies Group, 2006.

DeKoven, Marianne. *Rich and Strange: Gender, History, and Modernism*. Princeton, NJ: Princeton University Press, 1991.

Delphy, Christine. *Close to Home: A Materialist Analysis of Women's Oppression*. London: Verso, 2016.

Dewey, John. *Art as Experience*. New York: Minton, Balch, 1934.

Diaconoff, Suellen. *Through the Reading Glass: Women, Books, and Sex in the French Enlightenment*. Albany: State University of New York Press, 2005.

Dinshaw, Carolyn. "Temporalities." In *Middle English: Oxford Twenty-First Century Approaches to Literature*, edited by Paul Strohm, 107–23. Oxford: Oxford University Press, 2007.

Efron, John. "From Mitteleuropa to the Middle East: Orientalism through a Jewish Lens." *Jewish Quarterly Review* 94, no. 3 (2004): 490–520.

Felski, Rita. *The Gender of Modernity*. Cambridge, MA: Harvard University Press, 1995.

Ferguson, Frances. "Jane Austen, *Emma*, and the Impact of Form." *Modern Language Quarterly* 61, no. 1 (2000): 157–80.

Fernald, Anne. "Women's Fiction, New Modernist Studies, and Feminism." *Modern Fiction Studies* 59, no. 2 (2013): 229–40.

Ficowski, Jerzy. *Regions of the Great Heresy: Bruno Schulz, a Biographical Portrait*. New York: W. W. Norton, 2003.

Finkin, Jordan. *A Rhetorical Conversation: Jewish Discourse in Modern Yiddish Literature*. College Park: Penn State University Press, 2010.

Flaubert, Gustave. *Madam Bovari.* Translated by Dvora Baron. Tel Aviv: Sifriyat po'alim, 1966.

———. *Madame Bovary.* Edited by Margaret Cohen. Translated by Eleanor Marx Aveling and Paul DeMan. Norton Critical Edition. New York: Norton, 2005.

———. *Madame Bovary.* Paris: Flammarion, 1979.

Fogel, Dvoyre. *See* Vogel, Debora.

Fogel, Josh. "Fradl Shtok." *Yiddish Leksikon* (blog), August 12, 2019. https://yleksikon.blogspot.com/2019/08/fradl-shtok.html.

Forman, Freida, Ethel Raicus, and Sarah Silberstein Swartz, eds. *Found Treasures: Stories by Yiddish Women Writers.* Toronto: Second Story Press, 1994.

François, Anne-Lise. *Open Secrets: The Literature of Uncounted Experience.* Stanford, CA: Stanford University Press, 2008.

Freeze, ChaeRan. *Jewish Marriage and Divorce in Imperial Russia.* Waltham, MA: Brandeis University Press, 2001.

Frieden, Kenneth. *Classic Yiddish Fiction: Abramovtish, Sholem Aleichem, and I. L. Peretz.* Albany: State University of New York Press, 1995.

Frishman, David. "Mendele, zayn lebn un zayn verk." In *Kritik iber mendele mokher sforim.* Warsaw: Farlag Mendele, 1911.

Galili, Ziva. "Zionism in the Early Soviet State: Between Legality and Persecution." In *Revolution, Repression, and Revival: The Soviet Jewish Experience,* edited by Zvi Gitelman and Yaacov Ro'i, 37–67. New York: Rowman and Littlefield, 2007.

Gallagher, Catherine. "The Rise of Fictionality." In *The Novel,* edited by Franco Moretti, 1:336–63. Princeton, NJ: Princeton University Press, 2006.

Gilman, Sander. *The Jew's Body.* New York: Routledge, 1991.

Giżycki. *Biali i czarni: Fragmenty kolonjalne.* Warsaw: Gebethner and Wolff, 1934.

Glanz-Leyeles Aaron (A. Glanz). "Kultur un di froy." *Di fraye arbiter shtime,* October 10, 1915.

———. Papers. YIVO Institute for Jewish Research, New York.

———. "Temperament." *Der Tog,* December 7, 1919.

Glatstein, Jacob. "Tsu der biografye fun a dikhterin." *Tog-morgn-zhurnal,* Sunday supplement, September 19, 1965.

Glenn, Susan A. *Daughters of the Shtetl: Life and Labor in the Immigrant Generation.* Ithaca, NY: Cornell University Press, 1990.

Glickman, Rose. *Russian Factory Women: Workplace and Society, 1880–1914.* Reprint edition. Berkeley: University of California Press, 1986.

Gluzman, Michael. *The Politics of Canonicity: Lines of Resistance in Modernist Hebrew Poetry.* Stanford, CA: Stanford University Press, 2002.

Gluzman, Sarah. *El ha-gevul.* Tel Aviv: Hotsa'at Yisraelit, 1938.

Goldberg, Leah. "'Al Dvora Baron: Parashiyot." In *Ha-omets le-ḥulin,* 95–103. Tel Aviv: Sifriyat po'alim, 1975.

———. "Al ha-ḳomediyah ha-elohit." In *Mi-dor ume-'ever: Beḥinot u-te'amim be sifrut kelalit,* 82–122. Tel Aviv: Sifriyat po'alim, 1977.

———. *Avedot: Roman ganuz.* Edited by Giddon Ticotsky. Tel Aviv: Sifriyat po'alim, 2010.

———. "Eropah shelakhem." In *Ne'arot 'Ivriyot: Mikhteve Le'ah Goldberg min ha-provintsyah,* edited by Yfaat Weiss and Giddon Ticotsky, 291–95. Tel Aviv: Sifriyat po'alim, 2009.

———. "Le-or ha-rachamim." In *Ha-omets le-ḥulin*, 170–75. Tel Aviv: Sifriyat po'alim, 1975.

———. *Mikhtavim me-nesi'ah medumah*. Tel Aviv: Sifriyat po'alim, 2007.

———. "Pirḳei zikhronot meḳuṭa'im." In *Hekhal she-shaka': Ha-ḥinukh ha-'ivri be-Ḳovna mosadot ve-ishim*, edited by Y. Yablokovsky, 126–34. Tel Aviv: Irgun bogre ha-gimnasyon ha-'Ivri be-Ḳovna, 1962.

———. *Shirim*. Vol. 1. Tel Aviv: Sifriyat po'alim, 1986.

Goldman, Wendy Z. *Women, the State and Revolution: Soviet Family Policy and Social Life, 1917–1936*. Cambridge: Cambridge University Press, 1993.

Gollance, Sonia. "A Dance: Fradel Shtok Reconsidered." *In geveb*, December 3, 2017. https://ingeveb.org/articles/a-dance-fradel-shtok-reconsidered.

Gordinsky, Natasha. *Bi-sheloshah nofim: Yetsiratah ha-muḳdemet shel Le'ah Goldberg*. Jerusalem: Magnes Press, 2016.

———. "Zemani harut beshirai: Yetsiratah shel Le'ah Goldberg be-shanim 1935–1945." PhD diss., Hebrew University of Jerusalem, 2009.

Gornick, Vivian. "Radiant Poison." *Harpers*, September 2008. https://harpers.org/archive/2008/09/radiant-poison/.

Govrin, Nurith. *Ha-maḥatsit ha-rishonah: Dvora Baron*. Jerusalem: Mosad Bialik, 1988.

Grace-Pollack, Sophie. "Hashpa'ato shel shomer 'al ḳore' yidish." *Hulyot* 10 (2006): 69–79.

Grumberg, Karen. "Between the World and the Yishuv: The Translation of Knut Hamsun's *Markens Grøde* as a Zionist Sacred Text." *Prooftexts: A Journal of Jewish Literary History* 36, nos. 1–2 (2017): 111–36.

Guenther, Irene. "Magic Realism, New Objectivity, and the Arts during the Weimar Republic." In *Magical Realism: Theory, History, and Community*, edited by Lois Parkinson Zamora and Wendy B. Faris, 15–31. Durham, NC: Duke University Press, 1995.

Hagati-Chomsky, Michal. "Rahel Katznelson." In *Jewish Women: A Comprehensive Historical Encyclopedia*. December 31, 1999. Jewish Women's Archive. https://jwa.org/encyclopedia/article/katznelson-rahel.

Hammerman, Shaina, and Naomi Seidman. "Between Aunt and Niece: Grace Paley and the Jewish American 'Swerve.'" *Prooftexts: A Journal of Jewish Literary History* 32, no. 2 (2012): 176–202.

Harshav, Benjamin. *Language in Time of Revolution*. Stanford, CA: Stanford University Press, 1993.

———. *The Polyphony of Jewish Culture*. Stanford, CA: Stanford University Press, 2007.

Harshav, Benjamin, and Barbara Harshav. *American Yiddish Poetry: A Bilingual Anthology*. Stanford, CA: Stanford University Press, 2007.

Hasak-Lowy, Todd. *Here and Now: History, Nationalism, and Realism in Modern Hebrew Fiction*. Syracuse, NY: Syracuse University Press, 2008.

Hasan-Rokem, Galit. "The Wandering Jew: A Jewish Perspective." In *Proceedings of the Ninth World Congress of Jewish Studies*. Jerusalem: World Congress of Jewish Studies, 1986.

Hellerstein, Kathryn. *A Question of Tradition: Women Poets in Yiddish, 1586–1987*. Stanford, CA: Stanford University Press, 2014.

Hemus, Ruth. *Dada's Women*. New Haven, CT: Yale University Press, 2009.

Henig, Roni. "Life of the Non-Living: Nationalization, Language and the Narrative of 'Revival' in Modern Hebrew Literary Discourse." PhD diss. Columbia University, 2018.

Herzog, Dagmar. *Sexuality in Europe: A Twentieth-Century History*. Cambridge: Cambridge University Press, 2011.

Heschel, Susannah. *Abraham Geiger and the Jewish Jesus*. Chicago: University of Chicago Press, 1998.

Hess, Jonathan. *Germans, Jews, and the Claims of Modernity*. New Haven, CT: Yale University Press, 2002.

Hess, Tamar. "Empathy as the Origin of Narrative in Deborah Baron's Prose." Presented at the Association for Jewish Studies annual conference, Boston, 2018.

———. *Ḥeḳ-ha-em shel zikhronot: Nashim, oṭobiyografiyah yeha-'aliyah ha-sheniyah*. Or Yehuda: Dvir, 2014.

———. "Peri bedidutah: 'Al siaḥ ha-ohavim ha-episṭolari u-mikhtavim me-nesi'ah medumah le-Le'ah Goldberg." In *Pegishot 'im meshorret*, edited by Ruth Kartun-Blum and Anat Weisman, 152–66. Tel Aviv: Sifriyat po'alim, 2000.

Hever, Hannan. *Producing the Modern Hebrew Canon: Nation Building and Minority Discourse*. New York: NYU Press, 2002.

Hilf, Mary Asia, and Barbara Bourns. *No Time for Tears*. New York: T. Yoseloff, 1964.

Hoffman, Matthew B. *From Rebel to Rabbi: Reclaiming Jesus and the Making of Modern Jewish Culture*. Stanford, CA: Stanford University Press, 2007.

Holmes, Rachel. *Eleanor Marx: A Life*. New York: Bloomsbury, 2015.

Howe, Irving, and Eliezer Greenberg. *A Treasury of Yiddish Poetry*. New York: Holt, Rinehart and Winston, 1969.

Humphrey, Caroline. "Cosmopolitanism and Kosmopolitizm in the Political Life of Soviet Citizens." *FOCAAL——Journal of Global and Historical Anthropology* 44 (2004): 138–52.

Huyssen, Andreas. *After the Great Divide: Modernism, Mass Culture, Postmodernism*. Bloomington: Indiana University Press, 1987.

Hyman, Paula. "Two Models of Modernization: Jewish Women in the German and the Russian Empires." In *Jews and Gender: The Challenge to Hierarchy*, edited by Jonathan Frankel, 39–53. New York: Oxford University Press, 2000.

Irigaray, Luce. *This Sex Which Is Not One*. Translated by Catherine Porter. Ithaca, NY: Cornell University Press, 1985.

Jacobs, Adriana Ximena. *Strange Cocktail: Translation and the Making of Modern Hebrew Poetry*. Ann Arbor: University of Michigan Press, 2018.

Jelen, Sheila. *Intimations of Difference: Dvora Baron in the Modern Hebrew Renaissance*. Syracuse, NY: Syracuse University Press, 2007.

Jelen, Sheila, and Shachar Pinsker, eds. *Hebrew, Gender, and Modernity: Critical Responses to Dvora Baron's Fiction*. Bethesda: University Press of Maryland, 2000.

Johnston, Robert Harold. *New Mecca, New Babylon: Paris and the Russian Exiles, 1920–1945*. Montreal: McGill-Queen's Press, 1988.

Kamendish, Paula. *Mamas of Dada: Women of the European Avant-Garde*. Columbia: University of South Carolina Press, 2015.

Kaminsky, Ilya, and Katherine Towler. "An Interview with Poet and Fiction Writer Grace Paley." *Poets and Writers*, March 17, 2008. https://www.pw.org/content/interview_poet_and_fiction_writer_grace_paley.

Karpilove, Miriam. *Diary of a Lonely Girl, or The Battle against Free Love*. Translated by Jessica Kirzane. Syracuse, NY: Syracuse University Press, 2020.

Katznelson-Shazar, Rachel. *Divre Po'elet*. Tel Aviv: Hotsa'at Mo'etset ha-po'alot, 1930.

———. "'Im ha-sefer 'Ḳeṭanot.'" *Davar*, May 17, 1934.

———. *Vos arbeterins dertseyln: An erets yisroel bukh*. New York: Pioneer Women's Organization, 1932.

Kazin, Alfred. "The Jew as Modern Writer." *Commentary* 41, no. 4 (1966): 37–41.

Kellman, Ellen. "Fradel Shtok." *Jewish Women: A Comprehensive Historical Encyclopedia*. December 31, 1999. Jewish Women's Archive, https://jwa.org/encyclopedia/article/shtok-fradel.

Kenvin, Helene. "Fradel Shtok: Author and Poet." *Jewish Gen ShtetlLinks*. Accessed May 15, 2015. https://kehilalinks.jewishgen.org/SkalaPodol/FradelShtok.html.

Klepfisz, Irena. "Di Mames, Dos Loshn / The Mothers, the Language: Feminism, Yidishkayt, and the Politics of Memory." *Bridges* 4, no. 1 (1994): 12–47.

———. "Queens of Contradiction: A Feminist Introduction to Yiddish Women Writers." In *Found Treasures: Stories by Yiddish Women Writers*, edited by Freida Forman, Ethel Raicus, Sarah Silberstein Swartz, and Margie Wolfe, 21–62. Toronto: Second Story Press, 1994.

Korman, Ezra. *Yidishe dikhterins antologye*. Chicago: L. M. Shteyn, 1928.

Koshy, Susan. "Minority Cosmopolitanism." *PMLA* 126, no. 3 (2011): 592–609.

Kozłowska, Magdalena. "Did You Teach Us to Do Otherwise?" Young Women in the Tsukunft Youth Movement in Interwar Poland and Their Role Models." *Aspasia* 14, no. 1 (2020): 57–77.

Kress, Susan. "Women and Marriage in Abraham Cahan's Fiction." *Studies in American Jewish Literature*, no. 3 (1983): 26–39.

Kronfeld, Chana. *The Full Severity of Compassion: The Poetry of Yehuda Amichai*. Stanford, CA: Stanford University Press, 2016.

Krutikov, Mikhail. *Yiddish Fiction and the Crisis of Modernity, 1905–1914*. Stanford, CA: Stanford University Press, 2002.

Laity, Cassandra. "Editor's Introduction: Toward Feminist Modernisms." *Feminist Modernist Studies* 1, nos. 1–2 (2018). DOI:10.1080/24692921.2017.1390870.

Lee, Haiyan. *Revolution of the Heart: A Genealogy of Love in China, 1900–1950*. Stanford, CA: Stanford University Press, 2006.

Leftwich, Joseph. *The Golden Peacock: A Worldwide Treasury of Yiddish Poetry*. New York: T. Yoseloff, 1961.

Lempel, Blume. *Oedipus in Brooklyn and Other Stories*. Translated by Ellen Cassedy and Yermiyahu Ahron Taub. Simsbury, CT: Mandel Vilar Press, 2016.

Lieblich, Amia. *Conversations with Dvora: An Experimental Biography of the First Modern Hebrew Woman Writer*. Berkeley: University of California Press, 1997.

Lindenmeyer, Antje. "'I Am Prince Yussuf': Else Lasker-Schüler's Autobiographical Performance." *Biography: An Interdisciplinary Quarterly* 24, no. 1 (2001): 25–34.

Lionnet, Françoise, and Shu-mei Shih. *Minor Transnationalism*. Durham, NC: Duke University Press, 2005.

Litvak, Olga. "Khave and Her Sisters: Sholem Aleichem and the Lost Girls of 1905." *Jewish Social Studies* 15, no. 3 (2009): 1–38.

Loeffler, James. *Rooted Cosmopolitans: Jews and Human Rights in the Twentieth Century*. New Haven, CT: Yale University Press, 2018.

Lubin, Orly. *Ishah ḳoret ishah*. Haifa: University of Haifa Press, 2006.

———. "Tidbits from Nehama's Kitchen: Alternative Nationalism in Dvora Baron's *The Exiles*." In *Hebrew, Gender, and Modernity: Critical Responses to Dvora Baron's Fiction*, edited by Sheila E. Jelen and Schachar Pinsker. Bethesda: University Press of Maryland, 2007.

Łukaszewicz, Piotr. *Zrzeszenie Artystów Plastyków Artes 1929–1935*. Wrocław: Zakład Narodowy im. Ossolińskich, 1975.

Lupton, Deborah. *The Emotional Self: A Sociocultural Exploration*. London: SAGE Publications, 1998.

Lutz, Violet. "Fradl Shtok." *Yiddish-Modern Jewish Studies* 17, nos. 3–4 (2012): 91–103.

Lyons, Janet. *Manifestoes: A Provocation of the Minor*. Ithaca, NY: Cornell University Press, 1999.

Lyubas, Anastasiya. "Gender, Language, and Territory: *Tsushtayer* Literary Journal in Galicia and Contributions of Yiddish Women Writers." *Nashim: A Journal of Jewish Women's Studies and Gender Issues*, no. 37 (2020).

———. "Plasticity of Language in Debora Vogel's Modernist Poetics." PhD diss., State University of New York, Binghamton, 2018.

Mann, Barbara. "Material Visions: The Poetry and Collage of Leah Goldberg's Native Landscapes." *Journal of Jewish Identities* 7, no. 1 (2014): 163–86.

———. "Of Madonnas and Magdalenas: Reading Mary in Modernist Hebrew and Yiddish Women's Poetry." In *Leḳeṭ: Yiddish Studies Today*, edited by Marion Aptroot, Efrat Gal-Ed, Roland Gruschka, and Simon Neuberg, 49–68. Düsseldorf: Düsseldorf University Press, 2012.

———. "Picturing the Poetry of Anna Margolin." *Modern Language Quarterly* 63, no. 2 (2002): 501–36.

Mansbach, S. A. *Modern Art in Eastern Europe: From the Baltic to the Balkans, ca. 1890–1939*. Cambridge: Cambridge University Press, 1998.

Mantovan, Daniela, "Language and Style in *Nokh alemen* (1913): Bergelson's Debt to Flaubert." In *Dovid Bergeleson: From Modernism to Socialist Realism*, edited by Joseph Sherman and Gennady Estraikh, 89–112. Leeds: Legenda, 2007.

Mao, Douglas. *Solid Objects: Modernism and the Test of Production*. Princeton, NJ: Princeton University Press, 1998.

Mao, Douglas, and Rebecca Walkowitz. "The New Modenist Studies." *PMLA* 123, no. 3 (2008): 737–48.

Marchand, Suzanne L. *German Orientalism in the Age of Empire: Religion, Race, and Scholarship*. Cambridge: Cambridge University Press, 2009.

———. "Nazism, Orientalism, and Humanism." In *Nazi Germany and the Humanities*, edited by Anson Rabinbach and Wolfgand Bialis, 267–305. Oxford: One World, 2007.

Martin, Terry. *The Affirmative Action Empire: Nations and Nationalism in the Soviet Union, 1923–1939*. Ithaca, NY: Cornell University Press, 2001.

Mash, Yenta. *On the Landing*. Translated by Ellen Cassedy. De Kalb: Northern Illinois University Press, 2018.

McBride, Patrizia C. *The Chatter of the Visible: Montage and Narrative in Modern Germany*. Ann Arbor: University of Michigan Press, 2016.

Mendes-Flohr, Paul. *Divided Passion: Jewish Intellectuals and the Experience of Modernity*. Detroit, MI: Wayne State University Press, 1991.

———. "Zarathustra's Apostle: Martin Buber and the Jewish Renaissance." In *Nietzsche and Jewish Culture*, edited by Jacob Golomb, 233–43. London: Routledge, 1997.

Michaels, Leonard. "Conversation with Grace Paley." In *Conversations with Grace Paley*, edited by Gerhard Bach and Blaine Hall, 26–35. Jackson: University of Mississippi Press, 1997.

Michaelson, Patricia. *Speaking Volumes: Women, Reading, and Speech in the Age of Austen*. Stanford, CA: Stanford University Press, 2002.

Miller, Cristanne. *Cultures of Modernism: Marianne Moore, Mina Loy, and Else Lasker-Schüler*. Ann Arbor: University of Michigan Press, 2007.

Miller, D. A. *The Novel and the Police*. Berkeley: University of California Press, 1989.

Miller, Nancy K. "Starting Out in the Fifties: Grace Paley, Philip Roth, and the Making of a Literary Career,." *Contemporary Women's Writing* 3, no. 2 (2009): 135–42.

Mintz, Alan L. *"Banished from Their Father's Table": Loss of Faith and Hebrew Autobiography*. Bloomington: Indiana University Press, 1989.

Miron, Dan. *Bodedim be-mo'adam*. Tel Aviv: Am oved, 1987.

———. "The Dark Side of Sholem Aleichem's Laughter." *Derekh Judaica Urbinatensia* 1 (2003): 16–55.

———. "The Endless Cycle: The Poetic World of Dvora Baron." In *Hebrew, Gender, and Modernity: Critical Responses to Dvora Baron's Fiction*, edited by Sheila Jelen and Shachar Pinsker, 17–31. Bethesda: University Press of Maryland, 2007.

———. *Imahot meyasdot, aḥayot ḥorgot*. Tel Aviv: Ha-kibbutz ha-me'uchad, 1991.

Molodowsky, Kadia. *A Jewish Refugee in New York: Rivke Zilberg's Journal*. Translated by Anita Norich. Bloomington: Indiana University Press, 2019.

———. "Meydlekh, froyen, vayber, un . . . nevue." *Literarishe Bleter* 3, no. 22 (1927): 416.

Moss, Kenneth B. *Jewish Renaissance in the Russian Revolution*. Cambridge, MA: Harvard University Press, 2009.

Mufti, Aamir. "Auerbach in Istanbul: Edward Said, Secular Criticism, and the Question of Minority Culture." *Critical Inquiry* 25, no. 1 (1998): 95–125.

Naveh, Hannah, and Tsilah Abramovitz Ratner. *Tsenah, tsenah: Merḥav ha-nedunyah ba-sipurim me-et Devorah Baron, Y.D. Berḳovits ṿe-Ya'aḳov Shṭainberg*. Tel Aviv: Ha-kibbutz ha-me'uchad, 2015.

Neugroschel, Joachim, ed. and trans. *No Star Too Beautiful: An Anthology of Yiddish Stories from 1382 to the Present*. New York: W. W. Norton, 2002.

Newman, Zelda. "The Correspondence between Kadya Molodowsky and Rokhl Korn." *Women in Judaism* 8, no. 1 (2011): 1–26.

Niger, Shmuel. "Di Ertseylungen fun Fradl Shtok." *Tsukunft* (October 1920), 608–10.

Nivizky, M. "Rut mi-gadot ha-Volga." In *Elisheva': Ḳovets ma'amarim odot ha-meshoreret Elisehva'*, 15–18. Tel Aviv: Tomer, 1927.

Norich, Anita. "Grace Paley." In *Encyclopedia of Jewish Women.* March 20, 2009. Jewish Women's Archive. https://jwa.org/encyclopedia/article/paley-grace.

———. "Translating and Teaching Yiddish Prose by Women." *In geveb*, April 2020. https://ingeveb.org/blog/translating-and-teaching-yiddish-prose-by-women.

North, Michael. *The Dialect of Modernism: Race, Language, and Twentieth-Century Literature.* Oxford: Oxford University Press, 1998.

Novershtern, Avraham. "Ha-ḳolot ṿeha-makhela: Shirat nashim be-yidish ben shetei milḥamot ha-'olam." *Biḳoret u-farshanut*, no. 40 (2008).

Olgin, M. "Pesimizm." *Di Naye velt*, January 9, 1920.

Olmert, Dana. "Aḥarit devar." In *Simṭa'ot: Roman*, 348. Tel Aviv: Ha-kibbutz ha-me'uchad, 2008.

Pagis, Ada, ed. *Dvorah Baron: Mivḥar ma'amare biḳoret 'al yetsiratah* [Dvora Baron: A Selection of Critical Essays on Her Work]. Tel Aviv: Am oved, 1974.

Paley, Grace. *Enormous Changes at the Last Minute.* New York: Farrar, Straus and Giroux, 1974.

———. "Introduction to 'A Conversation with My Father.'" In *Fathers: Reflections by Daughters*, edited by Ursula Owen. New York: Pantheon Books, 1983.

———. *Just As I Thought.* New York: Farar, Straus, and Giroux, 1998.

Parush, Iris. "Readers in Cameo: Women Readers in Jewish Society of Nineteenth-Century Eastern Europe." *Prooftexts: A Journal of Jewish Literary History* 14, no. 1 (1994): 1–23.

———. *Reading Jewish Women: Marginality and Modernization in Nineteenth-Century Eastern European Jewish Society.* Waltham, MA: Brandeis University Press, 2004.

Pecora, Vincent P. *Secularization and Cultural Criticism: Religion, Nation, and Modernity.* Chicago: University of Chicago Press, 2006.

Peleg, Yaron. "Heroic Conduct: Homoeroticism and the Creation of Modern, Jewish Masculinities." *Jewish Social Studies* 13, no. 1 (2006): 31–58.

Pellegrini, Ann. *Performance Anxieties: Staging Psychoanalysis, Staging Race.* New York: Routledge, 1996.

Peretz, I. L. "Speech at the 1908 Czernowitz Language Conference." In *Selected Works of I. L. Peretz*, edited by Marvin Zuckerman and Marion Herbst, 384–87. Malibu: Simon/Pangloss, 1996.

Pérez, Ashley Hope. "Against 'Écriture Féminine': Flaubert's Narrative Aggression in 'Madame Bovary.'" *French Forum* 38, no. 3 (2013): 31–47.

Pinsker, Shachar. "The Construction of Secular and Religious in Modern Hebrew Literature." In *Religion or Ethnicity? Jewish Identities in Evolution*, edited by Zvi Gitelman, 221–38. New Brunswick, NJ: Rutgers University Press, 2009.

———. *Literary Passports: The Making of Modernist Hebrew Fiction in Europe.* Stanford, CA: Stanford University Press, 2010.

———. *A Rich Brew: How Cafés Created Modern Jewish Culture.* New York: New York University Press, 2018.

———. "Unraveling the Yarn: Intertexuality, Gender, and Cultural Critique in the Stories of Dvora Baron." *Nashim: A Journal of Jewish Women's Studies and Gender Issues*, no. 11 (2006): 244–79.

Pratt, Norma Fain. "Culture and Radical Politics: Yiddish Women Writers, 1890–1940." *American Jewish History* 70, no. 1 (1980): 68–90.

Prell, Riv-Ellen. "Why Jewish Princesses Don't Sweat: Desire and Consumption in Postwar American Jewish Culture." In *People of the Body: Jews and Judaism from an Embodied Perspective*, edited by Howard Eilberg-Schwartz, 329–59. Albany: State University of New York Press, 1992.

Presner, Todd Samuel. *Muscular Judaism: The Jewish Body and the Politics of Regeneration*. London: Routledge, 2007.

Quint, Alyssa. "'Yiddish Literature for the Masses'? A Reconsideration of Who Read What in Jewish Eastern Europe." *AJS Review* 29, no. 1 (2005): 61–89.

Rabinow, Paul. "Representations Are Social Facts: Modernity and Postmodernity in Anthropology.'" In *Writing Culture: The Poetics and Politics of Ethnography*, edited by James Clifford and George E. Marcus, 234–61. Berkeley: University of California Press, 1986.

Raider, Mark A., and Miriam B. Raider-Roth, eds. *The Plough Woman: Records of the Pioneer Women of Palestine, a Critical Edition*. Waltham, MA: Brandeis University Press, 2002.

Rakovsky, Puah. *My Life as a Radical Jewish Woman: Memoirs of a Zionist Feminist*. Edited by Paula Hyman. Translated by Barbara Harshav and Paula Hyman. Bloomington: Indiana University Press, 2001.

Rancière, Jacques. *Dissensus: On Politics and Aesthetics*. London: Bloomsbury, 2015.

———. *Film Fables / Jacques Rancière*. Translated by Emiliano Battista. Talking Images Series. Oxford: Berg, 2006.

———. *The Flesh of Words: The Politics of Writing*. Translated by Charlotte Mandell. Stanford, CA: Stanford University Press, 2004.

———. *The Politics of Aesthetics*. Translated by Gabriel Rockhill. London: Continuum, 2004.

———. *The Politics of Literature*. Translated by Julie Rose. Cambridge: Polity, 2011.

———. "Why Emma Bovary Had to Be Killed." *Critical Inquiry* 34, no. 2 (2008): 233–48.

Rappaport, Y. "'Vi a veverke in rod'" [Like a squirrel in a circle]. *Shoybns*, no. 4 (1936): 37–39.

Ravitch, Melekh. "'Den mir hobn zunshtn keyn andri in der velt': E. Korman *Yidishe dikhterins*." *Literarishe bleter*, 5, no. 42 (October 19, 1928): 830–831.

———. "Meydlekh, froyen, vayber—yidishe dikhterins." Literarishe bleter, 4, no. 21 (May 27, 1927): 395–396.

———. Papers. National Library of Israel, Jerusalem.

Raz-Krakotzkin, Amnon. "Orientalizm, mada'e ha-yahadut, ṿeha-ḥevrah ha-Yiśra'elit: Mispar he'arot." *Gama'ah* 3 (1998): 34–61.

———. "The Zionist Return to the West and the Mizrachi Jewish Perspective." In *Orientalism and the Jews*, edited by Ivan Davidson Kalmar and Derek Penslar, 162–81. Waltham, MA: Brandeis University Press, 2005.

Richards, Jill. *The Fury Archives: Female Citizenship, Human Rights, and the International Avant-Gardes*. New York: Columbia University Press, 2020.

Robbins, Bruce. *Perpetual War: Cosmopolitanism from the Viewpoint of Violence*. Durham, NC: Duke University Press, 2012.

Roh, Franz. "Magic Realism, Post-Expressionism." In *Magical Realism: Theory, History, Community*, edited by Lois Parkinson Zamora and Wendy B. Faris. Durham, NC: Duke University Press, 1995.

Rokem, Na'ama. *Prosaic Conditions: Heinrich Heine and the Spaces of Zionist Literature*. Evanston, IL: Northwestern University Press, 2013.

———. "Questioning *Weltliteratur*: Heinrich Heine, Leah Goldberg, and the Department of Comparative Literature at the Hebrew University of Jerusalem." *Prooftexts: A Journal of Jewish Literary History* 36, nos. 1–2 (2017): 217–39.

Rosenthal, Laura J. "Introduction: Recovering from Recovery." *The Eighteenth Century* 50, no. 1 (2009): 1–11.

Rosenwald, Lawrence. "On the Reception of Buber and Rosenzweig's Bible." *Prooftexts: A Journal of Jewish Literary History* 14, no. 2 (1994): 141–65.

Roskies, David. "Yiddish Popular Literature and the Female Reader." *Journal of Popular Culture* 10, no. 4 (1977): 852–58.

Said, Edward. *Orientalism*. New York: Vintage, 1978.

Sands, Philippe. *East West Street: On the Origins of "Genocide" and "Crimes against Humanity."* New York: Vintage Books, 2016.

Sartre, Jean-Paul. *What Is Literature and Other Essays*. Cambridge, MA: Harvard University Press, 1988.

Schachter, Allison. *Diasporic Modernisms: Hebrew and Yiddish Literature in the Twentieth Century*. New York: Oxford University Press, 2012.

———. "'A Lily among Bullfrogs': Dahlia Ravikovitch and the Field of Hebrew Poetry." *Prooftexts: A Journal of Jewish Literary History* 28, no. 3 (2008): 310–34.

———. "Men Reading Women: Secularism and Literary Modernity in the Writings of Abraham Cahan and Sholem Aleichem." *Jewish Quarterly Review* 111, no. 4 (2021), forthcoming.

———. "Modernist Indexicality: The Language of Gender, Race, and Domesticity in Hebrew and Yiddish Modernism." *MLQ* 72, no. 4 (2011): 493–520.

Schiller, Friedrich. *On the Aesthetic Education of Man*. Translated by Reginald Snell. New York: Frederick Ungar, 1964.

Scholem, Gershom. *Major Trends in Jewish Mysticism*. New York: Schocken, 1995.

Schor, Naomi. *Breaking the Chain: Women, Theory, and French Realist Fiction*. New York: Columbia University Press, 1985.

Schulz, Bruno. "Akacje kwitną." *Nasza Opinja*, no. 72 (1936).

———. *Księga listów*. Edited by Jerzy Ficowski. Krakow: Wydawnictwo literackie, 1975.

Scott, Bonnie Kime. "Introduction." In *The Gender of Modernism a Critical Anthology*. Edited by Bonnie Kime Scott, 1–18. Bloomigton: Indiana University Press, 1990.

Segal, Miryam. *A New Sound in Hebrew Poetry: Poetics, Politics, Accent*. Bloomington: Indiana University Press, 2010.

Seidman, Naomi. *Faithful Renderings: Jewish-Christian Difference and the Politics of Translation*. Chicago: University of Chicago Press, 2006.

———. "Gender and the Disintegration of the Shtetl." In *The Shtetl: New Evaluations*, edited by Steven Katz, 193–210. New York: NYU Press, 2007.

———. *A Marriage Made in Heaven: The Sexual Politics of Hebrew and Yiddish*. Berkeley: University of California Press, 1997.

———. *The Marriage Plot: Or, How Jews Fell in Love with Love, and with Literature*. Stanford, CA: Stanford University Press, 2016.

———. "Reading 'Queer' Ashkenaz: This Time from East to West." *TDR: The Drama Review* 55, no. 3 (2011): 50–56.

Serdatzky, Yente. *Geklibene verk*. New York: Hebrew Publishing Company, 1913.

Seshagiri, Urmila. "Mind the Gap! Modernism and Feminist Praxis." *Modernism/Modernity Print Plus Forum* 2, no. 2 (2017). doi:10.26597/mod.0022.

Shandler, Jeffrey. *Awakening Lives: Autobiographies of Jewish Youth in Poland before the Holocaust*. New Haven, CT: Yale University Press, 2002.

Shanes, Joshua. *Diaspora Nationalism and Jewish Identity in Habsburg Galicia*. Cambridge: Cambridge University Press, 2012.

Shapira, Anita. *Ha-halikhah 'al ḳav ha-ofeḳ*. Tel Aviv: Am oved, 1987.

———. *Land and Power: The Zionist Resort to Force, 1881–1948*. Stanford, CA: Stanford University Press, 1992.

———. *Yosef Haim Brenner: A Life*. Stanford, CA: Stanford University Press, 2015.

Shavit, Zohar. "The Status of Translated Literature in the Creation of Hebrew Literature in Pre-State Israel (the Yishuv Period)." *Meta: Journal Des Traducteurs / Meta: Translators' Journal* 43, no. 1 (1998): 46–53.

Shneer, David. *Yiddish and the Creation of Soviet Jewish Culture: 1918–1930*. Cambridge: Cambridge University Press, 2004.

Sholem Aleichem. *Tevye the Dairyman and Motl the Cantor's Son*. Translated by Aliza Shevrin. New York: Penguin, 2009.

Shtok, Fradl. "A Soykher Fun Fel" [A fur merchant]. *Forverts*, November 19, 1942.

———. *From the Jewish Provinces: The Selected Stories of Fradl Shtok*. Translated by Jordan D. Finkin and Allison Schachter. Evanston, IL: Northwestern University Press, 2021.

———. *Gezamelte Ertseylungen*. New York: Farlag nay tsayt, 1919.

———. *Musicians Only*. New York: Pelican Publishing Company, 1927.

———. "Vos iz poezye." In *Fun mentsh tsu mentsh: A zamlbukh fun poezye*. Edited by Moshe Leyb Halpern. New York: Farlag Nyu-York, 1915.

Socher, Abraham. *The Radical Enlightenment of Solomon Maimon: Judaism, Heresy, and Philosophy*. Stanford, CA: Stanford University Press, 2006.

Sokoloff, Namoi, Anne Lapidus Lerner, and Anita Norich, eds. *Gender and Text in Modern Hebrew and Yiddish Literature*. New York: Jewish Theological Seminary of America, 1992.

Sorkin, David. *The Transformation of German Jewry, 1780–1840*. Detroit, MI: Wayne State University Press, 1999.

Stahl, Neta. *Other and Brother: Jesus in the Twentieth Century Jewish Literary Landscape*. New York: Oxford University Press, 2013.

Swados, Harvey. "Good and Short." *Hudson Review* 12, no. 3 (1959): 454–59.

Szymaniak, Karolina. *Być agentem wiecznej idei: Przemiany poglądów estetycznych Debory Vogel* [To be an agent of an eternal idea: The transformation of Debora Vogel's aesthetic views]. Krakow: Universitas, 2006.

———. "On the Ice Floe: Rachel Auerbach—the Life of a Yiddishist Intellectual in Early Twentieth Century Poland." In *Catastrophe and Utopia: Jewish Intellectuals in Central and Eastern Europe in the 1930s and 1940s*, edited by

Ferenc Laczó and Joachim von Puttkamer, 304–52. Berlin: Walter de Gruyter, 2017.

Tabatshnik, A. *Dikhter un dikhtung*. New York: Dayid Ignatoy literatur fond, 1949.

———. "Fradl Shtok." In *Leksikon fun der nayer yidisher literatur*, edited by Shmuel Niger and Jacob Shatsky, 8:608. New York: Congress for Jewish Culture, 1981.

Taylor, Jacqueline. *Grace Paley: Illuminating the Dark Lives*. Austin: University of Texas Press, 1990.

———. "Interview: Grace Paley on Storytelling and Story Hearing." *Literature in Performance* 7 (1987): 46–57.

Thomason, Laura E. *The Matrimonial Trap: Eighteenth-Century Women Writers Redefine Marriage*. Lewisburg, PA: Bucknell University Press, 2014.

Ticotsky, Giddon. "Boker afel ba-birah: aharit devar." In *Avedot*, 317–53. Tel Aviv: Sifriyat po'alim, 2010.

Tir-Appelroit, Arza. "Ha-targum be-tselem uvi-demut." PhD diss., Tel Aviv University, 2004.

Torres, Anna Elena. "Circular Landscapes: Montage and Myth in Dvoyre Fogel's Yiddish Poetry." *Nashim: A Journal of Jewish Women's Studies and Gender Issues*, no. 35 (2019): 40–74.

Trachtenberg, Barry. *The Revolutionary Roots of Modern Yiddish, 1903–1917*. Syracuse, NY: Syracuse University Press, 2008.

Tran, Ben. "Negative Paradise: Rethinking Anglophone and World Literature as Literary Dubbing." *Modern Fiction Studies* 64, no. 1 (2018): 153–75.

Tsemach, Shlomo. "*Madam Bovari* be-'ivrit." *Moznayim* 30 (1931).

Underhill, Karen. *Bruno Schulz and Galician Jewish Modernity*. Bloomington: University of Indiana Press, 2021.

Veidlinger, Jeffrey. *The Moscow State Yiddish Theater: Jewish Culture on the Soviet Stage*. Bloomington: Indiana University Press, 2000.

Venuti, Lawrence. "Local Contingencies: Translation and National Identities." In *Nation, Language, and the Ethics of Translation*, edited by Sandra Berman and Michael Wood, 177–202. Princeton, NJ: Princeton University Press, 2005.

Vogel, Debora [Dvoyre Fogel]. *Akatsyes blien: Montazhn*. Lwów: POL, 1935.

———. "A por bamerkungen vegn mayn bikhl, *Akatsyes blien*." *Shoybn*, no. 5 (March–April 1937): 38–40.

———. *Blooming Spaces: The Collected Poetry, Prose, Critical Writing, and Letters of Debora Vogel*. Translated by Anastasiya Lyubas. Boston: Academic Studies Press, 2020.

———. "Die Geometrie Des Verzichts: Gedichte, Montagen, Essays, Briefe." Edited by Anna Maja Misiak. Wuppertal, Germany: Arco, 2015.

———. "Di literarishe gatung montazh." *Bodn* 3, nos. 3–4 (1934): 99–105.

———. "Literarishe montazh: An araynfir." *Inzl* 3 (1938): 6–7.

———. "Ludzkie egzotyki." *Przegląd Społeczny* 8, nos. 7–8 (1934): 150–59.

———. "Lwowska Juderia." In *Almanach i leksykon Zydowstwa Polskiego*, 1:88–98. Lwòw, 1937.

———. *Manekinen*. Warsaw-Lemberg: Farlag Tsushtayer, 1934.

———. "Romans djalektyki." *Przegląd Społeczny* 9, no. 10 (1935): 243–47.

———. "Vegn B. Alkvits opruf tsu ir bukh Akatsyes." *In zikh*, no. 17 (1935): 62–64.

Warning, Rainer. "Reading Irony in Flaubert." *Style* 19, no. 3 (1985): 304–16.

Weiman-Kelman, Zohar. *Queer Expectations: A Genealogy of Jewish Women's Poetry*. Albany: State University of New York Press, 2018.

Weiser, Kalman. *Jewish People, Yiddish Nation: Noah Prylucki and the Folkists in Poland*. Toronto: University of Toronto Press, 2011.

Weiss, Yfaat. "A Small Town in Germany: Leah Goldberg and German Orientalism in 1932." *Jewish Quarterly Review* 99, no. 2 (2009): 200–229.

Weissler, Chava. "'For Women and for Men Who Are Like Women': The Construction of Gender in Yiddish Devotional Literature." *Journal of Feminist Studies in Religion* 5, no. 2 (1989): 7–24.

Weitzner, Jacob. "Ha-ishah be-yetsiratah shel Shalom Aleichem: 'Iyun be-Ṭuvya ha-ḥalvan." *Ḥulyot* 33 (1996): 129–36.

White, Hayden. *The Content of the Form: Narrative Discourse and Historical Representation*. Baltimore, MD: Johns Hopkins University Press, 1987.

Wilson, Elizabeth. *Adorned in Dreams: Fashion and Modernity*. Rev. ed. New Brunswick, NJ: Rutgers University Press, 2003.

Wisse, Ruth R. *A Little Love in Big Manhattan*. Cambridge, MA: Harvard University Press, 1988.

———. *The Modern Jewish Canon: A Journey through Language and Culture*. New York: Free Press, 2000.

Wolff, Larry. *The Idea of Galicia: History and Fantasy in Habsburg Political Culture*. Stanford, CA: Stanford University Press, 2010.

Wood, Ghislaine. *The Surreal Body: Fetish and Fashion*. London: Victoria and Albert Museum, 2007.

Woolf, Virginia. *A Room of One's Own*. Orlando, FL: Harcourt, 2005.

Yeglin, Ofra. *Ulai mabaṭ aḥer: Ḳlasiyut modernit u-modernizm ḳlasi be-shirat Le'ah Goldberg*. Tel Aviv: Ha-kibbutz ha-me'uchad, 2002.

Young, Tory, and Jeff Wallace, eds. "The Future of Women in Modernism." Special issue, *Literature Compass* 10, no. 1 (2013).

Zakai, Orian. "Zion of Their Own: Hebrew Women's Nationalist Writing." PhD diss., University of Michigan, Ann Arbor, 2012.

Żarnowska, Anna. "Women's Political Participation in Inter-war Poland: Opportunities and Limitations." *Women's History Review* 13, no. 1 (2004): 57–68.

Ziarek, Ewa Płonowska. *Feminist Aesthetics and the Politics of Modernism*. New York: Columbia University Press, 2012.

Zierler, Wendy. *And Rachel Stole the Idols: The Emergence of Modern Hebrew Women's Writing*. Detroit: Wayne State University Press, 2004.

———. "Breaking the Idyll: Rereading Flaubert's *Madame Bovary* and Agnon's *Sippur Pashut* through Devorah Baron's 'Fradl.'" *Prooftexts: A Journal of Jewish Literary History* 37, no. 3 (2019): 607–41.

———. "Hava Shapiro's Letters to Reuven Brainin." *Nashim: A Journal of Jewish Women's Studies and Gender Issues*, no. 16 (2008): 67–97.

INDEX